The Religion and Theology Student Writer's Manual and Reader's Guide

Joel Hopko

Archdiocese of Santa Fe

Gregory M. Scott

University of Central Oklahoma Emeritus

Stephen M. Garrison

University of Central Oklahoma

ROWMAN & LITTLEFIELD

Lanham • Boulder • New York • London

Executive Editor: Nancy Roberts
Editorial Assistant: Megan Manzano
Senior Marketing Manager: Kim Lyons
Interior Designer: Ilze Lemesis
Cover Designer: Sally Rinehart

Credits and acknowledgments for material borrowed from other sources, and reproduced with permission, appear on the appropriate page within the text.

Published by Rowman & Littlefield
A wholly owned subsidiary of The Rowman & Littlefield Publishing Group, Inc.
4501 Forbes Boulevard, Suite 200, Lanham, Maryland 20706
www.rowman.com

Unit A, Whitacre Mews, 26-34 Stannary Street, London SE11 4AB, United Kingdom

British Library Cataloguing in Publication Information Available

Library of Congress Cataloging-in-Publication Data
Names: Hopko, Joel, author.
Title: The religion and theology student writer's manual and reader's guide / Joel Hopko, Archdiocese of Santa Fe,
     Gregory M. Scott, University of Central Oklahoma Emeritus, Stephen M. Garrison, University of Central Oklahoma.
Description: Lanham : Rowman & Littlefield, 2017. | Includes bibliographical references and index.
Identifiers: LCCN 2017024892 (print) | LCCN 2017039025 (ebook) | ISBN 9781538100967 (electronic) | ISBN
     9781538100943 (hardback : alk. paper) | ISBN 9781538100950 (pbk. : alk. paper)
Subjects: LCSH: Religion—Study and teaching. | Religion—Authorship. | Theology—Study and teaching. | Theology—
     Authorship. | Academic writing.
Classification: LCC BL41 (ebook) | LCC BL41 .H63 2017 (print) | DDC 200.7—dc23
LC record available at https://lccn.loc.gov/2017024892

Printed in the United States of America

BRIEF CONTENTS

CONTENTS

WELCOME TO THE GREATEST STORIES EVER TOLD

Perhaps you have read sacred scriptures your entire life up to the present, or maybe you are relatively unfamiliar with them. In either case, you are now engaged in serious study of the greatest stories ever told: chronicles of adventure, deceit, sacrifice, redemption, agony, epiphany, theophany, ecstasy, salvation, catharsis, and apocalypse. And now you are a participant—you have become a part of them—because stories, dead on dusty shelves, come alive as they enter your mind, and you have set out to give them this life.

Your job now is well removed from mere entertainment. The job you have chosen, by virtue of your enrollment in a religion or theology course, is to be an intellectual mechanic. You will take things apart, and you will put them back together again. In so doing, you will employ certain *skills*, as follows:

- observing religious and spiritual behavior
- analyzing texts
- interpreting intentions and meaning
- communicating your insights to others

The first purpose of this book is to help you develop these skills. Underlying all these activities, most fundamentally, is the skill of writing. Much in the way a funnel directs liquid to its intended container, writing refines and directs your thoughts into clear, capable, professional literary "vessels" through which you communicate with communities of scholars. And so this book invites and empowers you to join the particular community of skilled *observers*, *analysts*, and *interpreters* known as religion scholars and theologians.

The second purpose of this book is to help you appreciate and make use of the fact that *writing is the best method of learning*. Learning does not happen through reading alone. You must make the material you read *your own*. The most effective way of gaining ownership is to write your own version of what you have read. When you write your own version, you associate concepts in the new material with similar ones already in your mind. These associations give staying power to conceptions that would otherwise slip away.

This manual was written to help you *learn* religion and theology by *practicing* the scholarship of these disciplines and thereby making your own unique contribution to society's understanding of how we engage transcendence—and how we engage each other. We wish you all success!

Joel Hopko
Greg Scott
Steve Garrison

AS WE TEACH WRITING, YOU TEACH RELIGION AND THEOLOGY

Of the numerous insights afforded by the last three decades of research into student engagement and learning, one constantly recurs: The more *choices* students are offered, the better they learn. This book offers lots of choices. Among the features of this book are forty-four writing exercises from which to choose. You may select some, and students may select others.

Aside from helping motivate students to learn, this volume offers substantial material on *basic reading and writing skills*, and introductions to a broad array of subject matter and approaches to the study of religion and theology.

In addition, this book helps you deal with three problems commonly faced by teachers of religion:

- Students increasingly need *specific directions* to produce a good paper.
- Religion and theology scholars, as always, want to teach religion and theology, not English.
- Students do not yet understand how and why to avoid *plagiarism*.

How many times have you assigned papers in your religion classes and found yourself teaching the basics of writing, in terms of not only content but form and grammar as well? This text, which may either accompany the primary text you assign in any class or stand on its own, allows you to assign one of the types of papers described in part 3, with the knowledge that virtually everything the student needs to know, from grammar to sources of information to reference style, is in parts 1 and 2 of this single volume.

We hope you find *The Religion and Theology Student Writer's Manual and Reader's Guide* to be helpful to your students, and we wish you all success.

Joel Hopko
Greg Scott
Steve Garrison

1

READ AND WRITE TO UNDERSTAND RELIGION AND THEOLOGY

1.1 THE BENEFITS OF EFFECTIVE READING

Getting Started

It doesn't matter how good a reader you are right now, how much you enjoy reading, how often you read, what sorts of texts you like and what sorts you avoid, how fast you read, or how effective your level of retention is. The fact is that the remainder of your academic career—the remainder, in fact, of your life—would be made richer if you were better at reading than you are now. This book attempts to make you a better reader, first by offering you tips for improvement, suggestions aimed at enhancing your enjoyment and understanding of any text, and second by supplying you with exercises to improve your reading in the specific discipline of religion.

But why do we need improvement in writing? It's such a basic skill, something we all learned to do in grade school. Right?

Well, sort of. Our grade school teachers taught us the basics: how to distinguish words in the characters on a page and how to pace ourselves through a sentence or a paragraph to arrive at a coherent meaning. Without these fundamental skills, we couldn't read at all. That's what elementary school focuses on: giving us the basics.

The problem is, there is more to reading than just those first few steps. If there weren't, then we would all be able to read any text pretty much as well as anybody else. It goes without saying, however, that all of us read at different levels of comprehension and different levels of enjoyment, depending on what it is we're reading. We are all different people, each with our own preferences and unique set of experiences that resonate easily to certain stimuli and less easily to others.

Think of all the different worlds you inhabit, your favorite pastimes, hobbies, sports, school subjects. Each is its own world, with its own set of rules and traditions, modes of behavior and thought, and language. Do you remember the first time you watched a professional basketball game on television? The action on the court was no doubt dizzying, but so was the conversation by which the sportscasters and commentators explained each play as it happened. What's a "pick and roll"? A "double double"? Or, for that matter, a "triple double"? Why do some penalties allow for a free throw or two while others don't? Basketball is a world with its own rules and its own ways of thinking and speaking. How long did it take you to become comfortable in this world—to become an *insider*?

Christian theology is rich in jargon. A theologically educated Christian insider would be able to make some (if not complete) sense of the following sentence: "Her relatively eschatological hermeneutic colors her exegesis of non-apocalyptic pericopes."

To read well in virtually any subject, particularly in any school subject or profession, it is essential that you acknowledge to yourself, as you begin to read, that you are entering a new world, one inhabited by insiders and one that can be difficult to understand for people who aren't insiders.

Difficult, but not impossible.

It is possible for us to learn how to tailor our reading skills to texts in different disciplines, including those for which we do not have a natural affinity or a set of closely related personal experiences. It requires energy and imagination and, above all, a shift in attitude.

Whether you are reading a textbook chapter, a newspaper or magazine article, a journal essay, a book, or a blog, read on for some tips to help you master the text.

Read with Patience

Different texts require different degrees of patience from the reader. Be sure, when you undertake to read a text written in a discipline with which you have little familiarity, that you are willing to read carefully to allow the material—and the world from which it comes—to sink in. Reading with patience means being willing to perform certain prereading activities that can aid in your mastery of the text. Some of these activities are discussed below.

Reading with patience requires making sure to give yourself plenty of time to read the text. If it's a homework assignment, don't start reading for the first time the night before it's due. The sense of urgency—if not panic—that attends a rushed reading assignment can drive the material right out of your head before you can master it. Reading with patience also means eliminating distractions, such as the television blaring in the next room or a device driving songs through those earbuds you're wearing. Too many people in the apartment? Go find a coffee shop with only a few customers. Hit the library and find a comfortable chair in the reading room. Would a snack help or hurt your ability to immerse yourself in the text?

Reading with patience means arranging your environment to enhance the clarity of your reading experience. The optimal environment is different for different people. What if you actually find that television noise or music is a help to your reading? If so, use it, but be honest with yourself about the effect of any external stimulus on your reading. The point is to do whatever you can do to *reduce your resistance to reading*.

Clarify Your Goals Before You Begin to Read

What is it *exactly* that you hope reading this text will do for you? Are you merely looking for a few facts to shore up a point you are making in a paper? Are you cramming for a test? Are you working to establish a general understanding of a particular topic or the contours and details of a many-sided argument? Or are you merely reading to amuse yourself? Whatever the reasons that sent you to the text, remind yourself of them from time to time as you read, comparing what you are finding in the text to whatever it is you are hoping to find. Be ready to revise your goals depending on what you learn from the text. If, for example, you begin reading an article in *Islam Today* about the value of fasting on Ramadan, do you become interested in examining the cohesion-building effects of sacrificial rituals?

Explore the Text's Format

Reconnoiter before Diving In   You need to remember that the writer, whoever it is, wants you to understand his or her writing and has used a variety of devices to help you. If the text has headings and subheadings, read through them first to see if they give you a sense of the author's direction and purpose. Note any distinctions among the headings, some of which may use larger and/ or boldface type to underscore their organizational importance. Understanding the relationship among headings can help you determine the shape of the text's argument.

Are there illustrations? Graphs? Charts? Photographs or drawings? If so, a quick study of them will enhance your understanding of the text's goals and their potential usefulness to you.

Keep in Mind the Writer's Goals

Read carefully the first paragraph or first page of the text, looking for the writer's main idea and strategy for presenting it. Even if you don't find a specific thesis statement—a sentence or two explaining the purpose of the text—bear in mind that most writers will find a way to signal to you what it is they hope their text accomplishes. Sometimes the thesis is in the title, but in other works you may have to search for it. What, for example, is the thesis of the following (abridged) *New York Times* article, "Why Values Voters Value Donald Trump," by Daniel K. Williams?

> As the number of Republican politicians and conservative pundits who renounce Donald J. Trump continues to rise, one important contingent remains steadfast in its support: conservative white evangelicals.
>
> As late as May, a majority of evangelical leaders said they intended to vote against the thrice-married adulterer and longtime supporter of Planned Parenthood. But now white evangelicals are overwhelmingly backing Mr. Trump. . . .
>
> Why? Are they dupes or hypocrites?
>
> The answer is neither. Conservative evangelicals are fully aware of Mr. Trump's flaws, but they are supporting him anyway because they believe his election is the only way they can regain control of the Supreme Court.[1]

Remember, too, that there is always another goal the writer hopes to achieve with any piece of writing: *to change you*—by inviting you to step a little farther and

---

[1]   Daniel K. Williams, "Why Values Voters Value Donald Trump," *New York Times*, August 20, 2016, http://nyti.ms/2bvKvO7.

to look from a slightly different angle into the world of the text, whatever that world might be: religion, politics, cuisine, astronomy, sports, fashion design, music, animal physiology, higher mathematics, film history, or something else. The text is the writer's way of asking you to pass through a doorway into a possibly unfamiliar environment that, the writer is convinced, offers you a worthwhile experience. As you read and understand the text, you are becoming more of an insider in that particular environment and broadening the way you look at the world.

Take Notes

Jot Down Notes Based on Your Early Explorations of Text Features   Your assessment of critical features—headings, illustrations, the introduction—has no doubt set up expectations in your mind about the direction and content of the text. Quickly writing down those expectations, in a list perhaps, and then comparing these notes to what you find as you read the text can help bring it into sharp relief in your mind.

Note-Taking Strategies   Your goal in taking down notes is to help you remember those elements in the text that your reading tells you will be useful to you. Two strategies for effective note-taking stand out:

1. Restating the material from the text in your own language
2. Phrasing notes in a way that establishes a dialogue with the text's writer

Rephrase Noteworthy Material in Your Own Words   Any method of note-taking that requires you to rewrite the text in your own words also requires you to engage the text at its most basic level—that of its language. In order to restate the text, you must understand it. Merely copying the text's words doesn't require the level of engagement that restating does.

Likewise, underlining or highlighting text is usually not a very effective way to "own" the text. It's just too easy. You often find yourself highlighting so many passages that the marking loses its effectiveness. Also, highlighting the text doesn't force you to run the material through your own language-making processes, which means you don't participate in the making of meaning as significantly as you should.

Engage in a Give-and-Take with the Author   In addition to recasting the wording of the text into your own language in your notes, you can enhance your understanding by adopting a note format that actually establishes a dialogue with the author.

Ask Questions   Rather than simply finding equivalents for key words or phrases from the text, you might consider phrasing your note in the form of a question or a criticism aimed at the writer's argument. This sort of give-and-take allows you to clarify and control the range of expectations that occur to you as you read. It's a good way to keep your thinking about the text sharp. For example, after reading the *New York Times* article excerpted above, you might write: "Why do Christian conservatives want, above all, to change the membership of the Supreme Court? Is abortion the only issue that concerns them?"

It takes very little time to formulate useful questions about almost any text. Never forget the six basic questions: *Who? What? When? Where? Why? How?* Practice using these questions in the exploratory stages of your reading until asking them becomes reflexive as you read.

Once you have examined the obvious features of a text and formulated some basic questions, you're ready to read.

Observe How Sentence Structure Aids Understanding

Pay Attention to the Little Words   As we thread our way through the pages of any text, our movement is actually directed by little words, mostly prepositions and conjunctions. These little words don't add facts or narrative information but instead act as traffic signals preparing us for a shift in emphasis or direction. Note how *furthermore, however, on the contrary*, and *nevertheless* reinforce our interpretation of a preceding passage and prepare us to understand how the next passage will fit along with it.

Some words or phrases *add* the meaning of the coming passage to the last one: *also, and, furthermore, not only . . . but also, too*. And some *contrast* the preceding passage with the coming one: *but, despite, nevertheless, instead of, rather than, yet*. The phrase *of course* indicates that the next fact follows obviously from the last one, as does the word *obviously*. Words such as *if, provided*, and *unless* indicate that the truth contained in the passage you've just read may be challenged by what the next passage adds to the argument.

You know these little words so well that it's easy to overlook their usefulness as markers. Don't. They are extremely important to your reading, shoring up your confidence line by line and preparing your mind for the next passage.

Pay Attention to the Rhythms of the Sentences   Often writers invite you to anticipate the way a sentence will move, perhaps by repeating a word, a phrase, or a syntactical structure, setting up a rhythmic expectation in your mind that, when satisfied, adds greatly to your grasp of the passage's meaning.

In his brief address commemorating the establishment of a military cemetery at the Gettysburg Battlefield, Abraham Lincoln used the repetition of a syntactical pattern in order to stop the forward motion of his speech to shift its focus from the audience's participation in the ceremony to the sacrifice that had occasioned the need for the graveyard:

> But in a larger sense we can not dedicate—we can not consecrate—we can not hallow—this ground. The brave men, living and dead, who struggled here, have consecrated it, far above our poor power to add or detract.[2]

As You Read, Be Aware of Other Language Tools

Your writer will employ a range of devices calculated to make you feel comfortable in the world of the text. Look for them and allow them to do their work.

- An *analogy* is a comparison of two things that are similar in some important way. Expect to find your writer composing analogies in which some element of the world of the text—an element unfamiliar to a noninsider—is compared

---

[2]   Abraham Lincoln, "The Gettysburg Address," Abraham Lincoln Online, accessed March 25, 2016, http://abrahamlincolnonline.org/lincoln/speeches/gettysburg.htm.

with some element more common to everyday life. Here's an example, from Elisabeth Kübler-Ross: "People are like stained-glass windows. They sparkle and shine when the sun is out, but when the darkness sets in, their true beauty is revealed only if there is a light from within."[3]

Analogies can be helpful in clarifying concepts that are employed to explain social institutions and behavior. To what extent, for example, is it correct to call America a "melting pot"? To answer this question, you must do considerable research and clarify many concepts and definitions along the way.

- *Concrete details*—details that evoke and engage the senses—can often do more to communicate meaning and intent than the most elaborate abstract description.

Perhaps the most powerful oration delivered by an American religious leader in the last century was the Reverend Martin Luther King Jr.'s "I Have a Dream" speech, delivered at the March on Washington on August 28, 1963. Notice how King skillfully specifies the concrete details of his dream:

I say to you today, my friends, though, even though we face the difficulties of today and tomorrow, I still have a dream. It is a dream deeply rooted in the American dream.

I have a dream that one day this nation will rise up, live out the true meaning of its creed: "We hold these truths to be self-evident: that all men are created equal."

I have a dream that one day on the red hills of Georgia the sons of former slaves and the sons of former slave-owners will be able to sit down together at the table of brotherhood.

I have a dream that one day even the state of Mississippi, a state sweltering with the heat of injustice, sweltering with the heat of oppression, will be transformed into an oasis of freedom and justice.

I have a dream that my four little children will one day live in a nation where they will not be judged by the color of their skin but by the content of their character.

I have a dream . . . I have a dream that one day in Alabama, with its vicious racists, with its governor having his lips dripping with the words of interposition and nullification; one day right there in Alabama little black boys and black girls will be able to join hands with little white boys and white girls as sisters and brothers.

I have a dream today.[4]

Test Your Recollection

It is easy to forget material right after you've learned it, so as you read you'll need to stop occasionally and say back to yourself the material you have just acquired. Recite it to yourself *in your own words* to make sure you have truly assimilated the content. This recollection is an important part of the reading process, but it can be dangerous in that if you stop to recollect too often you can lose your sense of forward motion. So, no matter how often you find yourself stopping to recollect material, and it may happen frequently in a difficult text, try never to stop for long. Remember that the very next sentence may unravel the difficulty that has induced you to make a momentary stop. *Keep going.*

---

[3]   Elisabeth Kübler-Ross, "Quotes," Elisabeth Kübler-Ross Foundation, accessed March 25, 2016, http://www.ekrfoundation.org/quotes.

[4]   Martin Luther King Jr., "'I Have a Dream . . .' Speech by the Rev. Martin Luther King at the 'March on Washington,'" National Archives, accessed November 21, 2016, https://www.archives.gov/files/press/exhibits/dream-speech.pdf.

Reread

The single most effective strategy for mastering a text is to reread it. The first time through, you are finding your way, and the text's concepts, facts, and lines of argument are forming themselves in your mind as you read, which means you have difficulty anticipating the text's direction. To use an analogy, reading a challenging text for the first time is like driving down a twisting country road at night, one you have never traveled before, with only your car's headlights to guide you. But once you've experienced that road, you will be able to navigate it again more confidently, anticipating its tricky turns. The same thing happens when you reread a text. Having been there before, you now know where the argument is going and can see more clearly not only what the writer is trying to say but his or her motives for saying it.

Rereading as an aid to understanding a text is most effective once you have gotten through the *entire* text. Only then will you have experienced the entire shape of the writer's argument and can commit your entire attention to clarifying passages that were difficult during your first run-through.

Pacing Is Vital

How can you possibly pay attention to all the reading tips just discussed and get any sense at all out of the text they are trying to help you understand? Practice. Learning how to improve your reading effectiveness takes time. Try one or two of the suggestions often enough to incorporate them into your reading routine, and then move on to others. The more reading you do, the better you'll get at it, and the wider and more interesting your world will become.

Read&Write 1.1   Analyze a Sermon

In 1741, a Congregationalist pastor and leading figure of the Great Awakening revival (1730–1755) preached one of history's most famous sermons, "Sinners in the Hands of an Angry God." An excerpt from the sermon appears below. Read through it and then read it again, looking for the strategies discussed above for enhancing reader involvement.

I.   There is no want of power in God to cast wicked men into hell at any moment. Men's hands can't be strong when God rises up: The strongest have no power to resist him, nor can any deliver out of his hands. He is not only able to cast wicked men into hell, but he can most easily do it. Sometimes an earthly prince meets with a great deal of difficulty to subdue a rebel, that has found means to fortify himself, and has made himself strong by the numbers of his followers. But it is not so with God. There is no fortress that is any defense from the power of God. Though hand join in hand, and vast multitudes of God's enemies combine and associate themselves, they are easily broken in pieces: They are as great heaps of light chaff before the whirlwind; or large quantities of dry stubble before devouring flames. We find it easy to tread on and crush a worm that we see crawling on the earth; so 'tis easy for us to cut or singe a slender thread that anything hangs by; thus easy is it for God when he pleases to cast his enemies down to hell. What are we, that we should think to stand before him, at whose rebuke the earth trembles, and before whom the rocks are thrown down?

II. They deserve to be cast into hell; so that divine justice never stands in the way, it makes no objection against God's using his power at any moment to destroy them. Yea, on the contrary, justice calls aloud for an infinite punishment of their sins. Divine justice says of the tree that brings forth such grapes of Sodom, "Cut it down, why cumbreth it the ground" (*Luke 13:7*). The sword of divine justice is every moment brandished over their heads, and 'tis nothing but the hand of arbitrary mercy, and God's mere will, that holds it back.

III. They are *already* under a sentence of condemnation to hell. They don't only justly deserve to be cast down thither, but the sentence of the law of God, that eternal and immutable rule of righteousness that God has fixed between him and mankind, is gone out against them, and stands against them; so that they are bound over already to hell. *John 3:18*, "He that believeth not is condemned already." So that every unconverted man properly belongs to hell; that is his place; from thence he is. *John 8:23*, "Ye are from beneath." And thither he is bound; 'tis the place that justice, and God's Word, and the sentence of his unchangeable law assign to him.

IV. They are now the objects of that very *same* anger and wrath of God that is expressed in the torments of hell: and the reason why they don't go down to hell at each moment, is not because God, in whose power they are, is not then very angry with them; as angry as he is with many of those miserable creatures that he is now tormenting in hell, and do there feel and bear the fierceness of his wrath. Yea, God is a great deal more angry with great numbers that are now on earth, yea, doubtless with many that are now in this congregation, that it may be are at ease and quiet, than he is with many of those that are now in the flames of hell. So that it is not because God is unmindful of their wickedness, and don't resent it, that he don't let loose his hand and cut them off. God is not altogether such an one as themselves, though they may imagine him to be so. The wrath of God burns against them, their damnation don't slumber, the pit is prepared, the fire is made ready, the furnace is now hot, ready to receive them, the flames do now rage and glow. The glittering sword is whet, and held over them, and the pit hath opened her mouth under them.

V. The *devil* stands ready to fall upon them and seize them as his own, at what moment God shall permit him. They belong to him; he has their souls in his possession, and under his dominion. The Scripture represents them as his "goods" (*Luke 11:21*). The devils watch them; they are ever by them, at their right hand; they stand waiting for them, like greedy hungry lions that see their prey, and expect to have it, but are for the present kept back; if God should withdraw his hand, by which they are restrained, they would in one moment fly upon their poor souls. The old serpent is gaping for them; hell opens its mouth wide to receive them; and if God should permit it, they would be hastily swallowed up and lost.

VI. There are in the souls of wicked men those hellish *principles* reigning, that would presently kindle and flame out into hell fire, if it were not for God's restraints. There is laid in the very nature of carnal men a foundation for the torments of hell: There are those corrupt principles, in reigning power in them, and in full possession of them, that are seeds of hell fire. These principles are active and powerful, and exceeding violent in their nature, and if it were not for the restraining hand of God upon them, they would soon break out, they would flame out after the same manner as the same corruptions, the same enmity does in the hearts of damned souls, and would beget the same torments in 'em as they do in them.[5]

5   Jonathan Edwards, "Sinners in the Hands of an Angry God," Jonathan Edwards Center at Yale University, accessed November 21, 2016, http://edwards.yale.edu/archive?path=aHR 0cDovL2Vkd2FyZHMueWFsZS5lZHUvY2dpLWJpbi9uZXdwaGlsby9nZXRvYmplY3QucGw /Yy4yMTo0Ny53amVv.

1.2 READING RITUAL AND NARRATIVE

When we hear the word *ritual*, sets of standardized practices within formal events most readily come to mind: church services, marriages, and funerals. But if we give the word a bit more thought, its potential for meaning begins to expand. It's fair to say that, for millions of fans, a baseball game is virtually a religious experience. The pledge to the flag before the game begins; the repeated organ music themes, chants, and waves; hot dogs and Cracker Jacks; hats, shirts, and banners all constitute one great, glorious ritual. Furthermore, most of us would admit that we practice cherished and formalized daily rituals. A good portion of our activity is composed of actions that we perform in a standard or stylized manner at specified times and places and on specific days. When you sit down to study, is it usually at the same place and during the same time of day? If you work out at a gym, do you do the same set of exercises from one day to the next? Do you always sit in the same seat in each of your classes? One of this book's authors, Joel Hopko, confesses, "In fact, my daily rituals are so well known to my cat that he sits patiently waiting for me to get up, eat breakfast, or finish my shower so that he can accompany me on the next phase of my routine." Let's confess, too: We humans love rituals—formal, informal, religious, secular, serious, or fun.

Compared to most cultures, many Americans are serious about their formal rituals. Church services, marriages, and funerals may be pleasant, but they are most often serious, if not somber, events. The wedding may be beautiful, but the fun starts at the reception. Southern African American services are active and joyful in a manner unknown to most Yankee Presbyterians. And yet the rituals of some cultures can be even more raucously joyful still.

One such ritual is recorded in a rich and delightful spiritual narrative by ethnographer and poet John G. Neihardt (1881–1973). In the early 1930s, Neihardt traveled to the Pine Ridge Oglala Sioux Reservation in western South Dakota and had a series of conversations with Black Elk (1863–1950), an Oglala holy man who had participated in the Battle of Little Big Horn and had experienced the crushing defeat of Lakotan sovereignty and the demise of its culture. From his notes on these conversations, Neihardt wrote *Black Elk Speaks*, published in 1932. You should be aware that Neihardt has generated some controversy about the accuracy of some passages in the book, but on the whole, its content conforms to similar narratives. Below is reprinted, by permission, chapter 16 of *Black Elk Speaks*. Although much of this book will provide you practice in writing analytically, allow yourself the pleasure of letting your first reading of the story be appreciative and participatory. Be there. Imagine the sights, sounds, and fragrances. Join the fun.

A quick note of introduction is in order. In this story, Black Elk describes activities of the heyokas, a certain set of Sioux holy men. Heyokas often do all their daily activities backward. They ride horses facing the wrong direction. They cover themselves with dirt to get clean. They erect a tepee to disembark camp. Why? They constantly get their communities to take themselves less seriously, to see the silliness in many things they do, to discover insights about themselves that would never occur to them otherwise. In this story, Black Elk also provides a glimpse of the profoundly life-giving power of spiritual visions and how they can become sources of emotional renewal and happiness.

Twenty days passed, and it was time to perform the dog vision with heyokas. But before I tell you how we did it, I will say something about heyokas and the heyoka ceremony, which seems to be very foolish, but is not so.

Only those who have had visions of the thunder beings of the west can act as heyokas. They have sacred power and they share some of this with all the people, but they do it through funny actions. When a vision comes from the thunder beings of the west, it comes with terror like a thunder storm; but when the storm of vision has passed, the world is greener and happier; for wherever the truth of vision comes upon the world, it is like a rain. The world, you see, is happier after the terror of the storm.

But in the heyoka ceremony, everything is backwards, and it is planned that the people shall be made to feel jolly and happy first, so that it may be easier for the power to come to them. You have noticed that the truth comes into this world with two faces. One is sad with suffering, and the other laughs; but it is the same face, laughing or weeping. When people are already in despair, maybe the laughing face is better for them; and when they feel too good and are too sure of being safe, maybe the weeping face is better for them to see. And so I think that is what the heyoka ceremony is for.

There was a man by the name of Wachpanne (Poor) who took charge of this ceremony for me, because he had acted as a heyoka many times and knew all about it. First he told all the people to gather in a circle on the flat near Pine Ridge, and in the center, near a sacred tepee that was set there, he placed a pot of water which was made to boil by dropping hot stones from a fire into it. First, he had to make an offering of sweet grass to the west. He sat beside the fire with some sweet grass in his hand, and said: "To the Great Spirit's day, to that day grown old and wise, I will make an offering." Then, as he sprinkled the grass upon the fire and the sweet smoke arose, he sang:

This I burn as an offering.
Behold it!
A sacred praise I am making. A sacred praise I am making.
My nation, behold it in kindness!
The day of the sun has been my strength. The path of the moon shall be my robe.
A sacred praise I am making.
A sacred praise I am making.

Then the dog had to be killed quickly and without making any scar, as lightning kills, for it is the power of the lightning that heyokas have.

Over the smoke of the sweet grass a rawhide rope was held to make it sacred. Then two heyokas tied a slip noose in the rope and put this over the neck of the dog. Three times they pulled the rope gently, one at each end of the rope, and the fourth time they jerked it hard, breaking the neck. Then Wachpanne singed the dog and washed it well, and after that he cut away everything but the head, the spine and the tail. Now walking six steps away from the pot, one for each of the Powers, he turned to the west, offering the head and spine to the thunder beings, then to the north, the east and the south, then to the Spirit above and to Mother Earth.

After this, standing where he was, six steps away, he faced the pot and said: "In a sacred manner I thus boil this dog." Three times he swung it, and the fourth time he threw it so that it fell head first into the boiling water. Then he took the heart of the dog and did with it just what he had done with the head and spine.

During all this time, thirty heyokas, one for each day of a moon, were doing foolish tricks among the people to make them feel jolly. They were all dressed and painted in such funny ways that everybody who saw them had to laugh. One Side and I were fellow clowns. We had our bodies painted red all over and streaked with black lightning. The right sides of our heads were shaved, and the hair on the left side was left hanging long. This looked very funny, but it had a meaning; for when we looked toward where you are always facing (the south) the bare sides of our heads were toward the west, which showed that we were humble before the thunder beings who had given us power. Each of us carried a very long bow, so long that nobody could use it, and it was very crooked too. The arrows that we carried were very long and very crooked, so that it looked crazy to have them. We were riding sorrels with streaks of black lightning all over them, for we were to represent the two men of my dog vision.

Wachpanne now went into the sacred tepee, where he sang about the heyokas:

These are sacred,
These are sacred,
They have said,
They have said.
These are sacred,
They have said.

Twelve times he sang this, once for each of the moons.
Afterward, while the pot was boiling, One Side and I, sitting on our painted sorrels, faced the west and sang:

In a sacred manner they have sent voices.
Half the universe has sent voices.
In a sacred manner they have sent voices to you.

Even while we were singing thus, the heyokas were doing foolish things and making laughter. For instance, two heyokas with long crooked bows and arrows painted in a funny way, would come to a little shallow puddle of water. They would act as though they thought it was a wide, deep river that they had to cross; so, making motions, but saying nothing, they would decide to see how deep the river was. Taking their long crooked arrows, they would thrust these into the water, not downward, but flat-wise just under the surface. This would make the whole arrow wet. Standing the arrows up beside them, they would show that the water was far over their heads in depth, so they would get ready to swim. One would then plunge into the shallow puddle head first, getting his face in the mud and fighting the water wildly as though he were drowning. Then the other one would lunge in to save his comrade, and there would be more funny antics in the water to make the people laugh.

After One Side and I had sung to the west, we faced the pot, where the heart and the head of the dog had been boiling. With sharp pointed arrows, we charged on horseback upon the pot and past it. I had to catch the head upon my arrow and One Side had to catch the heart, for we were representing the two men I had seen in the vision. After we had done this, the heyokas all chased us, trying to get a piece of the meat, and the people rushed to the pot, trying to get a piece of the sacred flesh. Ever so little of it would be good for them, for the power of the west was in it now. It was like giving them medicine to make them happier and stronger.

When the ceremony was over, everybody felt a great deal better, for it had been a day of fun. They were better able now to see the greenness of the world, the wideness of the sacred day, the colors of the earth, and to set these in their minds.

The Six Grandfathers have placed in this world many things, all of which should be happy. Every little thing is sent for something, and in that thing there should be happiness and the power to make happy. Like the grasses showing tender faces to each other, thus we should do, for this was the wish of the Grandfathers of the World.[6]

While religious narrative serves to preserve and communicate religious experiences, religious ritual puts our natural affinity for ritual to use so that we can vividly remember and even *re-experience* special events. Unlike our personal rituals, which are largely unconscious, religious rituals are deeply intentional. Participants in a religious ritual pay strict attention to words, tones, settings, gestures, and bodily movements, seeking to immerse themselves in the original experience of awe or rapture. In this sense, religious rituals are the original *virtual reality* machines.

Read&Write 1.2 Appreciate the Lakota Heyoka Ceremony

Write an essay in which you reflect on the Lakota Heyoka Ceremony as depicted in *Black Elk Speaks*. To what extent does the book's account of the ceremony offer you insights into your own life? How and to what extent does the Lakota Heyoka Ceremony inspire you?

1.3 READING MYSTICAL EXPERIENCE AND THE SACRED

Most of us are familiar with déjà vu—a sense that we are repeating an experience we have had before—and some of us can recall an encounter with something we can only describe as supernatural. Incidents involving forces or aspects of experience that appear to clash with or transcend ordinary reality have been a basic aspect of human life from primitive times to the present. Anthropologist Lowell D. Holmes observes, "As we look around the world and see that all men are drawn to a belief in something greater than everyday reality, we find justification for asking why religion of some variety is found everywhere. . . . It appears that all religious behavior represents a response to the wonder and fear of the uncontrollable forces of nature."[7] This experience is often referred to as "mystical," "sacred," or "holy." These words are fitting because they capture something of the emotion created by the experience, but the latter two words have also developed connotations of "ethical perfection" or even "prissiness" that are less than adequate.

Clarifying this ambiguity, German theologian Rudolf Otto coined the term *numinous*. The word derives from the Latin *numen*, meaning "divine will" or "divine power," and captures a comprehensive array of feelings, including awe, wonder, rapture, and fascination. *Numinous* stands to *numen* as *ominous* stands to *omen*. While

---

[6] John G. Neihardt, *Black Elk Speaks: Being the Life Story of a Holy Man of the Oglalah Sioux, as Told through John G. Neihardt (Flaming Rainbow)* (Lincoln: University of Nebraska Press, 1988), 145–49.

[7] Lowell D. Holmes, *Anthropology: An Introduction* (New York: Ronald Press, 1965), 237.

ominous carries great emotional power, it is essentially negative—that is, it refers to something that induces fear or dread. Thus the two words, *numinous* and *ominous*, stand as poles of differing psychological and emotional experience.

The "sacred scriptures" of religions across the world are filled with descriptions and reactions to numinous encounters like that of Moses with the burning bush, that of Muhammad with the angel Gabriel, that of Paul with the resurrected Christ, or—in the *Bhagavad Gita*—Arjuna's encounter with the fearsome aspects of the god Krishna. But experiences of the numinous are hardly confined to scripture or antiquity. The behavior of people from every epoch, circumstance, and class testifies to our continuing human affinity for the numinous.

An interesting example of the emergence of a contemporary "sacred" tradition is provided by the devotions associated with the folk saint Juan Soldado ("Soldier Juan"). An article from the *Atlantic* details the astonishing cultic popularity that grew around an otherwise obscure individual who died in Tijuana in 1938. That year, the local economy was depressed due to the impact of the repeal of Prohibition in the United States and a new casino ban. Tijuana's cantinas and clubs were severely affected as the flow of US revelers slowed. Mass deportations of Mexican nationals from the States deepened the crisis. The rape and murder of an eight-year-old girl provided an added spark for tension within the community. When army private Juan Castillo Morales was identified as the suspect in the crime, the whole town erupted into fury. With mobs threatening to lynch Morales, a military tribunal tried him in a single night, and he was subjected to death by *ley de fuga*, a ritual practiced in Mexico in which a person condemned by a community is given a chance to escape but is shot in the attempt. Private Morales was compelled to run for his life toward the border as a firing squad took aim and brought him down, staining the ground where he fell with his blood. Sympathizers found that it was not possible to clean the blood from the area; declaring this to be a miracle, they built a shrine on the spot.[8]

The cult of Juan Soldado remained a local affair until the late twentieth century, when crowds of northbound migrants found themselves waylaid in Tijuana, unable to cross a US border that had become one of the most protected in the world. While stranded, many migrants discovered the shrine dedicated to Private Juan Castillo—known now as Juan Soldado—and, as they eventually continued their journeys, they carried his legend with them. Many individuals now attribute their successful migrations to prayers offered to the folk saint.[9]

Today many migrants face a modern-day *ley de fuga* as they desperately flee privation, criminal gangs, and hostile forces in an attempt to reach and cross the border. While official Catholicism cannot endorse an unauthorized saint, local priests like Father Jesus Arambarri bear witness to the power of the Soldado cult for those in need. Images of Juan Soldado have appeared across the American Southwest on murals and candles at shrines where prayers are offered in gratitude and in petition for those still trying to cross.[10]

[8] Levy Vonk, "Big in Mexico: The Migrants' Saint," *Atlantic*, June 2016, http://www.theatlantic.com /magazine/archive/2016/06/big-in-mexico/480759.

[9] Ibid.

[10] Ibid.

Read&Write 1.3 Explain the Popularity of Juan Soldado

In a two- or three-page paper explain the popularity of Juan Soldado and come to a conclusion about the extent to which the Soldado phenomenon is unique or else is a typical religious experience. Provide examples from established contemporary or historical religious traditions that support your argument.

1.4 READING SOCIAL COHESION AND ETHICS

Over the past two centuries—contrary to the predictions of many leading intellectuals of the nineteenth and early twentieth centuries, including Karl Marx, Ludwig Feuerbach, and Sigmund Freud—religion has not withered away but remains an integral part of the social, political, and cultural dynamics of the contemporary world. Indeed, over the course of the last century, research among archeologists, sociologists, and cultural anthropologists has fueled a growing consensus that religion plays a central role in the formation, continuation, and evolution of human society and that a primary reason for its success is its potency in providing social cohesion.

The powerful practicality of social cohesion cannot be underestimated. When they met in Philadelphia to draft the Constitution in 1787, the delegates to the Constitutional Convention knew they had one preeminent purpose: to devise a plan for government that would hold society together while preserving rights of conscience and a diversity of economic energies. The nation's second president, John Adams, spoke this widely shared sentiment:

> Suppose a nation in some distant Region should take the Bible for their only law Book, and every member should regulate his conduct by the precepts there exhibited! Every member would be obliged in conscience, to temperance, frugality, and industry; to justice, kindness, and charity towards his fellow men; and to piety, love, and reverence toward Almighty God. . . . What a Eutopia, what a Paradise would this region be.[11]

The pioneering work of sociologist Emile Durkheim (1858–1917) with Australian tribal groups led him to propose that religion serves as the glue that holds societies together. By the mid-twentieth century, anthropologist Lowell D. Holmes could observe that

> in nearly every society religion embodies an expression and reaffirmation of its central values . . . every society has its set of sanctions (action it approves) and taboos (actions it forbids), which are made more powerful by the threat of supernatural punishment. These acts are considered so important that some power greater than man must enforce them.[12]

[11] John Adams, *Diary and Autobiography of John Adams* (Cambridge, MA: Belknap Press of Harvard University Press, 1961), 3:9.
[12] Holmes, *Anthropology*, 246.

Holmes quotes his colleague Francis Hsu, to elaborate:

> Each society, in order to safeguard the individual and the group, has a particular set
> of symbols with which to express its corporate concern in the problems of existence.
> This concern has two facets: the solidarity of the group at any moment and the sur-
> vival of the group through time.[13]

Although these commentators do not deny that religious factionalism has often rup-
tured nations and increased antagonisms among them, the binding force of common belief has also often cemented alliances.

Read&Write 1.4   Explain How New Religious Movements Achieve Social Cohesion

In a seminal summary article published in the *Atlantic* addressing the continuing vitality
of new religious movements (NRMs), author Toby Lester provides many insights into the
mechanisms through which NRMs and religions in general thrive and provide social cohesion.[14] You will find access to Lester's article online through your campus library. While
reading this article, create a list of at least a dozen mechanisms that religions and religious
movements use to achieve social cohesion.

1.5   READING DOCTRINE

During the 2016 presidential election, considerable publicity was given to the split in
the normally nearly unanimous political position of America's Evangelicals between
supporters and opponents of Republican candidate Donald Trump. Not even the
best efforts of conservative Christian leadership could close this gap. Conservative
Christianity, which commands the allegiance of an energetic minority of America's
population, holds positions that reflect a reaction to a secular, postmodern, atom-
ized culture. Its intermittent political strength over the last several decades illustrates
the singularly effective role of religion in maintaining social cohesion over time. Yes,
political factions like the Vietnam antiwar movement or Bernie Sanders's political
reform movement come and go, but they lack the stamina of religions in this respect.

A common activity of all religions as they develop is to formulate core beliefs and
then establish distinctive practices and rules for ordering human life. These normative rules, called *doctrines* (i.e., teachings) or even *dogmas* (teachings formally issued
and considered definitive for the religion or organization), are often controversial.
And Evangelicals tend to formulate controversial doctrines that interface with public
policy, raising long-standing questions about the proper relationship of church and
state. Evangelicals managed, for example, to have some of their doctrines inserted
in the *Republican Platform 2016*, including positions against gay marriage, antigay

[13]   Ibid.
[14]   Toby Lester, "Oh, Gods!" *Atlantic*, February 2002, http://www.theatlantic.com/magazine
        /archive/2002/02/oh-gods/302412.

discrimination, and abortion; and for biblical studies in public schools. Here are excerpts from the platform document:

> The American family . . . is the foundation of civil society, and the cornerstone of the family is natural marriage, the union of one man and one woman. . . .
>
> We oppose government discrimination against businesses or entities which decline to sell items or services to individuals for activities that go against their religious views about such activities. . . .
>
> We support the appointment of judges who respect traditional family values and the sanctity of innocent human life. . . .
>
> A good understanding of the Bible being indispensable for the development of an educated citizenry, we encourage state legislatures to offer the Bible in a literature curriculum as an elective in America's high schools.[15]

Doctrines play a pivotal role within the broader context of the effects of religion in societies. Religions provide both social cohesion and opportunities for conflict and schisms. With respect to social cohesion, history affirms the beneficial role that religions continue to play. We need look no further than the deeply spiritual but nonsectarian Mohandas Gandhi, who saved more lives than any other single person in history. His successful nonviolent crusades liberated India from British colonial rule and prevented hundreds of thousands of Indian Hindus and Muslims from engaging in a bitter civil war. In addition, we may cite Pope Francis's offering desperately needed hope to millions of impoverished South Americans, continuing work based on Mother Teresa's efforts to comfort the poor, and the universally inspiring messages of the Dalai Lama. We also see how our communities benefit from a myriad of local religious organizations providing assistance and inspiration throughout the world. All these activities serve to bind communities in common purpose.

But the societal roles of religions change over time. Christianity has been both a persecuted outlaw sect and the state religion of the Roman Empire and many of its successor states. One effect of the Reformation was a revitalized discussion of the proper roles of the *ecclesiastical sword*, wielded by the church, and the *secular sword*, wielded by ruling monarchs. By the middle of the fifteenth century, papal supremacy was challenged when, in principalities across Europe, masses of people accepted the new doctrines of Protestant reformers Martin Luther, John Calvin, John Knox, and others, a situation calling for a new understanding of proper church-state relations. This ended a millennium of assumed Roman Catholic Church superiority to any secular powers, which had been seen not as independently inherent, but as deriving from ecclesiastical authority.

The Anabaptists, led by Menno Simons and others, preached complete church-state separation and the unequivocal superiority of their church over the state within their own Christian community. The other reformers, however, agreed that both religious and secular powers derived just authority from God, and, therefore, both had a viable role in managing society. But significant differences also arose. While Calvin saw no problem with a unified political-ecclesiastical power and the establishment of a rigid theocracy in the city of Geneva, Luther believed that placing the same people in positions of both ecclesiastical and secular authority would damage church and

---

[15] RNC Platform Committee, *Republican Platform 2016*, July 18, 2016, https://prod-cdn-static.gop .com/media/documents/DRAFT_12_FINAL[1]-ben_1468872234.pdf.

state. But Luther affirmed the unified action of both authorities in maintaining social order when disruptive social movements arose—such as the rebellion led by Thomas Muntzer—and he advocated acceptance of a common theology by both agencies.

The US Constitution instituted a program largely in accord with Luther's formulation. The First Amendment reads, "Congress shall make no law respecting an establishment of religion." This carefully worded phrase allowed for states to legislate established churches, which several did through the early decades of the nineteenth century. These churches, though supported by the states, had independent administrations.

In the twentieth century, breaking with Roman Catholicism's traditional insistence that *legitimate* secular governments were bound to establish and protect *only* the Roman Catholic faith, the Second Vatican Council issued a new understanding of church-state relations that affirmed the stand of Luther while advocating a cooperative church-state relationship to advance common goals.

> The Church, by reason of her role and competence, is not identified in any way with the political community nor bound to any political system. She is at once a sign and a safeguard of the transcendent character of the human person. The Church and the political community in their own fields are autonomous and independent from each other. Yet both, under different titles, are devoted to the personal and social vocation of the same men. The more that both foster sounder cooperation between themselves with due consideration for the circumstances of time and place, the more effective will their service be exercised for the good of all. For man's horizons are not limited only to the temporal order; while living in the context of human history, he preserves intact his eternal vocation.[16]

Events since the end of the twentieth century show that questions regarding the appropriate roles of church and state are far from confined to Christianity or the West. Throughout the Muslim world, Islamist parties have battled with more "secular" groups for control of nations, the implementation of *shari'a* law, or even the establishment of a Pan-Islamic "caliphate." A controversy over the legality of burkas, traditional Muslim female apparel, poses a dilemma for the French, who strongly advocate both personal freedom and rejection of the subjugation of women. Similar conflicts rock the modern state of Israel as hard-line elements within Judaism control social policy, notwithstanding the resistance of more moderate Israelis, including the state's original founders.

In India, a newly militant Hinduism seeks to impose its face on the national identity of a society long distinguished by tribalism and religious syncretism. In Sri Lanka and Myanmar, Buddhist militants challenge more secular status quos. Even Russia, long thought of as atheistic or secularist, has increasingly looked to the Orthodox faith to provide the foundation for its drive to reestablish its national and cultural identity.

So familiar church-state controversies continue. Let's look a bit more deeply into controversies generated by recent Evangelical political activism. As Evangelicals exercise their constitutional rights to engage public policy, they instigate a continuing stream of disputes. Are prayers at the local football game legitimate? Can a stone engraved with the Ten Commandments be placed on the lawn of a public

---

[16] *Pastoral Constitution on the Church in the Modern World, Gadium et Spes,* §76, December 7, 1965.

building? Does intelligent design deserve mention in science textbooks? Yes, doctrine-generated church-state controversies are alive and well. Kathy Gilsinan's article "The Church of the Flying Spaghetti Monster," published in the November 2016 issue of the *Atlantic* and reprinted here in its entirety, with permission, provides an entertaining example.

This spring, the Infrastructure Ministry in Brandenburg, Germany, found itself litigating what counts as religion. The ministry typically concerns itself with worldly issues like road signage. But then the Church of the Flying Spaghetti Monster (FSM) sought a road sign of the sort that local Catholic and Protestant churches receive from the German state.

The ensuing legal skirmish—a court ultimately sided with the Infrastructure Ministry, which argued that FSM wasn't "a recognized religious community"—was the outgrowth of a different controversy more than a decade ago and 5,000 miles away. In 2005, the Kansas Board of Education voted to let public schools teach the creationist theory of intelligent design alongside evolution, arguing, among other things, that you couldn't prove a supernatural being *hadn't* given rise to life. A 24-year-old with a degree in physics named Bobby Henderson responded on his website that you also couldn't prove a flying spaghetti monster hadn't created the universe. Why not teach that theory as well?

The Kansas board reversed itself within two years, but the semi-parodic Church of the Flying Spaghetti Monster has outlasted the dispute, spreading via the internet to countries around the world. As FSM has taken root in Europe, where evolution is fairly uncontroversial, its purpose has shifted somewhat, with followers using it to test the relationship between Church and state in countries ranging from relatively secular France to heavily Catholic Poland.

There's no official count of Church membership in Europe (or anywhere else), but "Pastafarian" Facebook pages from countries across the Continent have accumulated thousands of likes, while, country by country, FSM members have waged and even won legal battles for the privileges enjoyed by other religions. Along the way, something funny has happened to a movement founded in large part to critique organized religion: It's gotten organized, and has taken on both the trappings and some of the social functions of a real religion.

FSM has its own iconography (the deity features, in addition to spaghetti, two meatballs and a pair of eyes) as well as a Sabbath (Friday, because "our god was faster than the other gods, and he finished with the creation of Earth earlier"). The flagship German church, in Brandenburg, features a weekly mass modeled on the Catholic celebration, but with noodles and beer in place of bread and wine. FSM officiants even conduct weddings in several countries; this year, New Zealand became the first to legally recognize these marriages.

In Austria, a onetime church leader named Niko Alm started a tradition of "religious headgear" (an overturned colander), winning the right to wear it in his ID photo. "Headgear is not allowed in driver's licenses, except for religious reasons," he explained. "So I invented a religious reason." Since then, he told me, the headgear has been adopted in "virtually every country that has Pastafarianism"—with some countries allowing it in official photos. Even as a US court this year denied a Nebraska prisoner's request to practice the Pastafarian faith, ruling FSM a parody and not a religion, the Netherlands chamber of commerce went the other way, becoming the first country to grant Pastafarians "official status." Alm says there is "high variation" in Church practices by country, save for some common elements like pirate costumes and beer. Austrian Pastafarians, he said, don't do a weekly service like Brandenburg's Nudelmasse; instead, "we meet, like, three or four times a year and drink beer." And whereas the Austrian Church concentrates on changing laws, he maintains that the British "only do the fun parts." In Russia, where the Church is particularly active, eight Pastafarians were detained for holding an unauthorized "pasta procession" in 2013; on a more recent visit to the country, Alm "signed hundreds of colanders."

FSM's big idea, in Russia as in Kansas, is that "nothing is inherently sacred; it's sacred by virtue of the fact that people agree that it's sacred," says Douglas Cowan, a religious-studies professor at Renison University College, in Canada. As if to underscore the point, the Church may be the only one in the world with a God-back guarantee: If you're not satisfied, Henderson has pointed out, "your old religion will most likely take you back."[17]

To be sure, Pastafarian theology is a parody of the doctrines of major religions. While injecting some humor into doctrinal disputes, Pastafarians are nevertheless serious. Their doctrines ridicule traditional religions. Finding intelligent design (a doctrine often accompanied by a denial of human-made climate change) to be a dangerous attack on science, Pastafarians direct their doctrinal arrows to the heart and soul of traditional religion—namely, the existence of traditional scriptural gods.[18]

Read&Write 1.5   Explore Doctrinal Options for the Separation of Church and State

Advancing political agendas, Pastafarian doctrines pose important legal and constitutional questions for American governments. Here are three clusters of such questions:

- *Did the Kansas Board of Education, in 2005, by voting to let public schools teach the theory of intelligent design, create an unconstitutional establishment of religion?* Is intelligent design inherently a religious doctrine? Is a court or other government body qualified to determine whether intelligent design is science? Is a court or other government body qualified to determine whether astrology is science? Is Bobby Henderson's response to the board's argument—that if you can argue that you can't prove a supernatural being did *not* create the universe, then you can argue that you also can't prove a Flying Spaghetti Monster did *not* create the universe—a valid argument?
- *To what extent is Pastafarianism a religion?* Legal status as a religion provides certain privileges, including nonprofit tax status and support for conscientious objection. Can just any group of "colander-capped beer-drinking noodle-eaters" claim status as a church and thereby gain the privileges that accompany that status?
- *What constitutes legitimate religious doctrine?* Does a theology have to embrace a single god? Christians reject all gods except the one attested to in the Bible. Muslims reject all gods but Allah. Numerous religions worldwide accept all gods (*pantheism*). Can a case be made that Pastafarians, who reject all gods, have a legitimate theology? Can science—an epistemological and ontological belief system—be a legitimate theology?

---

[17]   Kathy Gilsinan, "Big in Europe: The Church of the Flying Spaghetti Monster," *Atlantic*, November 2016, 23.

[18]   Bobby Henderson, *The Gospel of the Flying Spaghetti Monster* (New York: Villard, 2006).

Your objective in this exercise is challenging. You will find more information about Pastafarian doctrine on a variety of websites. In his book, *The Gospel of the Flying Spaghetti Monster*, Bobby Henderson provides a thorough exposition of Pastafarian theology. In an essay of up to ten pages, answer the following questions:

1. Did the Kansas Board of Education, by voting in 2005 to let public schools teach the theory of intelligent design, create an unconstitutional establishment of religion?
2. To what extent is Pastafarianism a legitimate religion?
3. What constitutes legitimate religious doctrine, and does Pastafarian doctrine qualify?

2

READ AND WRITE

EFFECTIVELY

Writing is a way of ordering your experience. Think about it. No matter what you are writing—it may be a paper for your comparative religions class, a short story, a limerick, a grocery list—you are putting pieces of your world together in new ways and making yourself freshly conscious of those pieces. This is one of the reasons why writing is so hard. From the infinite welter of data that your mind continually processes and locks in your memory, you are selecting only certain items significant to the task at hand, relating them to other items, and phrasing them with a new coherence. You are mapping a part of your universe that has hitherto been unknown territory. You are gaining a little more control over the processes by which you interact with the world around you.

This is why the act of writing, no matter what its result, is never insignificant. It is always *communication*—if not with another human being, then with yourself. It is a way of making a fresh connection with your world.

Writing, therefore, is also one of the best ways to learn. This statement may sound odd at first. If you are an unpracticed writer, you may share a common notion that the only purpose of writing is to express what you already know or think. According to this view, any learning that you as a writer might have experienced has already occurred by the time your pen meets the paper; your task is thus to inform and even surprise the reader. But, if you are a practiced writer, you know that at any moment as you write, you are capable of surprising yourself. And it is that surprise that you look for: the shock of seeing what happens in your own mind when you drop an old, established opinion into a batch of new facts or bump into a cherished belief from a different angle. Writing synthesizes new understanding for the writer. E. M. Forster's famous question, "How do I know what I think until I see what I say?"[1] is one that all of us could ask. We make meaning as we write, jolting ourselves by little, surprising discoveries into a larger and more interesting universe.

A Simultaneous Tangle of Activities

One reason that writing is difficult is that it is not actually a single activity at all but a process consisting of several activities (that will be discussed later in this chapter).

---

[1]   E. M. Forster, *Aspects of the Novel* (New York: Harvest, 1956), 101.

The activities can overlap, with two or more sometimes operating simultaneously as you labor to organize and phrase your thoughts. The writing process, an often-frustrating search for both meaning and the best way to articulate that meaning, tends to be sloppy for everyone.

Frustrating though that search may sometimes be, it need not be futile. Remember this: The writing process uses skills that we all have. In other words, the ability to write is not some magical competence bestowed on the rare, fortunate individual. We are all capable of phrasing thoughts clearly and in a well-organized fashion. But learning how to do so takes practice.

The one sure way to improve your writing is to write.

One of the toughest but most important jobs in writing is to maintain enthusiasm for your writing project. Such commitment may sometimes be hard to achieve, given the difficulties that are inherent in the writing process and that worsen when the project is unappealing at first glance. How, for example, can you be enthusiastic about having to write a paper comparing the meditative practices of Hinduism and Buddhism when you have never once thought about meditation and can see no use in doing so now?

Sometimes unpracticed student writers fail to assume responsibility for keeping themselves interested in their writing. No matter how hard it may seem at first to drum up interest in your topic, you have to do it—that is, if you want to write a paper you can be proud of, one that contributes useful material and a fresh point of view to the topic. One thing is guaranteed: If you are bored with your writing, your reader will be, too. So what can you do to keep your interest and energy level high?

Challenge yourself. Think of the paper not as an assignment but as a piece of writing that has a point to make. To get this point across persuasively is the real reason you are writing, not because a teacher has assigned you a project. If someone were to ask you why you are writing your paper and your immediate, unthinking response is, "Because I've been given a writing assignment" or "Because I want a good grade" or some other nonanswer along these lines, your paper may be in trouble.

If, on the other hand, your first impulse is to explain the challenge of your main point—"I'm writing to show how culture affects theology"—then you are thinking usefully about your topic.

Maintain Self-Confidence

Having confidence in your ability to write well about your topic is essential for good writing. This does not mean that you will always know what the result of a particular writing activity will be. In fact, you must cultivate your ability to tolerate a high degree of uncertainty while weighing evidence, testing hypotheses, and experimenting with organizational strategies and wording. Be ready for temporary confusion and for seeming dead ends, and remember that every writer faces these obstacles. Out of your struggle to combine fact with fact and to buttress conjecture with evidence, order will arise.

Do not be intimidated by the amount and quality of work that others have already done in your field of inquiry. The array of opinion and evidence that confronts you in the literature can be confusing. But remember that no important topic is ever exhausted. There are always gaps, questions that have not been satisfactorily explored in either the published research or the prevailing popular opinion. It is in these gaps that you establish your own authority, your own sense of control.

Remember that the various stages of the writing process reinforce each other. Establishing a solid motivation strengthens your sense of confidence about the project, which in turn influences how successfully you organize and write. If you start out well, use good work habits, and allow ample time for the various activities to coalesce, you should produce a paper that will reflect your best work, one that your audience will find both readable and useful.

2.1   GET INTO THE FLOW OF WRITING

The Nature of the Process

As you engage in the writing process, you are doing many things at once. While planning, you are, no doubt, defining the audience for your paper at the same time that you are thinking about its purpose. As you draft the paper, you may organize your next sentence while revising the one you have just written. Different parts of the writing process overlap, and much of the difficulty of writing occurs because so many things happen at once. Through practice—in other words, through *writing*—it is possible to learn to control those parts of the process that can in fact be controlled and to encourage those mysterious, less controllable activities.

No two people go about writing in exactly the same way. It is important to recognize the routines, modes of thought as well as individual exercises, that help you negotiate the process successfully. It is also important to give yourself as much time as possible to complete the process. Procrastination is one of the writer's greatest enemies. It saps confidence, undermines energy, and destroys concentration. Writing regularly and following a well-planned schedule as closely as possible often make the difference between a successful paper and an embarrassment.

Although the various parts of the writing process are interwoven, there is naturally a general order in the work of writing. You have to start somewhere! What follows is a description of the various stages of the writing process—planning, drafting, revising, editing, and proofreading—along with suggestions on how to approach each most successfully.

Plan   Planning includes all activities that lead to the writing of the first draft of a paper. The particular activities in this stage differ from person to person. Some writers, for instance, prefer to compile a formal outline before writing the draft. Others perform brief writing exercises to jump-start their imaginations. Some draw diagrams; some doodle. Later, we will look at a few starting strategies, and you can determine which may help you.

Now, however, let us discuss certain early choices that all writers must make during the planning stage. These choices concern *topic*, *purpose*, and *audience*, elements that make up the writing context, or the terms under which we all write. Every time you write, even if you are only writing a diary entry or a note to the mail carrier, these elements are present. You may not give conscious consideration to all of them in each piece of writing that you do, but it is extremely important to think carefully about them when writing a religion paper. Some or all of these defining elements may be dictated by your assignment, yet you will always have a degree of control over them.

Select a Topic No matter how restrictive an assignment may seem, there is no reason to feel trapped by it. Within any assigned subject you can find a range of topics to explore. What you are looking for is a topic that engages your own interest. Let your curiosity be your guide. If, for example, you have been assigned the subject of comparing an important ritual from one faith with that from another, then guide yourself to find some issue concerning the topic that interests you. (For example, how do the Jewish bar mitzvah and the Catholic confirmation, both foundational confirmation rituals, compare in terms of the rigor entailed by preparation for the event? How do the doctrinal bases of these two rituals differ?) Any good topic comes with a set of questions; you may well find that your interest increases if you simply begin asking questions. One strong recommendation: Ask your questions *on paper*. Like most mental activities, the process of exploring your way through a topic is transformed when you write down your thoughts as they come, instead of letting them fly through your mind unrecorded. Remember the words of Louis Agassiz: "A pen is often the best of eyes."[2]

Although it is vital to be interested in your topic, you do not have to know much about it at the outset of your investigation. In fact, having too heartfelt a commitment to a topic can be an impediment to writing about it; emotions can get in the way of objectivity. It is often better to choose a topic that has piqued your interest yet remained something of a mystery to you—a topic discussed in one of your classes, perhaps, or mentioned on television or in a conversation with friends.

Narrow the Topic The task of narrowing your topic offers you a tremendous opportunity to establish a measure of control over the writing project. It is up to you to hone your topic to just the right shape and size to suit both your own interests and the requirements of the assignment. Do a good job of it, and you will go a long way toward guaranteeing yourself sufficient motivation and confidence for the tasks ahead. However, if you do not do it well, somewhere along the way you may find yourself directionless and out of energy.

Generally, the first topics that come to your mind will be too large for you to handle in your research paper. For example, the subject of the immigration of Muslim refugees from Syria generates many news reports. Yet despite all the attention, there is still plenty of room for you to investigate the topic on a level that has real meaning for you and that does not merely recapitulate the published research. What about an analysis of how Syrian immigrants contribute to the cultural life of American communities?

The problem with most topics is not that they are too narrow or have been too completely explored, but rather that they are so rich that it is often difficult to choose the most useful way to address them. Take some time to narrow your topic. Think through the possibilities that occur to you and, as always, jot down your thoughts.

Students in an undergraduate course on mysticism were told to write an essay of 2,500 words on one of the issues shown below. Next to each general topic is an example of how students narrowed it into a manageable paper topic.

---

[2] Catherine Owens Pearce, *A Scientist of Two Worlds: Louis Agassiz* (Philadelphia: Lippincott, 1958), 106.

General Topic	Narrowed Topic
Seeking God	Techniques for experiencing the divine
Qualities of Divinity	Personalities of gods
Varieties of revelation	Mystical visions
Emotional benefits of mystical experience	Contentment

EXERCISE

Without doing research, see how you can narrow the general topics shown below.

Example

General topic	The Amish as community builders
Narrowed topics	The benefits of solidarity in Amish communities
	Pressures to conform to religious norms in Amish communities
	Maintaining traditions in Amish communities

General Topics

ritual	Islam	faith
sin	salvation	stewardship
theology	Scripture	saints
absolution	Heaven	epiphany

Find a Thesis   As you plan your writing, be on the lookout for an idea that can serve as your thesis. A *thesis* is not a fact, which can be immediately verified by data, but an assertion worth discussing, an argument with more than one possible conclusion. Your thesis sentence will reveal to your reader not only the argument you have chosen but also your orientation toward it and the conclusion that your paper will attempt to prove.

In looking for a thesis, you are doing many jobs at once:

- You are limiting the amount and kind of material that you must cover, thus making them manageable.
- You are increasing your own interest in the narrowing field of study.
- You are working to establish your paper's purpose, the reason you are writing about your topic. (If the only reason you can see for writing is to earn a good grade, then you probably won't!)
- You are establishing your notion of who your audience is and what sort of approach to the subject might best catch its interest.

In short, you are gaining control over your writing context. For this reason, it is a good idea to come up with a thesis early on, a *working thesis*, that will very probably change as your thinking deepens but will allow you to establish a measure of order in the planning stage.

The Thesis Sentence The introduction of your paper will contain a sentence that expresses the task that you intend to accomplish. This *thesis sentence* communicates your main idea, the one you are going to prove, defend, or illustrate. It sets up an expectation in the reader's mind that it is your job to satisfy. But, in the planning stage, a thesis sentence is more than just the statement that informs your reader of your goal: It is a valuable tool to help you narrow your focus and confirm in your own mind your paper's purpose.

Developing a Thesis Students in a class on Islam were assigned a twenty-page paper on an aspect of the historical development of the religion. The choice of the aspect was left to the students. One, Nora Shuttlebee, decided to investigate the relationship between economics and the development of factions within the first half millennium of Islamic history. Her first working thesis was as follows:

> Shia and Sunni Muslims have similar theologies but different ethnic traditions, which express themselves in political and economic competitions.

The problem with this thesis, as Nora found out, was that it was not an idea that could be argued, but rather a fact that could be easily corroborated by the sources she began to consult. As she read reports from such groups as the Islamic Research Foundation and the Islamic Research Institute and talked with representatives from local Muslim groups, she began to get interested in efforts to strengthen ties within Islamic sects and traditions. Nora's second working thesis was as follows:

> Cultural competitions among Muslims in Sunni-dominated nations wherein Shia Muslims are persecuted create substantial challenges for NGOs working toward reconciliation.

While her second thesis narrowed the topic somewhat and gave Nora an opportunity to use material from her research, there was still no real comment attached to it. It still stated a bare fact, easily proved. At this point, Nora became interested in the even narrower topic of how groups seeking reconciliation focus their energies on political equality for Shias. As Nora explored the success or failure of various reconciliation efforts, she began to focus on a central problem for the reconciliation activists. As a result, Nora developed her third working thesis:

> Because NGOs working for Muslim reconciliation are quickly labeled as fronts for pro-Shia interests in Western countries, an increased focus on efforts to educate Sunni populations about the benefits of reconciliation would be helpful to all concerned.

Note how this thesis narrows the focus of Nora's paper even further than the other two had, while also presenting an arguable hypothesis. It tells Nora what she has to do in her paper, just as it tells her readers what to expect.

At some time during your preliminary thinking on a topic, you should consult a library to see how much published work on your issue exists. This search has at least two benefits:

1. It acquaints you with a body of writing that will become very important in the research phase of your paper.
2. It gives you a sense of how your topic is generally addressed by the community of scholars you are joining. Is the topic as important as you think it is? Has there been so much research on the subject as to make your inquiry, in its present formulation, irrelevant?

As you go about determining your topic, remember that one goal of your religion writing in college is always to enhance your own understanding of religious traditions, to build an accurate model of the way religions work. Let this goal help you direct your research into those areas that you know are important to your knowledge of the discipline.

Define a Purpose   There are many ways to classify the purposes of writing, but in general most writing is undertaken either to inform or to persuade an audience. The goal of informative, or expository, writing is simply to impart information about a particular subject, whereas the aim of persuasive writing is to convince your reader of your point of view on an issue. The distinction between expository and persuasive writing is not hard and fast, and most writing in religion has elements of both types. Most effective writing, however, is clearly focused on either exposition or persuasion. An assignment to interview a local religious leader is clearly expository, because you will try to present clearly a person's comments and views. But an assignment to apply exegetical methods to three pericopes calls on you to interpret part of a religious text; therefore, you will need to persuade. When you begin writing, consciously select a primary approach of exposition or persuasion, and then set out to achieve that goal. Remember, as you do so, that this initial determination of focus may, like any other aspect of the paper, change as your exploration of the topic deepens.

Read&Write 2.1   Explain or Persuade

Can you tell from the titles of these two papers, both on the same topic, which is an **expository** paper and which is a **persuasive** paper?

1. Recent Developments in Taoism
2. Why Taoism Is Adopting More Traditional Institutional and Liturgical Practices

Learn What You Want to Say   By the time you write your final draft, you must have a very sound notion of the point you wish to argue. If, as you write that final draft, someone were to ask you to state your thesis, you should be able to give a satisfactory answer with a minimum of delay and no prompting. If, on the other hand, you have to hedge your answer because you cannot easily express your thesis, you may not yet be ready to write a final draft. You may have to write a draft or two or engage in various prewriting activities to form a secure understanding of your task.

EXERCISE   Knowing What You Want to Say

Two writers have been asked to state the thesis of their papers. Which one better understands the writing task?

Writer 1: "My paper is about American Muslims."

Writer 2: "My paper argues that efforts by American Muslims to find acceptance in American communities meet substantial, unwarranted resistance from American fundamentalist Christians."

Watch Out for Bias! There is no such thing as pure objectivity. You are not a machine. No matter how hard you may try to produce an objective paper, the fact is that every choice you make as you write is influenced to some extent by your personal beliefs and opinions. In other words, what you tell your readers is truth is influenced, sometimes without your knowledge, by a multitude of factors: your environment, upbringing, and education; your attitude toward your audience; your religious and political affiliations; your race and gender; your career goals; and your ambitions for the paper you are writing. The influence of such factors can be very subtle, and it is something you must work to identify in your own writing as well as in the writing of others in order not to mislead or to be misled. Remember that one of the reasons for writing is *self-discovery*. The writing you will do in religion classes—as well as the writing you will do for the rest of your life—will give you a chance to discover and confront honestly your own views on your subjects. Responsible writers keep an eye on their own biases and are honest about them with their readers.

Define Your Audience In any class that requires you to write, you may sometimes find it difficult to remember that the point of your writing is not simply to jump through the technical hoops imposed by the assignment. Rather, the point is *communication*—the transmission of your knowledge and your conclusions to readers in a way that suits you. Your task is to pass on to your readers the spark of your own enthusiasm for your topic. Readers who were indifferent to your topic before reading your paper should look at it in a new way after finishing it. This is the great challenge of writing: to enter into a reader's mind and leave behind both new knowledge and new questions.

It is tempting to think that most writing problems would be solved if the writer could view the writing as if another person had produced it. The discrepancy between the understanding of the writer and that of the audience is the single greatest impediment to accurate communication. To overcome this barrier, you must consider your audience's needs. By the time you begin drafting, most, if not all, of your ideas will have begun to attain coherent shape in your mind, so that virtually any words with which you try to express those ideas will reflect your thought accurately—to you. Your readers, however, do not already hold the conclusions that you have so painstakingly achieved. If you omit from your writing the material that is necessary to complete your readers' understanding of your argument, they may well be unable to supply that information themselves.

The potential for misunderstanding is present for any audience, whether it is made up of general readers, experts in the field, or your professor, who is reading in part to see how well you have mastered the constraints that govern the relationship between writer and reader. Make your presentation as complete as possible, bearing in mind your audience's knowledge of your topic.

2.2   THINK CREATIVELY

We have discussed various methods of selecting and narrowing the topic of a paper. As your focus on a specific topic sharpens, you will naturally begin to think about the kinds of information that will go into the paper. In the case of papers that do not require formal research, this material will come largely from your own recollections. Indeed, one of the reasons instructors assign such papers is to convince you of the incredible richness of your memory, the vastness and variety of the "database" that you have accumulated and that, moment by moment, you continue to build.

So vast is your hoard of information that it can sometimes be difficult to find within it the material that would best suit your paper. In other words, finding out what you already know about a topic is not always easy. *Invention*, a term borrowed from classical rhetoric, refers to the task of discovering, or recovering from memory, such information. As we write, we go through some sort of invention procedure that helps us explore our topic. Some writers seem to have little problem coming up with material; others need more help. Over the centuries, writers have devised different exercises that can help locate useful material housed in memory. We will look at a few of these briefly.

Freewriting

Freewriting is an activity that forces you to get something down on paper. There is no waiting around for inspiration. Instead, you set a time limit—perhaps three to five minutes—and write for that length of time without stopping, not even to lift the pen from the paper or your hands from the keyboard. Focus on the topic, and do not let the difficulty of finding relevant material stop you from writing. If necessary, you may begin by writing, over and over, some seemingly useless phrase, such as, "I cannot think of anything to write," or perhaps the name of your topic. Eventually, something else will occur to you. (It is surprising how long a three-minute period of freewriting can seem to last!) At the end of the freewriting, look over what you have produced for anything you might be able to use. Much of the writing will be unusable, but there might be an insight or two that you did not know you had.

In addition to its ability to help you recover usable material from your memory for your paper, freewriting has certain other benefits. First, it takes little time, which means that you may repeat the exercise as often as you like. Second, it breaks down some of the resistance that stands between you and the act of writing. There is no initial struggle to find something to say; you just write.

For his introductory world religions class, Mitchell Staats had to write a paper on some aspect of Hinduism. Mitchell, who felt his understanding of Hinduism was slight, began the job of finding a topic that interested him with two minutes of freewriting. Thinking about Hinduism, Mitchell typed slowly but steadily for this period without stopping. Here is the result of his freewriting:

Okay okay Hinduism. Hindu, what does that mean? Like was Hindu a god? Or was Irving K. Hindu—or whoever—the religion's founder? Does the word "Hindu" mean, "He who contemplates his navel?" Boy, am I ignorant! Are Hindus those guys in orange robes who used to make a nuisance of themselves in airports? Is it those guys who drive taxis in NYC?. All I know is stereotypes. Sacred cows. Big Indian temples with monks who hum all day. Ari Krishna and George Harrison. Maybe find a good overview, something better than Wikipedia. Find out how many Hindus there are and where they live. Find out their basic beliefs. Do they still have a rigid caste system? Are the untouchables a problem for Eliot Ness? Maybe find out the core beliefs and read some of the important scriptures? Lots of research to do. Where to start?

Brainstorming

Brainstorming is simply the process of making a list of ideas about a topic. It can be done quickly and at first without any need to order items in a coherent pattern. The point is to write down everything that occurs to you as quickly and briefly as possible, using individual words or short phrases. Once you have a good-sized list of items, you can then group them according to relationships that you see among them. Brainstorming thus allows you to uncover both ideas stored in your memory and useful associations among those ideas.

A professor in a sociology of religion course at the University of California–Irvine asked his students to write a seven-hundred-word paper, in the form of a letter to be published in a local newspaper, providing readers information about the religious practices of Latino immigrants. One student, Courtney Wittey, started thinking about the assignment by brainstorming. First, she simply wrote down anything about life in society that occurred to her:

demographics of settlement	religion and the American Dream
religious beliefs	religious faith and deportation
poverty's effect on their religion	religious communities and celebrations
religion's role in reducing poverty	effective and thriving parishes
religion and immigrant family life	the political effects of religion
religious communities and economic opportunity	the relationship of religion and patterns of discrimination

Thinking through her list, Courtney decided to create two new separate lists: one devoted to contributions of religion to aspects of California Latino immigrant life, and the other, to remaining challenges to California Latino immigrant life. At this point she decided to discard some items that were redundant or did not seem to have much potential.

Contributions	Challenges
cohesion	competition with nonimmigrants
support	discrimination
tradition	injustice
familiarity	low voter turnout
faith and common beliefs	language acquisition

At this point, Courtney decided that her topic would be about the ways in which religion supported the efforts of immigrants to be successful in California. Which items on her lists would be relevant to her paper?

Asking Questions

It is always possible to ask most or all of the following questions about any topic: *Who? What? When? Where? Why? How?* They force you to approach the topic as a journalist does, setting it within different perspectives that can then be compared.

A professor asked her class on American Christianity to write a paper describing the effects of theology and beliefs on membership growth within three selected denominations over the last half century. One student developed the following questions as he began to think about a thesis:

Who are some popular religious leaders?
What specific beliefs affect their success?
What benefits do their belief systems provide?
What commitments do the belief systems entail?
When during the life cycle of denominations is leadership most important to the membership?
Where do the denominations come from?
Who benefits the most and the least from these denominations?

Can you think of other questions that would make for useful inquiry?

Maintaining Flexibility

As you engage in invention strategies, you are also performing other writing tasks. You are still narrowing your topic, for example, as well as making decisions that will affect your choice of tone or audience. You are moving forward on all fronts, with each decision you make affecting the others. This means that you must be flexible enough to allow for adjustments in your understanding of the paper's development and of your goal. Never be so determined to prove a particular theory that you fail to notice when your own understanding of it changes. Stay objective.

Read&Write 2.2   Freewrite

Religious revivals and similar movements occasionally have a variety of effects on society as a whole. In the mid-1980s, conservative Christians, led by Jerry Falwell and Pat Robertson in particular, invigorated their political efforts with an antiabortion and anti-LGBT agenda. Liberal Christians, led by *Sojourners* magazine editor Jim Wallis, attempted to counter the Right's agenda with emphases on inclusiveness and the problems of the poor. The political effects of these movements continue to wax and wane, changing focus somewhat over time.

Find a newspaper, online or in print, and select an article that provides information about a religious movement or revival. Following the sample in this chapter, do some freewriting. The objective of your freewriting is to establish an initial approach to understanding the viability and strength of the movement you have selected.

2.3   ORGANIZE YOUR WRITING

The structure of any religion paper is governed by a formal pattern. When rigid external controls are placed on their writing, some writers feel that their creativity is hampered by a kind of "paint-by-numbers" approach to structure. It is vital to the success of your paper that you never allow yourself to be overwhelmed by the pattern rules for any type of paper. Remember that such controls exist not to limit your creativity, but to make the paper immediately and easily useful to its intended audience. It is as necessary to write clearly and confidently in a position paper or a policy analysis paper as in a term paper for English literature, a résumé, a short story, or a job application cover letter.

A paper that contains all the necessary facts but presents them in an ineffective order will confuse rather than inform or persuade. Although there are various methods of grouping ideas, none is potentially more effective than outlining. Unfortunately, no organizing process is more often misunderstood.

The Importance of Outlining

Outline for Yourself   Outlining can do two jobs. First, it can force you, the writer, to gain a better understanding of your ideas by arranging them according to their interrelationships. There is one primary rule of outlining: Ideas of equal weight are placed on the same level within the outline. This rule requires you to determine the relative importance of your ideas. You must decide which ideas are of the same type or order, and into which subtopic each idea best fits.

If, in the planning stage, you work to arrange your ideas in a coherent outline, you will greatly enhance your grasp of the topic. You will have linked your ideas logically together and given a basic structure to the body of the paper. This sort of subordinating and coordinating activity is difficult, however, and as a result, inexperienced writers sometimes begin to write their first draft without an effective outline, hoping for the best. This hope is usually unfulfilled, especially in complex papers involving research.

EXERCISE Organizing Thoughts

Rodrigo, a student in a course on Religious Missions and Evangelism, researched the effectiveness of the mission programs of both the Latter-day Saints and the Assemblies of God in his state and came up with the following facts and theories. Number them in logical order:

____ A growing number of young prospective converts in the state do not possess the basic background knowledge of Christian beliefs held by members in previous generations.

____ As reported by the Mormons, the number of newly recruited members in the state increased from 1,291 in 2005 to 15,272 in 2015, whereas the Assemblies reported a decrease of 10 percent in new recruits over the same period.

____ While the Mormons reported that their recruitment was accomplished by young missionaries canvassing neighborhoods, the Assemblies reported that individual pastors and evangelists were their main recruitment agents.

____ As a whole, according to a Pew Trust study, the number of Americans who regularly attend church declined by 6.5 percent during that decade.

____ In general, the first fifteen years of the twenty-first century has seen a decline in successful recruitment to religious organizations.

Outline for Your Reader   The second job an outline can perform is to serve as a reader's blueprint of the paper, summarizing its points and their interrelationships.

By consulting your outline, a busy reader can quickly get a sense of your paper's goal and the argument you have used to promote it. The clarity and coherence of the outline help determine how much attention your audience will give to your ideas.

As religion students, you will be given a great deal of help with the arrangement of your material into an outline to accompany your paper. A look at the format presented below will show you how strictly a formal outline is structured. But, although you must pay close attention to these requirements, do not forget how powerful a tool an outline can be in the early planning stages of your paper.

The Formal Outline Pattern   Following this pattern accurately during the planning stage of your paper helps guarantee that your ideas are placed logically:

Thesis sentence (precedes the formal outline)

I. First main idea
   A. First subordinate idea
      1. Reason, example, or illustration
         a. Supporting detail
         b. Supporting detail
         c. Supporting detail
      2. Reason, example, or illustration
         a. Supporting detail
         b. Supporting detail
         c. Supporting detail
   B. Second subordinate idea
II. Second main idea

Notice that each level of the paper must have more than one entry; for every A there must be at least a B (and, if required, a C, a D, and so on), and for every 1 there must be, at least, a 2. This arrangement forces you to *compare ideas*, looking carefully at each one to determine its place among the others. The insistence on assigning relative values to your ideas is what makes an outline an effective organizing tool.

Read&Write 2.3   Write a Paper Outline

This is a relatively simple exercise, but it does require some thought. Start by perusing today's newspaper (local or national). When you come to an article that interests you, stop. Suppose the article is like the one below, by William Yardley, partially reprinted here from the *New York Times*:

Pastors in Northwest Find Focus in "Green"

MILLWOOD, WA—State auditors told Millwood Community Presbyterian Church last summer to close its farmers' market on the church parking lot or the lot could no longer be claimed as tax-exempt. Without hesitation, the church kept the market and paid the $700 in annual taxes.

Money is tight, but the locally raised beef and vegetables and, most important, the environmentally minded customers had become central to the 90-year-old church's ministry. . . .

Across the Northwest, where church attendance has long been low but concern for the environment high, some church leaders and parishioners are ringing doorbells to inform neighbors—many of whom have never stepped inside the sanctuary down the street—about ways to conserve energy and lower their utility bills. Some view the new push as a way to revitalize their congregations and reconnect with their nearby community.[3]

Think. What is it about the article that interests you? Is it the role of religion in addressing concerns for the environment? Is it new ways of making religion relevant in society?

Now, following the outline format described in this chapter section, write an outline of a paper you might write because you read this article. Your outline will not *summarize* the article, although a short summary might be included in your paper. Your paper outline might look something like this:

Green Pastors and Congregation Growth

I. Mainline Protestant churches and Roman Catholic dioceses have witnessed declines in membership over the past three decades.
    A. Religious idealism has been primarily the province of conservative denominations.
        1. Abortion and homosexuality have energized conservatives.
        2. Reagan-economic Republicans and social conservatives joined forces.
    B. Mainline concerns faded with economic prosperity declines in the 1970s.
        1. Poverty lost its appeal as a motivating force.
        2. Civil rights victories weakened as a compelling force.
        3. The Vietnam conflict and the oil crisis diverted attention from traditional mainline causes.

II. Global warming is of increasing concern in the population as a whole.
    A. Liberals see global warming as a major concern.
        1. Coastal cities where liberals live are most vulnerable to climate change.
        2. Hurricane Katrina and the 2016 floods in Louisiana are garnering attention to environmental causes.
    B. Mainline churches are intensifying their construction of environmental problems as spiritual issues.
        1. Stewardship of resources is a primary concern.
        2. Global warming will affect the poor in disproportionate numbers.

III. Mainline churches are finding that environmental concerns boost membership.
    A. The environment provides an opening for domestic missions.
        1. Prospects easily accept information on how to preserve the environment.
        2. Farmers' markets present opportunities to publicize church activities.
    B. Churches are in a unique position to take advantage of environmental concerns.
        1. Unlike organizations like the Sierra Club, churches are neighborhood-oriented.
        2. Churches can offer multiple opportunities for people to serve their communities.

---

[3] William Yardley, "Pastors in Northwest Find Focus in 'Green,'" *New York Times*, January 15, 2010, http://www.nytimes.com/2010/01/16/us/16church.html.

2.4 DRAFT, REVISE, EDIT, AND PROOFREAD

Write the Rough Draft

After planning comes the writing of the first draft. Using your thesis and outline as direction markers, you must now weave your amalgam of ideas, data, and persuasion strategies into logically ordered sentences and paragraphs. Although adequate pre-writing may facilitate drafting, it still will not be easy. All writers establish their own individual methods of encouraging themselves to forge ahead with the draft, but here are some general tips:

- Remember that this is a rough draft, not the final paper. At this stage, it is not necessary that every word be the best possible choice. Do not put that sort of pressure on yourself. You must not allow anything to slow you down now. Writing is not like sculpting in stone, where every chip is permanent; you can always go back to your draft and add, delete, reword, and rearrange. *No matter how much effort you have put into planning, you cannot be sure how much of this first draft you will eventually keep.* It may take several drafts to get one that you find satisfactory.

- Give yourself sufficient time to write. Do not delay the first draft by telling yourself there is still more research to do. You cannot uncover all the material there is to know on a particular subject, so do not fool yourself into trying. Remember that writing is a process of discovery. You may have to begin writing before you can see exactly what sort of research you need to do. Keep in mind that there are other tasks waiting for you after the first draft is finished, so allow for them as you determine your writing schedule.

    More important, give yourself time to write, because the more time that passes after you have written a draft, the better your ability to view it with objectivity. It is very difficult to evaluate your writing accurately soon after you complete it. You need to cool down, to recover from the effort of putting all those words together. The "colder" you get on your writing, the better you are able to read it as if it were written by someone else and thus acknowledge the changes you will need to make to strengthen the paper.

- Stay sharp. Keep in mind the plan you created as you narrowed your topic, composed a thesis sentence, and outlined the material. But if you begin to feel a strong need to change the plan a bit, do not be afraid to do so. Be ready for surprises dealt you by your own growing understanding of your topic. Your goal is to record your best thinking on the subject as accurately as possible.

Paragraph Development   There is no absolute requirement for the structure of any paragraph in your paper except that all its sentences must be clearly related to each other and each must carry *one step further* the job of saying what you want to say about your thesis. In other words, any sentence that simply restates something said in another sentence anywhere else in the paper is a waste of your time and the reader's. It isn't unusual for a paragraph to have, somewhere in it, a *topic* sentence that serves as the key to the paragraph's organization and announces the paragraph's connection to the paper's thesis. But not all paragraphs need topic sentences.

What all paragraphs in the paper *do* need is an organizational strategy. Here are four typical organizational models, any one of which, if you keep it in mind, can help you build a coherent paragraph:

- *Chronological organization:* The sentences of the paragraph describe a series of events or steps or observations as they occur over time. This happens, then that, and then that.
- *Spatial organization:* The sentences of the paragraph record details of its subject in some logical order: top to bottom, up to down, outside to inside.
- *General-to-specific organization:* The paragraph starts with a statement of its main idea and then goes into detail as it discusses that idea.
- *Specific-to-general organization:* The paragraph begins with smaller, nuts-and-bolts details, arranging them into a larger pattern that, by the end of the paragraph, leads to the conclusion that is the paragraph's main idea.

These aren't the only organizational strategies available to you, and, of course, different paragraphs in a paper can use different strategies, though a paragraph that employs more than one organizational plan is risking incoherence. The essential thing to remember is that each sentence in the paragraph must bear a logical relationship to the one before it and the one after it. This notion of *interconnectedness* can prevent you from getting off track and stuffing extraneous material in your paragraphs.

Like all other aspects of the writing process, paragraph development is a challenge. But remember, one of the helpful facts about paragraphs is that they are relatively small, especially compared to the overall scope of your paper. Each paragraph can basically do only one job—handle or help handle a single idea, which is itself only a part of the overall development of the larger thesis idea. That paragraphs are small and aimed at a single task means that it is relatively easy to revise them. By focusing clearly on the single job a paragraph does and filtering out all the paper's other claims for your attention, you should gain enough clarity of vision during the revision process to understand what you need to do to make that paragraph work better.

Authority   To be convincing, your writing must be authoritative—that is, you must sound as if you have complete confidence in your ability to convey your ideas in words. Sentences that sound stilted or that suffer from weak phrasing or the use of clichés are not going to win supporters for the positions that you express in your paper. So a major question becomes, *How can I sound confident?*

Below are some points to consider as you work to convey to your reader that necessary sense of authority.

Level of Formality   Tone is one of the primary methods by which you signal to the readers who you are and what your attitude is toward them and toward your topic. Your major decision is which level of language formality is most appropriate to your audience. The informal tone you would use in a letter to a friend might well be out of place in a paper on the Albigensian Heresy written for your history-of-religion professor. Remember that tone is only part of the overall decision that you make about how to present your information. Formality is, to some extent, a function of individual word choices and phrasing. For example, is it appropriate to use contractions such as *isn't* or *they'll?* Would the strategic use of a sentence fragment for effect be out of place? The use of informal language, the personal *I*, and the second-person *you* are traditionally forbidden—for better or worse—in certain kinds of writing. Often, part of the challenge of writing a formal paper is simply how to give your prose impact while staying within the conventions.

Jargon One way to lose readers quickly is to overwhelm them with *jargon*—phrases that have a special, usually technical meaning within your discipline but that are unfamiliar to the average reader. The very occasional use of jargon may add an effective touch of atmosphere, but anything more than that will severely dampen a reader's enthusiasm for the paper. Often the writer uses jargon to impress the reader by sounding lofty or knowledgeable. Unfortunately, all that jargon usually does is cause confusion. In fact, the use of jargon indicates a writer's lack of connection to the audience.

Theological writing can be a haven for jargon. Perhaps writers of scholarly textual interpretations believe their readers are all completely attuned to their terminology. Or some may hope to obscure controversial information in confusing language. In other cases, the problem could simply be unclear thinking by the writer. Whatever the reason, the fact is that religion papers can sometimes sound like prose made by machines to be read by machines.

Some students may feel that, to be accepted as religion scholars, their papers should conform to the practices of their published peers. This is a mistake. Remember that it is never better to write a cluttered or confusing sentence than a clear one, and burying your ideas in jargon defeats the effort that you went through to form them.

EXERCISE Revising Jargon

What words in the following sentence from an article in a religion journal are jargon? Can you rewrite the sentence to clarify its meaning?

> The hermeneutics of Christian anarchy are anathema to the presbytery and the exegetical imprecision of the analysis of the pericopes in question reflects antediluvian conceptual precepts.

Clichés In the heat of composition, as you are looking for words to help you form your ideas, it is sometimes easy to plug in a *cliché*—a phrase that has attained universal recognition by overuse.

Note: Clichés differ from jargon in that clichés are part of the general public's everyday language, whereas jargon is specific to the language of experts in a field.

Our vocabularies are brimming with clichés:

It's raining cats and dogs.
That issue is as dead as a doornail.
It's time for the archbishop to face the music.
Angry voters made a beeline for the ballot box.

The problem with clichés is that they are virtually meaningless. Once colorful means of expression, they have lost their color through overuse, and they tend to bleed energy and color from the surrounding words. When revising, replace clichés with fresh wording that more accurately conveys your point.

Descriptive Language   Language that appeals to readers' senses will always engage their interest more fully than language that is abstract. This is especially important for writing in disciplines that tend to deal in abstracts, such as religion. The typical religion paper, with its discussions of ritual, doctrine, or eschatology, is usually in danger of floating off into abstraction, with each paragraph drifting farther away from the felt life of the readers. Whenever appropriate, appeal to your readers' sense of sight, hearing, taste, touch, or smell.

EXERCISE Using Descriptive Language

Which of these two sentences is more effective?

1. The American Roman Catholic bishops are more liberal than the pope on some issues.
2. While the pope has expressed a need for increased attention to the problems of the poor, the American Roman Catholic bishops are more liberal than the pope on the need to redistribute wealth, to allow women a greater role in church offices, and to welcome the LGBT community to the parishes.

Bias-Free and Gender-Neutral Writing   Language can be a very powerful method of either reinforcing or destroying cultural stereotypes. By treating the sexes in subtly different ways in your language, you may unknowingly be committing an act of discrimination. A common example is the use of the pronoun *he* to refer to a person whose gender has not been identified.

Some writers, faced with this dilemma, alternate the use of male and female personal pronouns; others use the plural to avoid the need to use a pronoun of either gender:

Sexist: A priest should always treat his bishop with respect.

Corrected: A priest should always treat his or her bishop with respect.

Or: Priests should always treat their bishops with respect.

Sexist: Man is a spiritual animal.

Corrected: People are spiritual animals.

Remember that language is more than the mere vehicle of your thoughts. Your words shape perceptions for your readers. How well you say something will profoundly affect your readers' responses to what you say. Sexist language denies to many of your readers the basic right to fair and equal treatment. Make sure your writing does not reflect this form of discrimination.

Revise

After all the work you have gone through writing it, you may feel "married" to the first draft of your paper. However, revision is one of the most important steps in ensuring your paper's success. Although unpracticed writers often think of revision as little more than making sure all the *i*'s are dotted and *t*'s are crossed, it is much more than that. Revising is *reseeing* the essay, looking at it from other perspectives, trying always to align your view with the one that will be held by your audience. Research indicates that we are actually revising all the time, in every phase of the writing process, as we reread phrases, rethink the placement of an item in an outline, or test a new topic sentence for a paragraph. Subjecting your entire hard-fought draft to cold, objective scrutiny is one of the toughest activities to master, but it is absolutely necessary. You must make sure that you have said everything that needs to be said clearly and logically. One confusing passage will deflect the reader's attention from where you want it to be. Suddenly the reader has to become a detective, trying to figure out why you wrote what you did and what you meant by it. You do not want to throw such obstacles in the path of understanding.

Here are some tips to help you with revision:

1. Give yourself adequate time for revision. As discussed above, you need time to become "cold" on your paper in order to analyze it objectively. After you have written your draft, spend some time away from it. Then try to reread it as if someone else had written it.

2. Read the paper carefully. This is tougher than it sounds. One good strategy is to read it aloud yourself or to have a friend read it aloud while you listen. (Note, however, that friends are usually not the best critics. They are rarely trained in revision techniques and are often unwilling to risk disappointing you by giving your paper a really thorough examination.)

3. Have a list of specific items to check. It is important to revise in an orderly fashion, in stages, first looking at large concerns, such as the overall organization, and then at smaller elements, such as paragraph or sentence structure.

4. Check for unity—the clear and logical relation of all parts of an essay to its thesis. Make sure that every paragraph relates well to the whole of the paper and is in the right place.

5. Check for coherence. Make sure there are no gaps between the various parts of the argument. Look to see that you have adequate transitions everywhere they are needed. *Transitional elements* are markers indicating places where the paper's focus or attitude changes. Such elements can take the form of one word—*however, although, unfortunately, luckily*—or an entire sentence or a paragraph: *In order to fully appreciate the importance of religion as a cohesion-generating presence in South American communities, it is necessary to examine briefly the Roman Catholic church's role in helping Mexican citizens resist the influence of drug cartels.*

   Transitional elements rarely introduce new material. Instead, they are direction pointers, either indicating a shift to new subject matter or signaling how the writer wishes certain material to be interpreted by the reader. Because you, the writer, already know where and why your paper changes direction and how you want particular passages to be received, it can be very difficult for you to catch those places where transition is needed.

6. Avoid unnecessary repetition. Two types of repetition can annoy a reader: repetition of content and repetition of wording.

   Repetition of content occurs when you return to a subject you have already discussed. Ideally, you should deal with a topic once, memorably, and then move on to your next subject. Organizing a paper is a difficult task, however, which usually occurs through a process of enlightenment in terms of purposes and strategies, and repetition of content can happen even if you have used prewriting strategies. What is worse, it can be difficult for you to be aware of the repetition in your own writing. As you write and revise, remember that any unnecessary repetition of content in your final draft is potentially annoying to your readers, who are working to make sense of the argument they are reading and do not want to be distracted by a passage repeating material they have already encountered. You must train yourself, through practice, to look for material that you have repeated unnecessarily.

Repetition of wording occurs when you overuse certain phrases or words. This can make your prose sound choppy and uninspired, as the following examples demonstrate:

> The archdiocese's report on liturgical reform will surprise a number of people. A number of people will want copies of the report.

> The Rabbi said at a press conference that he is happy with the report. He will circulate it to the local news agencies in the morning. He will also make sure that the temple leadership has copies.

> I became upset when I heard how the task force on rabbinical education had voted. I called the chairman and expressed my reservations about the committee's decision. I told him I felt that he had let the teachers and students of the region's synagogues down. I also issued a press statement.

The last passage illustrates a condition known by composition teachers as the *I-syndrome*. Can you hear how such duplicated phrasing can hurt a paper? Your language should sound fresh and energetic. Before you submit your final draft, make sure to read through your paper carefully, looking for such repetition.

However, not all repetition is bad. You may wish to repeat a phrase for rhetorical effect or special emphasis: *I came. I saw. I conquered.* Just make sure that any repetition in your paper is intentional, placed there to produce a specific effect.

Edit

Editing is sometimes confused with the more involved process of revising. But editing is done later in the writing process, after you have wrestled through your first draft—and maybe your second and third—and arrived at the final draft. Even though your draft now contains all the information you want to impart and has the information arranged to your satisfaction, there are still many factors to check, such as sentence structure, spelling, and punctuation.

It is at this point that an unpracticed writer might be less than vigilant. After all, most of the work on the paper is finished, as the "big jobs" of discovering, organizing, and drafting information have been completed. But watch out! Editing is as important as any other part of the writing process. Any error that you allow in the final draft will count against you in the mind of the reader. This may not seem fair, but even a minor error—a misspelling or the confusing placement of a comma—will make a much greater impression on your reader than perhaps it should. Remember that everything about your paper is your responsibility, including performing even the supposedly little jobs correctly. Careless editing undermines the effectiveness of your paper. It would be a shame if all the hard work you put into prewriting, drafting, and revising were to be damaged because you carelessly allowed a comma splice!

Most of the revision tips given above hold for editing as well. It is best to edit in stages, looking for only one or two kinds of errors each time you reread the paper. Focus especially on errors that you remember committing in the past. If, for instance, you know that you tend to misplace commas, go through your paper looking at each comma carefully. If you have a weakness for writing unintentional sentence fragments, read each sentence aloud to make sure that it is indeed a complete sentence. Have you accidentally shifted verb tenses anywhere, moving from past to present tense for no reason? Do all the subjects in your sentences agree in number with their verbs? *Now is the time to find out.*

Watch out for *miscues*—problems with a sentence that the writer simply does not see. Remember that your search for errors is hampered in two ways:

1. As the writer, you hope not to find any errors in your work. This desire can cause you to miss mistakes when they do occur.
2. Because you know your material so well, it is easy, as you read, to unconsciously supply missing material—a word, a piece of punctuation—as if it were present.

How difficult is it to see that something is missing in the following sentence?

Unfortunately, lay leaders often have too little knowledge the principles of hermeneutics.

We can guess that the missing word is probably *of*, which should be inserted after *knowledge*. It is quite possible, however, that the writer of the sentence, while rereading the text, would automatically supply the missing *of* as if it were on the page. This is a miscue, which can be hard for writers to spot because they are so close to their material.

One tactic for catching mistakes in sentence structure is to read the sentences aloud, starting with the last one in the paper and then moving to the next-to-last, then to the previous sentence, and thus going backward through the paper (reading each sentence in the normal, left-to-right manner, of course) until you reach the first sentence of the introduction. This backward progression strips each sentence of its rhetorical context and helps you focus on its internal structure.

Editing is the stage in which you finally answer those minor questions that you had put off when you were wrestling with wording and organization. Any ambiguities regarding the use of abbreviations, italics, numerals, capital letters, titles (When do you capitalize the title *president*, for example?), hyphens, dashes (usually created on a typewriter or computer by striking the hyphen key twice), apostrophes, and quotation marks must be cleared up now. You must also check to see that you have used the required formats for footnotes, endnotes, margins, page numbers, and the like.

Guessing is not allowed. Sometimes unpracticed writers who realize that they do not quite understand a particular rule of grammar, punctuation, or format do nothing to fill that knowledge gap. Instead they rely on guesswork and their own logic—which is not always up to the task of dealing with so contrary a language as English—to get them through problems that they could solve if they referred to a writing manual. Remember that it does not matter to the reader why or how an error shows up in your writing. It only matters that you have dropped your guard. You must not allow a careless error to undo all the good work that you have done.

Proofread

Before you hand in the final version of your paper, it is vital that you check it one more time to make sure there are no errors of any sort. This job is called *proofreading*, or *proofing*. In essence, you are looking for many of the same things you had checked for during editing, but now you are doing it on the last draft, which is about to be submitted to your audience. Proofreading is as important as editing; you may have missed an error that you still have time to find, or an error may have been introduced when the draft was recopied or typed for the last time. Be aware that, sometimes, sending a file from one computer to another can strip formatting commands from the draft, removing such items as italics or tab settings. Like every other stage of the writing process, proofreading is your responsibility.

At this point, you must check for typing mistakes: transposed or deleted letters, words, phrases, or punctuation. If you have had the paper professionally typed, you still must check it carefully. Do not rely solely on the typist's proofreading. If you are creating your paper on a computer or a word processor, it is possible for you to unintentionally insert a command that alters your document drastically by slicing out a word, line, or sentence at the touch of a key. Make sure such accidental deletions have not occurred.

Above all else, remember that your paper represents you. It is a product of your best thinking, your most energetic and imaginative response to a writing challenge. If you have maintained your enthusiasm for the project and worked through the stages of the writing process honestly and carefully, you should produce a paper you can be proud of, one that will serve its readers well.

Read&Write 2.4   Discover Your Own Style

Here is another opportunity to do some self-reflection. On December 31, 2010, His Holiness the Dalai Lama, religious leader of Tibet, made a pronouncement on "Countering Stress and Depression." He said, in part:

> As human beings we are gifted with this wonderful human intelligence. Besides that, all human beings have the capacity to be very determined and to direct that strong sense of determination in whatever direction they like. So long as we remember that we have this marvelous gift of human intelligence and a capacity to develop determination and use it in positive ways, we will preserve our underlying mental health. Realizing we have this great human potential gives us a fundamental strength. This recognition can act as a mechanism that enables us to deal with any difficulty, no matter what situation we are facing, without losing hope or sinking into feelings of low self-esteem.
>
> I write this as someone who lost his freedom at the age of 16, then lost his country at the age of 24. Consequently, I have lived in exile for more than 50 years during which we Tibetans have dedicated ourselves to keeping the Tibetan identity alive and preserving our culture and values.[4]

Your writing project is to reflect upon and respond, in a personal essay of 750 to 1,000 words, to the Dalai Lama's message. Let this be an opportunity for you to know yourself better.

---

[4]   The Dalai Lama, "Countering Stress and Depression," The Office of His Holiness the 14th Dalai Lama, December 31, 2010, https://www.dalailama.com/messages/compassion-and-human-values/countering-stress-and-depression.

3

PRACTICE THE CRAFT
OF SCHOLARSHIP

3.1 THE COMPETENT WRITER

Good writing places your thoughts in your readers' minds in exactly the way you want them to be there. Good writing tells your readers just what you want them to know without telling them anything you do not want them to know. This may sound odd, but the fact is that writers must be careful not to let unwanted messages slip into their writing. Look, for example, at the passage below, taken from a paper discussing sermons on the problems of homelessness. Hidden within the prose is a message that jeopardizes the paper's success. Can you detect the message?

> Recent homilies delivered on the subject of homeless families have had little to say about the particular problems dealt with in this paper. Because few of these homilies address the problem of mental illness.

Chances are, when you reached the end of the second "sentence," you felt that something was missing and perceived a gap in logic or coherence, so you went back through both sentences to find the place where things had gone wrong. The text following the first sentence is actually not a sentence at all. It does have certain features of a sentence—for example, a subject (*few*) and a verb (*address*)—but its first word (*Because*) subordinates the entire clause that follows, taking away its ability to stand on its own as a complete idea. The second "sentence," which is properly called a *subordinate clause*, merely fills in some information about the first sentence, telling us why recent homilies delivered on the subject of homeless families have had little to say about the particular problems dealt with in this paper.

The sort of error represented by the second "sentence" is commonly called a *sentence fragment*, and it conveys to the reader a message that no writer wants to send: that the writer either is careless or, worse, has not mastered the language. Language errors such as fragments, misplaced commas, or shifts in verb tense send out warnings in readers' minds. As a result, readers lose some of their concentration on the issue being discussed; they become distracted and begin to wonder about the language competency of the writer. The writing loses effectiveness.

> **Note:** Whatever goal you set for your paper—whether to persuade, describe, analyze, or speculate—you must also set one other goal: to display language competence. If your paper does not meet this goal, it will not completely achieve its other aims. Language errors spread doubt like a virus; they jeopardize all the hard work you have done on your paper.

Language competence is especially important in religion. Anyone who doubts this should remember the beating that Vice President Dan Quayle took in the press for misspelling the word *potato* at a 1992 spelling bee. His error caused a storm of humiliating publicity for the hapless Quayle, adding to an impression of his general incompetence.

Correctness Is Relative

Although they may seem minor, the sort of language errors we are discussing—often called *surface errors*—can be extremely damaging in certain kinds of writing. Surface errors come in a variety of types, including misspellings, punctuation problems, grammar errors, and the inconsistent use of abbreviations, capitalization, and numerals. These errors are an affront to your readers' notions of correctness, and therein lies one of the biggest problems with surface errors. Different audiences tolerate different levels of correctness. You know that you can get away with surface errors in, say, a letter to a friend, who will probably not judge you harshly for them, whereas those same errors in a job application letter might eliminate you from consideration for the position. Correctness depends to an extent on context.

Another problem is that the rules governing correctness shift over time. What would have been an error to your grandmother's generation—for example, the splitting of an infinitive or the ending of a sentence with a preposition—is taken in stride by most readers today.

So how do you write correctly when the rules shift from person to person and over time? Here are some tips.

Consider Your Audience   One of the great risks of writing is that even the simplest of choices regarding wording or punctuation can sometimes prejudice your audience against you in ways that may seem unfair. For example, look again at the old grammar rule forbidding the splitting of infinitives. After decades of telling students to never split an infinitive (something just done in this sentence), most composition experts now concede that a split infinitive is *not* a grammar crime. But suppose you have written a position paper trying to convince your church elders of the need to visit elderly members of the congregation, and half of the elders—the people you wish to convince—remember their eighth-grade grammar teacher's warning about splitting infinitives. How will they respond when you tell them, in your introduction, that elders are obligated "to frequently visit" elderly members because of their relative distance from their families? How much of their attention have you suddenly lost because of their automatic recollection of what is now a nonrule? It is possible, in other words, to write correctly and still offend your readers' notions of language competence.

Make sure that you tailor the surface features and the degree of formality of your writing to the level of competency that your readers require. When in doubt, take a conservative approach. Your audience may be just as distracted by a contraction as by a split infinitive.

Aim for Consistency When dealing with a language question for which there are different answers—such as whether to use a comma before the conjunction in a series of three (*the bishop's speech addressed medical care, housing for the poor, and the job situation*)—always use the same strategy throughout your paper. If, for example, you avoid splitting one infinitive, avoid splitting *all* infinitives.

Have Confidence in What You Know About Writing!

It is easy for unpracticed writers to allow their occasional mistakes to shake their confidence in their writing ability. The fact is, however, that most of what we know about writing is correct. We are all capable, for example, of writing grammatically sound phrases, even if we cannot list the rules by which we achieve coherence. Most writers who worry about their chronic errors make fewer mistakes than they think. Becoming distressed about errors makes writing even more difficult.

Read&Write 3.1 Correct a Sentence Fragment

See how many ways you can rewrite this so-called two-sentence passage to eliminate the fragment and make the passage syntactically correct.

> Although married couples often both work full-time, women do most of the housework. Except when the men work second or third shifts.

3.2 AVOID ERRORS IN GRAMMAR AND PUNCTUATION

As various composition theorists have pointed out, the word *grammar* has several definitions. One meaning is "the formal patterns in which words must be arranged in order to convey meaning." We learn these patterns very early in life and use them spontaneously, without thinking. Our understanding of grammatical patterns is extremely sophisticated, even though few of us can actually cite the rules by which the patterns work. Patrick Hartwell tested grammar learning by asking native English speakers of different ages and levels of education, including high school teachers, to arrange these words in natural order:

French the young girls four

Everyone could produce the natural order for this phrase: *the four young French girls*. Yet none of Hartwell's respondents was able to cite the rules that govern the order of the words.[1]

---

[1] Patrick Hartwell, "Grammar, Grammars, and the Teaching of Grammar," *College English* 47 (February 1985): 105–27.

Eliminate Chronic Errors   But if just thinking about our errors has a negative effect on our writing, how do we learn to write more correctly? Perhaps the best answer is simply to write as often as possible. Give yourself lots of practice in putting your thoughts into written shape—and then in revising and proofing your work. As you write and revise, be honest—and patient—with yourself. Chronic errors are like bad habits; getting rid of them takes time.

You probably know of one or two problem areas in your writing that you could have eliminated but have not yet done so. Instead, you may have fudged your writing at critical points, relying on half-remembered formulas from past English classes or trying to come up with logical solutions to your writing problems. (*Reminder:* The English language does not always work in a way that seems logical.) You may have simply decided that comma rules are unlearnable or that you will never understand the difference between the verbs *lay* and *lie*. And so you guess, and you come up with the wrong answer a good part of the time. What a shame, when just a little extra work would give you mastery over those few gaps in your understanding and boost your confidence as well.

Instead of continuing with this sort of guesswork and living with the holes in your knowledge, why not face the problem areas now and learn the rules that have heretofore escaped you? What follows is a discussion of those surface features of writing in which errors most commonly occur. You will probably be familiar with most if not all the rules discussed, but there may well be a few you have not yet mastered. Now is the time to do so.

Apostrophes

An apostrophe is used to show possession. When you wish to say that something belongs to someone or something, you add either an apostrophe and an *s* or an apostrophe alone to the word that represents the owner(s).

When the owner is singular (a single person or thing), the apostrophe precedes an added *s*:

> According to Sister Amelia's secretary, the senior staff meeting has been canceled.

> The lay educator's friends challenged the bishop's policy in the last episcopal meeting.

> Somebody's Qur'an was left in the auditorium.

The same rule applies if the word showing possession is a plural that does not end in *s*:

> The women's society sponsored several benefit concerts during their annual charity drive.

> Father Garrity has proven himself a tireless worker for improved children's services.

When the word expressing ownership is a plural ending in *s*, the apostrophe follows the *s*:

> The new initiation ceremony was discussed at the club secretaries' conference.

There are two ways to form the possessive for two or more nouns:

1. To show joint possession (both nouns owning the same thing or things), the last noun in the series is possessive:

The rabbi and the music director's invitations were sent out yesterday.

2. To indicate that each noun owns an item or items individually, each noun must show possession:

Pastor Scott's and Pastor MacKay's speeches took different approaches to the same problem.

The importance of the apostrophe is obvious when you consider the difference in meaning between the following two sentences:

Be sure to pick up the volunteer's bags on your way to the airport.

Be sure to pick up the volunteers' bags on your way to the airport.

In the first sentence, you have only one volunteer to worry about, whereas in the second, you have at least two!

Capitalization

Here is a brief summary of some hard-to-remember capitalization rules:

1. You may, if you choose, capitalize the first letter of the first word in a sentence that follows a colon. However, make sure you use one pattern consistently throughout your paper:

Our instructions are explicit: *D*o not allow anyone into the conference without an identification badge.

Our instructions are explicit: *d*o not allow anyone into the conference without an identification badge.

2. Capitalize *proper nouns* (names of specific people, places, or things) and *proper adjectives* (adjectives made from proper nouns). A common noun following a proper adjective is usually not capitalized, nor is a common adjective preceding a proper adjective (such as *a*, *an*, or *the*):

Proper Nouns	Proper Adjectives
Pentateuch	Pentateuchal command
Iraq	the Iraqi ambassador
Shakespeare	a Shakespearean tragedy

Proper nouns include:

- *Names of monuments and buildings:* St. Peter's Basilica, Masjid al-Haram, the Wailing Wall
- *Historical events, eras, and certain terms concerning calendar dates:* the Diaspora, Easter, Ramadan, December, Diwali
- *Parts of the country:* North, Southwest, Eastern Seaboard, the West Coast, New England

Note: When words like **north**, **south**, **east**, **west**, and **northwest** are used to designate direction rather than geographical region, they are not capitalized, as in **We drove east to Boston and then made a tour of the East Coast.**

- *Words referring to race, religion, and nationality:* Islam, Muslim, Caucasian, White (or white, depending on context), Asian, Negro, Black (or black, depending on context), Slavic, Arab, Jewish, Hebrew, Buddhism, Buddhists, Southern Baptists, the Bible, the Qur'an, American
- *Names of languages:* English, Chinese, Latin, Sanskrit
- *Titles of corporations, institutions, universities, and organizations:* Dow Chemical, General Motors, the National Endowment for the Humanities, Baylor University, Colby College, Kiwanis Club, Diocese of Santa Fe, American Association of Retired Persons, Oklahoma State Senate

Note: Some words once considered proper nouns or adjectives have, over time, become common and are no longer capitalized, such as *french fries, pasteurized milk, arabic numerals,* and *italics.*

3. Titles of individuals may be capitalized if they precede a proper name; otherwise, titles are usually not capitalized:

The Punjab community honored Archaka Prasha.
The Punjab honored the archaka from Chennai.
We phoned Pastor Jessup, who arrived shortly afterward.
We phoned the pastor, who arrived shortly afterward.
A story on Cardinal Layton's health appeared in yesterday's paper.
A story on the cardinal's health appeared in yesterday's paper.
Pope Francis's visit to Argentina was a public relations success.
The pope's visit to Argentina was a public relations success.

When Not to Capitalize   In general, do not capitalize nouns when your reference is nonspecific. For example, you would not capitalize *the archbishop*, but you would capitalize *Archbishop York*. The second reference is as much a title as it is a term of identification, whereas the first reference is a mere identifier. Likewise, there is a difference in degree of specificity between *the state treasury* and *the Texas State Treasury*.

Note: The meaning of a term may change somewhat depending on its capitalization. What, for example, might be the difference between a *Democrat* and a *democrat*? When capitalized, the word refers to a member of a specific political party; when not capitalized, it refers to someone who believes in the democratic form of government.

Capitalization depends to some extent on the context of your writing. For example, if you are writing a policy analysis for a specific religious institution, you may capitalize words and phrases that refer to that corporation—such as *Board of Directors, Chairman of the Board*, and *the Institute*—that would not be capitalized in a paper written for a more general audience. Likewise, in some contexts, it is not unusual to see the titles of certain powerful officials capitalized even when not accompanying a proper noun:

The Cardinal took few members of his staff to the funeral service with him.

Colons

We all know certain uses for the colon. A colon can, for example, separate the parts of a statement of time (*4:25 a.m.*), separate chapter and verse in a biblical quotation (*John 3:16*), and close the salutation of a business letter (*Dear Pastor Keaton:*). But the colon has other, less well-known uses that can add extra flexibility to sentence structure.

The colon can introduce into a sentence certain kinds of material, such as a list, a quotation, or a restatement or description of material mentioned earlier:

List

The building committee's research proposal promised to do three things: (1) establish the extent of the problem, (2) examine several possible solutions, and (3) estimate the cost of each solution.

Quotation

In his sermon, the pastor challenged us with these words: "How will your committee's work make a difference in the life of our congregation?"

Restatement or Description

Ahead of us, according to the priest's chief of staff, lay the biggest job of all: convincing our constituents of the plan's benefits.

Commas

The comma is perhaps the most troublesome of all marks of punctuation, no doubt because its use is governed by so many variables, such as sentence length, rhetorical emphasis, and changing notions of style. The most common problems are outlined below.

The Comma Splice   A *comma splice* is the joining of two complete sentences with only a comma:

A complaint is merely an accusation against a church official, actual removal from office usually requires a vote by the Presbytery.

A negligent worker who has been effectively motivated is no longer a problem for the church, he has become an asset.

It might be possible for the congregation to raise money on the sale of baked goods, however, such a move would be criticized by the local baker.

In each of these passages, two complete sentences (also called *independent clauses*) have been spliced together only by a comma, which is an inadequate break between the two sentences.

One foolproof way to check your paper for comma splices is to read the structures on both sides of each comma carefully. If you find a complete sentence on each side, and if the sentence following the comma does not begin with a coordinating conjunction (*and, but, for, nor, or, so, yet*), then you have found a comma splice.

Simply reading the draft to try to "hear" the comma splices may not work because the rhetorical features of your prose—its *movement*—may make it hard to detect this kind of error in sentence completeness. There are five commonly used ways to correct comma splices:

1. Place a period between the two independent clauses:

   INCORRECT A prospective pastor receives many benefits from his or her affiliation with a denomination, there are liabilities as well.

   CORRECT A prospective pastor receives many benefits from his or her affiliation with a denomination. There are liabilities as well.

2. Place a comma and a coordinating conjunction (*and, but, for, or, nor, so, yet*) between the independent clauses:

   INCORRECT The elder's speech described the major differences of opinion over the church donation situation, it also suggested a possible course of action.

   CORRECT The elder's speech described the major differences of opinion over the church donation situation, and it also suggested a possible course of action.

3. Place a semicolon between the independent clauses:

   INCORRECT Some people feel that the diocese should play a large role in establishing a housing program for the homeless, many others disagree.

   CORRECT Some people feel that the diocese should play a large role in establishing a housing program for the homeless; many others disagree.

4. Rewrite the two clauses as one independent clause:

   INCORRECT Television ads played a large part in temple outreach, however they were not the deciding factor in gaining new members.

   CORRECT Television ads played a large but not a decisive role in gaining new members.

5. Change one of the independent clauses into a dependent clause by beginning it with a subordinating word (*although, after, as, because, before, if, though, unless, when, which, where*), which prevents the clause from being able to stand on its own as a complete sentence.

   INCORRECT The bake sale was held last Tuesday, there was a poor community turnout.

   CORRECT When the bake sale was held last Tuesday, there was a poor community turnout.

Commas in a Compound Sentence A *compound sentence* is composed of two or more independent clauses—that is, two complete sentences. When these two clauses are joined by a coordinating conjunction, the conjunction should be preceded by a comma to signal the reader that another independent clause follows. (This is method 2 for fixing a comma splice, described above.) When the comma is missing, the reader is not expecting to find the second half of a compound sentence and may be distracted from the text.

As the following examples indicate, the missing comma is especially a problem in longer sentences or in sentences in which other coordinating conjunctions appear. Notice how the comma sorts out the two main parts of the compound sentence, eliminating confusion:

INCORRECT	The archbishop promised to visit the hospital and investigate the problem and then he called the press conference to a close.
CORRECT	The archbishop promised to visit the hospital and investigate the problem, and then he called the press conference to a close.
INCORRECT	The ethics review board can neither make policy nor enforce it nor can its members serve on auxiliary church committees.
CORRECT	The ethics review board can neither make policy nor enforce it, nor can its members serve on auxiliary church committees.

An exception to this rule arises in shorter sentences, where the comma may not be necessary to make the meaning clear:

The executive director phoned and we thanked him for his support.

However, it is never wrong to place a comma after the conjunction between independent clauses. If you are the least bit unsure of your audience's notion of "proper" grammar, it is a good idea to take the conservative approach and use the comma:

The temple finance director phoned, and we thanked him for his support.

Commas with Restrictive and Nonrestrictive Elements   A *nonrestrictive element* is a part of a sentence—a word, phrase, or clause—that adds information about another element in the sentence without restricting or limiting its meaning. Although this information may be useful, the nonrestrictive element is not needed for the sentence to make sense. To signal its inessential nature, the nonrestrictive element is set off from the rest of the sentence with commas.

The failure to use commas to indicate the nonrestrictive nature of a sentence element can cause confusion. See, for example, how the presence or absence of commas affects our understanding of the following sentence:

The gardener was talking with the volunteer coordinator, who won the outstanding service award last year.

The gardener was talking with the volunteer coordinator who won the outstanding service award last year.

Can you see that the comma changes the meaning of the sentence? In the first version of the sentence, the comma makes the information that follows it incidental: *The gardener was talking with the volunteer coordinator, who happened to have won the service award last year.* In the second version of the sentence, the information following the title *volunteer coordinator* is vital to the sense of the sentence; it tells us specifically *which* volunteer coordinator—presumably there are more than one—the gardener was addressing. Here, the lack of a comma has transformed the material following the phrase *volunteer coordinator* into a *restrictive element*, which means that it is necessary to our understanding of the sentence.

Be sure that you make a clear distinction in your paper between nonrestrictive and restrictive elements by setting off the nonrestrictive elements with commas.

Commas in a Series   A series is any two or more items of a similar nature that appear consecutively in a sentence. These items may be individual words, phrases, or clauses. In a series of three or more items, the items are separated by commas:

> The priest, the rabbi, and the imam all attended the ceremony.

> Because of the new zoning regulations, all church fundraising activities must be moved out of the neighborhood, all nonprofit organizations must apply for recertification and tax status, and the two local parishes must repave their parking lots.

The final comma in the series, the one before *and*, is sometimes left out, especially in newspaper writing. This practice, however, can make for confusion, especially in longer, complicated sentences like the second example above. Here is the way this sentence would read without the final, or serial, comma:

> Because of the new zoning regulations, all church fundraising activities must be moved out of the neighborhood, all non-profit organizations must apply for recertification and tax status and the two local parishes must repave their parking lots.

Notice that, without a comma, the division between the second and third items in the series is not clear. This is the sort of ambiguous structure that can cause a reader to backtrack and lose concentration. You can avoid such confusion by always using that final comma. Remember, however, that if you do decide to include it, do so consistently; make sure it appears in every series in your paper.

Misplaced Modifiers

A *modifier* is a word or group of words used to describe—or modify—another word in the sentence. A *misplaced modifier*, sometimes called a dangling modifier, appears at either the beginning or the end of a sentence and seems to be describing some word other than the one the writer obviously intended. The modifier therefore "dangles," disconnected from what it truly modifies. It is often hard for the writer to spot dangling modifiers, but readers can—and will—find them, and the result can be disastrous for the sentence, as the following examples demonstrate:

INCORRECT	Flying low over Beverly Hills, the Oral Roberts's mansion was seen.
CORRECT	Flying low over Beverly Hills, we saw Oral Roberts's mansion.
INCORRECT	Worried about the cost of the menu, the dessert was eliminated by the committee.
CORRECT	Worried about the cost of the menu, the committee eliminated the dessert.
INCORRECT	To lobby for prison reform, a lot of effort went into the television ads.
CORRECT	The lobby group put a lot of effort into the television ads advocating prison reform.
INCORRECT	Stunned, the television broadcast the defeated senator's concession speech.
CORRECT	The television broadcast the stunned senator's concession speech.

Note that, in the first two incorrect sentences above, the confusion is largely due to the use of *passive-voice* verbs: "Oral Roberts's mansion *was seen*"; "the dessert *was eliminated*." Often, although not always, a dangling modifier results because the actor in the sentence—*we* in the first sentence, and *the committee* in the second—is either distanced from the modifier or obliterated by the passive-voice verb. It is a good idea to avoid using the passive voice unless you have a specific reason for doing so.

One way to check for dangling modifiers is to examine all modifiers at the beginning or end of your sentences. Look especially for *to be* phrases or for words ending in *-ing* or *-ed* at the start of the modifier. Then see if the modified word is close enough to the phrase to be properly connected.

Parallelism

Series of two or more words, phrases, or clauses within a sentence should have the same grammatical structure, a situation called *parallelism*. Parallel structures can add power and balance to your writing by creating a strong rhetorical rhythm. Here is a famous example of parallelism from the preamble to the US Constitution. (The capitalization follows that of the original eighteenth-century document. Parallel structures have been italicized.)

> We the People of the United States, in Order to *form a more perfect Union*, *establish Justice*, *insure domestic Tranquillity*, *provide for the common defence*, *promote the general Welfare*, and *secure the Blessings of Liberty to ourselves and our Posterity*, do *ordain* and *establish* this Constitution for the United States of America.

There are actually two series in this sentence: the first, composed of six phrases, each of which completes the infinitive phrase beginning with the word *to* (*to form*, [*to*] *establish*, [*to*] *insure*, [*to*] *provide*, [*to*] *promote*, and [*to*] *secure*); the second, consisting of two verbs (*ordain* and *establish*). These parallel series appeal to our love of balance and pattern, and they give an authoritative tone to the sentence. The writer, we feel, has thought long and carefully about the matter at hand and has taken firm control of it.

Because we find a special satisfaction in balanced structures, we are more likely to remember ideas phrased in parallelisms than in less highly ordered language. For this reason, as well as for the sense of authority and control that they suggest, parallel structures are common in political utterances:

> We hold these truths to be self-evident, that all men are created equal, that they are endowed by their Creator with certain unalienable rights, that among these are life, liberty, and the pursuit of happiness.
>
> —The Declaration of Independence, 1776

> Ask not what your country can do for you, ask what you can do for your country.
>
> —John F. Kennedy, Inaugural Address, 1961

Faulty Parallelism   If the parallelism of a passage is not carefully maintained, the writing can seem sloppy and out of balance. Scan your writing to make sure that all series and lists have parallel structures. The following examples show how to correct faulty parallelisms:

INCORRECT	The bishop promises not only *to reform* the missions program but also *the giving of raises* to all church employees. (Connective structures such as *not only . . . but also* and *both . . . and* introduce elements that should be parallel.)
CORRECT	The bishop promises not only *to reform* the missions program but also *to give* raises to all church employees.
INCORRECT	The cost *of doing nothing* is greater than the cost *to renovate* the chapel.
CORRECT	The cost *of doing nothing* is greater than the cost *of renovating* the chapel.
INCORRECT	Here are the items on the committee's agenda: (1) *to discuss* the new maintenance fee; (2) *to revise* the wording of the church charter; (3) *a vote* on the church business manager's request for an assistant.
CORRECT	Here are the items on the committee's agenda: (1) *to discuss* the new maintenance fee; (2) *to revise* the wording of the church charter; (3) *to vote* on the church business manager's request for an assistant.

Fused (Run-On) Sentences

A *fused sentence* is one in which two or more independent clauses (passages that can stand as complete sentences) have been run together without the aid of any suitable connecting word, phrase, or punctuation. There are several ways to correct a fused sentence:

INCORRECT	The parish business committee members were exhausted they had debated for two hours.
CORRECT	The parish business committee members were exhausted. They had debated for two hours. (The clauses have been separated into two sentences.)
CORRECT	The parish business committee members were exhausted; they had debated for two hours. (The clauses have been separated by a semicolon.)
CORRECT	The parish business committee members were exhausted, having debated for two hours. (The second clause has been rephrased as a dependent clause.)
INCORRECT	Our cost analysis impressed the committee it also convinced them to reconsider their action.
CORRECT	Our cost analysis impressed the committee and also convinced them to reconsider their action. (The second clause has been rephrased as part of the first clause.)
CORRECT	Our cost analysis impressed the committee, and it also convinced them to reconsider their action. (The clauses have been separated by a comma and a coordinating word.)

Although a fused sentence is easily noticeable to the reader, it can be maddeningly difficult for the writer to catch. Unpracticed writers tend to read through the fused spots, sometimes supplying the break that is usually heard when sentences are spoken. To check for fused sentences, read the independent clauses in your paper carefully, making sure that there are adequate breaks among all of them.

Pronouns

Its* Versus *It's Do not make the mistake of trying to form the possessive of *it* in the same way that you form the possessive of most nouns. The pronoun *it* shows possession by simply adding an *s*.

> The youth pastor selected a campsite on its merits.

The word *it's* is a contraction of *it is*:

> It's the most expensive program ever launched by the church school committee.

What makes the *its/it's* rule so confusing is that most nouns form the singular possessive by adding an apostrophe and an *s*:

> The archbishop's decision startled the congregation.

When proofreading, any time you come to the word *it's*, substitute the phrase *it is* while you read. If the phrase makes sense, you have used the correct form. For example, if you have used the word *it's*:

> The newspaper article was misleading in it's analysis of the temple's education program.

then read it as *it is*:

> The newspaper article was misleading in it is analysis of the temple's education program.

If the phrase makes no sense, substitute *its* for *it's*:

> The newspaper article was misleading in its analysis of the temple's education program.

Vague Pronoun References Pronouns are words that take the place of nouns or other pronouns that have already been mentioned in your writing. The most common pronouns include *he*, *she*, *it*, *they*, *them*, *those*, *which*, and *who*. You must make sure there is no confusion about the word to which each pronoun refers:

> The priest said that he would support our bill if the archbishop would also back it.

The word that the pronoun replaces is called its *antecedent*. To check the accuracy of your pronoun references, ask yourself, "To what does the pronoun refer?" Then answer the question carefully, making sure that there is not more than one possible antecedent. Consider the following example:

> Several special interest groups decided to defeat the new church construction proposal. This became the turning point of the pastor's construction campaign.

To what does the word *this* refer? The immediate answer seems to be the word *proposal* at the end of the previous sentence. It is more likely that the writer was referring to the attempt of the special interest groups to defeat the construction proposal, but there is no word in the first sentence that refers specifically to this action.

The pronoun reference is thus unclear. One way to clarify the reference is to change the beginning of the second sentence:

> Several special interest groups decided to defeat the new church construction proposal. Their attack on the proposal became the turning point of the pastor's construction campaign.

> Here is another example:

> When the bishop appointed his brother Ken to the position of business manager, he had little idea how bad the budget deficit was.

To whom does the word *he* refer? It is unclear whether the writer is referring to the bishop or his brother. One way to clarify the reference is simply to repeat the antecedent instead of using a pronoun:

> When the bishop appointed his brother Ken to the position of business manager, Ken had little idea how bad the budget deficit was.

Pronoun Agreement A pronoun must agree with its antecedent in both gender and number, as the following examples demonstrate:

> Pastor Smith said that he appreciated our club's support in the church fundraising campaign.

> One reporter asked the new reporter what she would do if the editor offered her a promotion.

> Having listened to our proposal, the coach decided to put it into effect within the week.

> Engineers working on the chapel construction project said they were pleased with the renovation so far.

Certain words, however, can be troublesome antecedents because they may look like plural pronouns but are actually singular:

anyone	each	either	everybody	everyone
nobody	no one	somebody	someone	

A pronoun referring to one of these words in a sentence must be singular, too:

INCORRECT   Each of the women in the support group brought their children.

CORRECT   Each of the women in the support group brought her children.

INCORRECT   Has everybody received their ballot?

CORRECT   Has everybody received his or her ballot? (The two gender-specific pronouns are used to avoid sexist language.)

CORRECT   Have all the delegates received their ballots? (The singular antecedent has been changed to a plural one.)

A Shift in Person

It is important to avoid shifting unnecessarily among first person (*I, we*), second person (*you*), and third person (*she, he, it, one, they*). Such shifts can cause confusion:

INCORRECT	Most people [third person] who apply for church office find that if you [second person] tell the truth during your interview, you will gain the elders' respect.
CORRECT	Most people who apply for church office find that if they tell the truth during their interviews, they will gain the elders' respect.
INCORRECT	One [third person singular] cannot tell whether they [third person plural] are suited for church office until they decide to apply.
CORRECT	One cannot tell whether one is suited for church office until one decides to apply.

Quotation Marks

It can be difficult to remember when to use quotation marks and where they go in relation to other punctuation. When faced with these questions, unpracticed writers often try to rely on logic rather than on a rule book, but the rules do not always seem to rely on logic. The only way to make sure of your use of quotation marks is to memorize the rules. Luckily, there are not many.

Use quotation marks to enclose direct quotations that are no longer than one hundred words or eight typed lines:

> In his farewell address to the Cleveland diocese, the bishop warned, "The great rule of conduct for us with regard to Muslims is, in extending our welcome, to have with them as little disagreement as possible."

Longer quotations, called *block quotations*, are placed in a double-spaced indented block, without quotation marks:

> Rabbi Lowey clearly explained his motive for continuing the temple outreach program in his August 22, 2016, response to David Levine's open letter:

> I would save the outreach program. I would save it the shortest way under the temple bylaws. The sooner full participation can be restored, the nearer the temple will be the temple as it was. If there be those who would not save the temple unless they could at the same time save the outreach program, I do not agree with them. If there be those who would not save the outreach program unless they could at the same time stay within the budget, I do not agree with them.

Use single quotation marks to set off quotations within quotations:

> "I intend," said the imam, "to use in my speech a line from the poem 'Home Burial.'"

Note: When the quote occurs at the end of the sentence, both the single and double quotation marks are placed outside the period.

Use quotation marks to set off titles of the following:

> Short poems (those not printed as a separate volume)
> Short stories
> Articles or essays

Songs

Episodes of television or radio shows

Use quotation marks to set off words or phrases used in special ways:

- To convey irony:

  The "spiritual" church administration has done nothing but cater to local business.

- To indicate a technical term:

  To "sermonize" is to attempt to persuade in an obnoxious way. The last notable failed attempt to sermonize occurred just last week in choir practice.

(Once the term is defined, it is not placed in quotation marks again.)

Quotation Marks in Relation to Other Punctuation   Place commas and periods *inside* closing quotation marks:

"My beloved congregation," said the pastor, "there are tough times ahead of us."

Place colons and semicolons *outside* closing quotation marks:

In his sermon on slothfulness, the rabbi warned against "an encroaching indolence"; he was referring to Pokémon Go.

There are several victims of the imam's campaign to "Turn Back the Clock": the homeless, the elderly, the mentally impaired.

Use the context to determine whether to place question marks, exclamation points, and dashes inside or outside closing quotation marks. If the punctuation is part of the quotation, place it inside the quotation mark:

"When will choir director make up its mind?" asked the baritone.

The demonstrators shouted, "Free the hostages!" and "No more slavery!"

If the punctuation is not part of the quotation, place it outside the quotation mark:

Which president said, "We have nothing to fear but fear itself"?

Note that although the quote is a complete sentence, you do not place a period after it. There can only be one piece of *terminal punctuation* (punctuation that ends a sentence).

Semicolons

The semicolon is a little-used punctuation mark that you should learn to incorporate into your writing strategy because of its many potential applications. For example, a semicolon can be used to correct a comma splice:

INCORRECT   The mosque leadership left the meeting in good spirits, their demands were met.

CORRECT | The mosque leadership left the meeting in good spirits; their demands were met.

INCORRECT | Several guests at the fundraiser had lost their invitations, however, we were able to seat them anyway.

CORRECT | Several guests at the fundraiser had lost their invitations; however, we were able to seat them anyway.

It is important to remember that conjunctive adverbs such as *however, therefore,* and *thus* are not coordinating words (such as *and, but, or, for, so, yet*) and cannot be used with a comma to link independent clauses. If the second independent clause begins with *however,* it must be preceded by either a period or a semicolon. As you can see from the second example above, connecting two independent clauses with a semicolon instead of a period preserves the suggestion that there is a strong relationship between the clauses.

Semicolons can also separate items in a series when the series items themselves contain commas:

> The temple newspaper account of the rally stressed the march, which drew the biggest crowd; the rabbi's speech, which drew tremendous applause; and the party in the park, which lasted for hours.

Avoid misusing semicolons. For example, use a comma, not a semicolon, to separate an independent clause from a dependent clause:

INCORRECT | Students from the youth ministry volunteered to answer phones during the pledge drive; which was set up to generate money for the new arts center.

CORRECT | Students from the youth ministry volunteered to answer phones during the pledge drive, which was set up to generate money for the new arts center.

Do not overuse semicolons. Although they are useful, too many semicolons in your writing can distract your readers' attention. Avoid monotony by using semicolons sparingly.

Sentence Fragments

A *fragment* is an incomplete part of a sentence that is punctuated and capitalized as if it were an entire sentence. It is an especially disruptive error because it obscures the connections that the words of a sentence must make in order to complete the reader's understanding.

Students sometimes write fragments because they are concerned that a sentence needs to be shortened. Remember that cutting the length of a sentence merely by adding a period somewhere often creates a fragment. When checking a piece of writing for fragments, it is essential that you read each sentence carefully to determine whether it has (1) a complete subject and a verb; and (2) a subordinating word before the subject and verb, which makes the construction a subordinate clause rather than a complete sentence.

Some fragments lack a verb:

INCORRECT	The chairperson of our committee, receiving a letter from the parish examiner. (Watch out for words that look like verbs but are being used in another way—in this example, the word *receiving*.)
CORRECT	The chairperson of our committee received a letter from the parish examiner.

Some fragments lack a subject:

INCORRECT	Our study shows that there is broad support for improvement in the child-care ministry. And in the food kitchen.
CORRECT	Our study shows that there is broad support for improvement in the child-care ministry and in the food kitchen.

Some fragments are subordinate clauses:

INCORRECT	After the latest edition of the newspaper came out. (This clause has the two major components of a complete sentence: a subject [*edition*] and a verb [*came*]. Indeed, if the first word [*After*] were deleted, the clause would be a complete sentence. But that first word is a *subordinating word*, which prevents the following clause from standing on its own as a complete sentence. Watch out for this kind of construction. It is called a *subordinate clause*, and it is not a sentence.)
CORRECT	After the latest edition of the newspaper came out, the editor's secretary was overwhelmed with phone calls. (A common method of correcting a subordinate clause that has been punctuated as a complete sentence is to connect it to the complete sentence to which it is closest in meaning.)
INCORRECT	Several members asked for copies of the prophet's proclamation. Which called for reform of the program for the poor.
CORRECT	Several representatives asked for copies of the prophet's proclamation, which called for reform of the program for the poor.

Spelling

We all have problems spelling certain words that we have not yet committed to memory. But most writers are not as bad at spelling as they believe they are. Usually an individual finds only a handful of words troubling. It is important to be as sensitive as possible to your own particular spelling problems—and to keep a dictionary handy. There is no excuse for failing to check spelling.

What follows are a list of commonly confused words and a list of commonly misspelled words. Read through the lists, looking for those words that tend to give you trouble. If you have any questions, consult your dictionary.

Commonly Confused Words

accept/except
advice/advise
affect/effect
aisle/isle
allusion/illusion
an/and
angel/angle
ascent/assent
bare/bear
brake/break
breath/breathe
buy/by
capital/capitol
choose/chose
cite/sight/site
complement/compliment
conscience/conscious
corps/corpse
council/counsel
dairy/diary
descent/dissent
desert/dessert
device/devise
die/dye
dominant/dominate
elicit/illicit
eminent/immanent/
   imminent

envelop/envelope
every day/everyday
fair/fare
formally/formerly
forth/fourth
hear/here
heard/herd
hole/whole
human/humane
its/it's
know/no
later/latter
lay/lie
lead/led
lessen/lesson
loose/lose
may be/maybe
miner/minor
moral/morale
of/off
passed/past
patience/patients
peace/piece
personal/personnel
plain/plane
precede/proceed
presence/presents
principal/principle

quiet/quite
rain/reign/rein
raise/raze
reality/realty
respectfully/respectively
reverend/reverent
right/rite/write
road/rode
scene/seen
sense/since
stationary/stationery
straight/strait
taught/taut
than/then
their/there/they're
threw/through
too/to/two
track/tract
waist/waste
waive/wave
weak/week
weather/whether
were/where
which/witch
whose/who's
your/you're

Commonly Misspelled Words

acceptable
accessible
accommodate
accompany
accustomed
acquire
against
annihilate
apparent
arguing
argument
authentic
before
begin
beginning
believe
benefited

bulletin
business
cannot
category
committee
condemn
courteous
definitely
dependent
desperate
develop
different
disappear
disappoint
easily
efficient
environment

equipped
exceed
exercise
existence
experience
fascinate
finally
foresee
forty
fulfill
gauge
guaranteed
guard
harass
hero
heroes
humorous

hurried	parallel	secession
hurriedly	parole	secretary
hypocrite	peaceable	senseless
ideally	performance	separate
immediately	pertain	sergeant
immense	practical	shining
incredible	preparation	significant
innocuous	probably	sincerely
intercede	process	skiing
interrupt	professor	stubbornness
irrelevant	prominent	studying
irresistible	pronunciation	succeed
irritate	psychology	success
knowledge	publicly	successfully
license	pursue	susceptible
likelihood	pursuing	suspicious
maintenance	questionnaire	technical
manageable	realize	temporary
meanness	receipt	tendency
millennial	received	therefore
mischievous	recession	tragedy
missile	recommend	truly
necessary	referring	tyranny
nevertheless	religious	unanimous
no one	remembrance	unconscious
noticeable	reminisce	undoubtedly
noticing	repetition	until
nuisance	representative	vacuum
occasion	rhythm	valuable
occasionally	ridiculous	various
occurred	roommate	vegetable
occurrences	satellite	visible
omission	scarcity	without
omit	scenery	women
opinion	science	
opponent	secede	

Read&Write 3.2 Proofread for the Pope

You're on the staff of the Holy See. Pope Francis is about to make one of the most important speeches of his papacy, and it's your job to proofread the text before it can be printed for the world to read. There are fifteen errors embedded in the excerpt of the speech that appears below. As you locate the errors, circle them with a pencil. When you have finished, check the error key that follows the excerpt. Below the error key you'll find a copy of this excerpt from Pope Francis's speech as it was originally published, without the embedded errors. (Note that the published address does not use serial commas, that is, commas that separate the final two items in a series of three or more items. An example occurs in the fifth sentence of the second paragraph, in which no comma appears after the word "ideology": "in a religion, an ideology or an economic system.")

An Excerpt from "Pope Francis's Address to Congress,"
September 24, 2015 [with inserted errors]

This year marks the one hundred and fiftieth anniversary of the assassination President Abraham Lincoln, the guardian of liberty, who labored tirelessly that "this nation, under God, [might] have a new birth of freedom". Building a future of freedom requires love of the common good and cooperation in a spirit of subsidiarity and solidarity.

All of us is quite aware of, and deeply worried by, the disturbing social and political situation of the world today. Our world is increasingly a place of violent conflict. Hatred and brutal atrocities, committed even in the name of God and of religion. We know that no religion is immune from forms of individual delusion or ideological extremism. This means that we must be especially attentive to every type of fundamentalism, whether religious or of any other kind. A delicate balance is required to combat violence perpetrated in the name a religion, an ideology or an economic system, while also safeguarding religious freedom, intellectual freedom and individual freedoms. But there is another temptation which we must especially guard against: the simplistic reductionism which sees only good or evil; or, if you will, the righteous and sinners. The contemporary world, with it's open wounds which affect so many of our brothers and sisters; demands that we confront every form of polarization which would divide it into these two camps. We know that in the attempt to be freed of the enemy without, we can be tempted to feed the enemy within. To imitate the hatred and violence of tyrants and murderers are the best way to take their place, that is something which you, as a people, reject.

Our response must instead be one of hope and healing, of peace and justice. We are asked to summon the courage and the intelligence to resolve today's many geopolitical and economic crises. Even in the developed world, the effects of unjust structures and actions are all too aparent. Our efforts must aim at restoring hope, writing wrongs, maintaining commitments, and thus promoting the well-being of individuals and of peoples. We must move forward together, as one, in a renewed spirit of fraternity and solidarity. Cooperating generously for the common good.

The challenges facing us today calls for a renewal of that spirit of cooperation, which has accomplished so much good throughout the history of the United States. The complexity, the gravity and the urgency of these challenges demanded that we pool our resources and talents, and resolve to support one another, with respect for our differences and our convictions of conscious.

Error Key to Excerpt from the Pope's Address to Congress

The letters, words, and punctuation in **bold font** and <u>underlined</u> below indicate locations of grammar, spelling, and other errors. You can also check the original, error-free copy that follows, to find the correct forms of grammar and usage.

This year marks the one hundred and fiftieth anniversary of the **assassination President** Abraham Lincoln, the guardian of liberty, who labored tirelessly that "this nation, under God, [might] have a new birth of freedom<u>".</u> Building a future of freedom requires love of the common good and cooperation in a spirit of subsidiarity and solidarity.

All of us **is** quite aware of, and deeply worried by, the disturbing social and political situation of the world today. Our world is increasingly a place of violent **conflict. Hatred** and brutal atrocities, committed even in the name of God and of religion. We know that no religion is immune from forms of individual delusion or ideological extremism. This means that we must be especially attentive to every type of fundamentalism, whether religious or of any other kind. A delicate balance is required to combat violence perpetrated in the **name a** religion, an ideology or an economic system, while also safeguarding religious freedom, intellectual freedom and individual freedoms. But there is another temptation which we must especially guard against: the simplistic reductionism which sees only good or evil; or, if you will, the righteous and sinners. The contemporary world, with **it's** open wounds which affect so many of our brothers and **sisters; demands** that we confront every form of polarization which would divide it into these two camps. We know that in the attempt to be freed of the enemy without, we can be tempted to feed the enemy within. To imitate the hatred and violence of tyrants and murderers **are** the best way to take their **place, that** is something which you, as a people, reject.

Our response must instead be one of hope and healing, of peace and justice. We are asked to summon the courage and the intelligence to resolve today's many geopolitical and economic crises. Even in the developed world, the effects of unjust structures and actions are all too **aparent**. Our efforts must aim at restoring hope, **writing** wrongs, maintaining commitments, and thus promoting the well-being of individuals and of peoples. We must move forward together, as one, in a renewed spirit of fraternity and **solidarity. Cooperating** generously for the common good.

The challenges facing us today **calls** for a renewal of that spirit of cooperation, which has accomplished so much good throughout the history of the United States. The complexity, the gravity and the urgency of these challenges **demanded** that we pool our resources and talents, and resolve to support one another, with respect for our differences and our convictions of **conscious**.

Excerpt of Original Address of the Pope

This year marks the one hundred and fiftieth anniversary of the assassination of President Abraham Lincoln, the guardian of liberty, who labored tirelessly that "this nation, under God, [might] have a new birth of freedom." Building a future of freedom requires love of the common good and cooperation in a spirit of subsidiarity and solidarity.

All of us are quite aware of, and deeply worried by, the disturbing social and political situation of the world today. Our world is increasingly a place of violent conflict, hatred and brutal atrocities, committed even in the name of God and of religion. We know that no religion is immune from forms of individual delusion or ideological extremism. This means that we must be especially attentive to every type of fundamentalism, whether religious or of any other kind. A delicate balance is required to combat violence perpetrated in the name of a religion, an ideology or an economic system, while also safeguarding religious freedom, intellectual freedom and individual freedoms. But there is another temptation which we must especially guard against: the simplistic reductionism which sees only good or evil; or, if you will, the righteous and sinners. The contemporary world, with its open wounds which affect so many of our brothers and sisters, demands that we confront every form of polarization which would divide it into these two camps. We know that in the attempt to be freed of the enemy without, we can be tempted to feed the enemy within. To imitate the hatred and violence of tyrants and murderers is the best way to take their place. That is something which you, as a people, reject.

Our response must instead be one of hope and healing, of peace and justice. We are asked to summon the courage and the intelligence to resolve today's many geopolitical and economic crises. Even in the developed world, the effects of unjust structures and actions are all too apparent. Our efforts must aim at restoring hope, righting wrongs, maintaining commitments, and thus promoting the well-being of individuals and of peoples. We must move forward together, as one, in a renewed spirit of fraternity and solidarity, cooperating generously for the common good.

The challenges facing us today call for a renewal of that spirit of cooperation, which has accomplished so much good throughout the history of the United States. The complexity, the gravity and the urgency of these challenges demand that we pool our resources and talents, and resolve to support one another, with respect for our differences and our convictions of conscience.[2]

3.3 FORMAT YOUR PAPER PROFESSIONALLY

Your format makes your paper's first impression. Justly or not, accurately or not, it announces your professional competence—or lack of competence. A well-executed format implies that your paper is worth reading. More important, however, a proper format brings information to your readers in a familiar form that has the effect of setting their minds at ease. Your paper's format should therefore impress your readers with your academic competence as a religion scholar by following accepted professional standards. Like the style and clarity of your writing, your format communicates messages that are often more readily and profoundly received than the content of the document itself.

The formats described in this chapter conform with generally accepted standards in the discipline of religion, including instructions for the following elements:

General page formats
Title page
Abstract
Outline of contents
Table of contents
List of tables, illustrations, and figures
Text
Chapter Headings
Reference page
Appendices

---

[2] Holy See Press Office, "11—USA—Washington—24.09.2015—09.20: Congress of the United States of America Visit," United States Conference of Catholic Bishops, accessed November 28, 2016, http://www.usccb.org/about/leadership/holy-see/francis/papal-visit-2015/media-resources/upload/11-EN-congressional-address.pdf.

Except for special instructions from your instructor, follow the directions in this manual exactly.

General Page Formats

Religion assignments should be printed on 8.5-by-11-inch premium white bond paper, 20 pound or heavier. Do not use any other size or color except to comply with special instructions from your instructor, and do not use off-white or poor quality (draft) paper. Religion that is worth the time to write and read is worth good paper.

Always submit to your instructor an original typed or computer-printed manuscript. Do not submit a photocopy! Always make a second paper copy and back up your electronic copy for your own files in case the original is lost.

Margins, except in theses and dissertations, should be one inch on all sides of the paper. Unless otherwise instructed, all papers should be double-spaced in a twelve-point word-processing font or typewriter pica type. Typewriter elite type may be used if another is not available. Select a font that is plain and easy to read, such as Helvetica, Courier, Garamond, or Times Roman. Do not use script, stylized, or elaborate fonts.

Page numbers should appear in the upper right-hand corner of each page, starting immediately after the title page. No page number should appear on the title page or on the first page of the text. Page numbers should appear one inch from the right side and one-half inch from the top of the page. They should proceed consecutively beginning with the title page (although the first number is not actually printed on the title page). You may use lowercase roman numerals (i, ii, iii, iv, v, vi, vii, viii, ix, x, and so on) for the pages, such as the title page, table of contents, and table of figures, that precede the first page of text, but if you use them, the numbers must be placed at the center of the bottom of the page.

Ask your instructor about bindings. In the absence of further directions, do not bind your paper or enclose it within a plastic cover sheet. Place one staple in the upper left-hand corner, or use a paper clip at the top of the paper. Note that a paper to be submitted to a journal for publication should not be clipped, stapled, or bound in any form.

Title Page

The following information will be centered on the title page:

> Title of the paper
> Name of writer
> Course name, section number, and instructor
> College or university
> Date

Accomplishments of the Ozark Christian Church Missions Program

by

Nicole Ashley Linscheid

Contemporary American Religions

REL 213

Dr. Elia Baelish

Galilee Free University

September 30, 2017

As the sample title page above shows, the title should clearly describe the problem addressed in the paper. If the paper discusses youth programs in Albemarle County churches, for example, the title "Youth Programs Conducted by Albemarle County Churches" is professional, clear, and helpful to the reader. "Albemarle County," "Youth Programs," and "Churches" are all too vague to be effective. Also, the title should not be "cute." A cute title may attract attention for a play on Broadway, but it will detract from the credibility of a paper in religion. "Inadequate Solid Waste Disposal Facilities in Denver" is professional. "Down in the Dumps" is not.

Abstract

An abstract is a brief summary of a paper written primarily to allow potential readers to see if the paper contains information of sufficient interest for them to read. People conducting research want specific kinds of information, and they often read dozens of abstracts looking for papers that contain relevant data. Abstracts have the designation "Abstract" centered near the top of the page. Next is the title, also centered, followed by a paragraph that precisely states the paper's topic, research and analysis methods, and results and conclusions. The abstract should be written in one paragraph of no more than 150 words. Remember, an abstract is not an introduction; instead, it is a summary, as demonstrated in the sample below.

Abstract

Bertrand Russell's View of Mysticism

This paper reviews Bertrand Russell's writings on religion, mysticism, and science, and defines his perspective of the contribution of mysticism to scientific knowledge. Russell drew a sharp distinction between what he considered to be (1) the essence of religion, and (2) dogma or assertions attached to religion by theologians and religious leaders. Although some of his writings, including *Why I Am Not a Christian*, appear hostile to all aspects of religion, Russell actually asserts that religion, freed from doctrinal encumbrances, not only fulfills certain psychological needs but evokes many of the most beneficial human impulses. He believes that religious mysticism generates an intellectual disinterestedness that may be useful to science, but that it is not a source of a special type of knowledge beyond investigation by science.

Outline of Contents

The job of this outline is described in section 2.3 above: It serves as a blueprint for the paper, summarizing its goal and giving a sense of the argument's shape.

I. The problem is that parking facilities at Oak Ridge Parish Park have deteriorated as a result of normal wear, adverse weather, and vandalism, and are inadequate to meet parishioner demand.
   A. Only one major renovation has occurred since 1967, when the parking lot was opened.
   B. The parish maintenance department estimates that 10,000 square feet of new parking space and repairs on current surfaces would cost about $43,700.

II. The parish maintenance committee has given extensive consideration to three possible solutions.
   A. Do nothing. Parishioners will continue to park on neighboring streets, but no immediate outlay of parish funds will be necessary.
   B. Make all repairs immediately. Parishioners will enjoy immediate and increased use of facilities. $43,700 in funds will be needed. Sources include: (1) parish funds, (2) episcopate funds, (3) revenue bonds, and (4) a grant from the archdiocese.
   C. Make repairs according to a priority list over a five-year period, using a combination of general church revenues and a $20,000 loan. Parishioners will enjoy the most needed improvements immediately. The loan will require Church approval by the Episcopacy.

III. The recommendation of this report is that alternative C be adopted by the parish council. The benefit/cost analysis demonstrates that residents will be satisfied if basic improvements are made immediately. The parish council should, during its May 15 meeting, (1) adopt a resolution of intent to commit $5,000 per year for five years from the parish fund dedicated to this purpose and (2) approve for submission to the episcopacy in November 2017 an application for a $20,000 loan.

Table of Contents

A table of contents does not provide as much information as an outline, but it does include the titles of the major divisions and subdivisions of a paper. Tables of contents are not normally required in student papers or in papers presented at professional meetings, but they may be included. They are normally required, however, in books, theses, and dissertations. The table of contents should consist of the chapter or main section titles, and the headings used in the text, with one additional level of titles along with their page numbers, as the sample below demonstrates.

List of Tables, Illustrations, and Figures

If your paper includes tables, illustrations, or figures, include a page after the table of contents and list each one by the name for it that is used in the paper's text. List the items in the order in which they appear in the paper, along with their page numbers. You may list tables, illustrations, and figures together under the title "Figures" (and refer to them all as "figures" in the text), or, if you have more than a half page of entries, you may have separate lists for tables, illustrations, and figures (and title them accordingly in the text).

	Figures	
1.	Population Growth in Five Amish Communities, 1990–2016	1
2.	Amish Populations by State, 1980 and 2016	3
3.	Amish Community Expenditures, January–June 2015	6
4.	Educational Reforms at the Amish Communities in Pennsylvania	11
5.	Amish Enterprises, 1980–2015	21
6.	Gross Sales, Amish Products, 1900–2015	22
7.	California Amish Relocations, 1960–2015	35
8.	Amish Settlements in Illinois	37
9.	Amish Arts, 2016	39
10.	Amish Productivity after World War II	42

Text

Ask your instructor for the number of pages required for the paper you are writing. Follow the general page formats given in this chapter.

Chapter Headings

Your paper should include no more than three levels of headings:

1. *Primary*, which should be centered, in boldface, and use headline-style capitalization (each word except articles, prepositions, and conjunctions capitalized)
2. *Secondary*, which begins at the left margin, in boldface, and also uses headline-style capitalization
3. *Tertiary*, which also begins at the left margin and uses headline style capitalization, but is underlined instead of boldfaced, and followed immediately by a period and the first line of the succeeding text

The following illustration shows the proper use of chapter headings:

The Mormon Temple (Primary Heading)

Worship Spaces in the Mormon Temple (Secondary Heading)

<u>Rules for conducting worship</u>. The first rule states that only certified members . . . (Tertiary Heading)

Reference Page

The format for references is discussed in detail in the source citation information that is presented later in this chapter.

Tables   Tables are used in the text to show relationships among data, to help the reader come to a conclusion or understand a certain point. Tables that show simple results or "raw" data should be placed in an appendix. Tables should not reiterate the content of the text. They should say something new, and they should stand on their own. In other words, the reader should be able to understand the table without reading the text. Clearly label the columns and rows in the table. Each word in the title (except articles, prepositions, and conjunctions) should be capitalized. The source of the information should be shown immediately below the table, not in a footnote or endnote. A sample table is shown below.

TABLE 3.1

Projections of the Religious Organization Membership of Selected States, 2020–2035 (in thousands)

State	2020	2025	2030	2035
Alabama	2,251	2,631	2,956	3,224
Illinois	4,051	4,266	4,808	4,440
Maine	459	485	462	423
New Mexico	860	916	900	912
Oklahoma	1,171	1,491	1,789	2,057
Tennessee	2,627	2,966	2,162	2,662
Virginia	3,997	4,124	3,921	4,466

Source: Parkfest Statistics

Illustrations and Figures   Illustrations are not normally inserted in the text of a religion paper or even in an appendix unless they are necessary to explain the content. If illustrations are necessary, do not paste or tape photocopies of photographs or similar materials to the text or the appendix. Instead, photocopy each one on a separate sheet of paper and center it, along with its typed title, within the normal margins of the paper. The format of illustration titles should be the same as that for tables and figures.

Figures in the form of charts and graphs may be very helpful in presenting certain types of information.

Appendices Appendices are reference materials provided for the convenience of the reader at the back of the paper, after the text. Providing information that supplements the important facts in the text, they may include maps, charts, tables, and other selected documents. Do not place materials that are merely interesting or decorative in your appendix. Use only items that will answer questions raised by the text or are necessary to explain the text. Follow the guidelines for formats for tables, illustrations, and figures when adding material in an appendix. At the top center of the page, label your first appendix "Appendix A," your second appendix "Appendix B," and so on. Do not append an entire government report, journal article, or other publication, but only the portions of such documents that are necessary to support your paper. The source of the information should always be evident on the appended pages.

Read&Write 3.3 Explain the Data in This Table

Study the information in the table below and write a "Data Interpretation Essay" in which you *interpret* what this table tells you and speculate on what the cultural implications of its data might be.

Religious Affiliation in America: 1990, 2001, and 2008, from the US Census (in thousands)

Religious Group	1990	2001	2008
Adult population total	**175,440**	**207,983**	**228,182**
Christian total	151,225	159,514	173,402
Catholic	46,004	50,873	57,199
Baptist	33,964	33,820	36,148
Protestant—no denomination supplied	17,214	4,647	5,187
Methodist/Wesleyan	14,174	14,039	11,366
Lutheran	9,110	9,580	8,674
Christian—no denomination supplied	8,073	14,190	16,834
Presbyterian	4,985	5,596	4,723
Pentecostal/Charismatic	3,116	4,407	5,416
Episcopalian/Anglican	3,043	3,451	2,405
Mormon/Latter-day Saints	2,487	2,697	3,158
Churches of Christ	1,769	2,593	1,921
Jehovah's Witness	1,381	1,331	1,914
Seventh-day Adventist	668	724	938
Assemblies of God	617	1,105	810
Holiness/Holy	610	569	352
Congregational/United Church of Christ	438	1,378	736

(continued)

Religious Affiliation in America: 1990, 2001, and 2008, from the US Census (*Continued*)

Religious Group	1990	2001	2008
Church of the Nazarene	549	544	358
Church of God	590	943	663
Orthodox (Eastern)	502	645	824
Evangelical/Born Again	546	1,088	2,154
Mennonite	235	346	438
Christian Science	214	194	339
Church of the Brethren	206	358	231
Nondenominational	194	2,489	8,032
Disciples of Christ	144	492	263
Reformed/Dutch Reform	161	289	206
Apostolic/New Apostolic	117	254	970
Quaker	67	217	130
Christian Reform	40	79	381
Foursquare Gospel	28	70	116
Independent Christian Church	25	71	86
Other Christian	105	254	206
Other Religions	5,853	7,740	8,796
Jewish	3,137	2,837	2,680
Muslim	527	1,104	1,349
Buddhist	404	1,082	1,189
Unitarian/Universalist	502	629	586
Hindu	227	766	582
Native American	47	103	186
Sikh	13	57	78
Wiccan	8	134	342
Pagan	(NA)	140	340
Spiritualist	(NA)	116	426
Other unclassified	991	774	1,030
No religion specified	14,331	29,481	34,169
Atheist	*	902	1,621
Agnostic	1,186*	991	1,985
Humanist	29	49	90
No Religion	13,116	27,486	30,427
Refused to reply to question	4,031	11,246	11,815

Source: US Census Bureau, "Self-Described Religious Identification of Adult Population," *Statistical Abstract of the United States: 2012*, Section 1: Population, Table 75, revised November 23, 2015, http://www.census.gov/library /publications/2011/compendia/statab/131ed/population.html.

* Atheist included in Agnostic.

3.4 CITE YOUR SOURCES PROPERLY

One of your most important jobs when you write a research paper is to document your use of source material carefully and clearly. Failure to do so will cause your reader confusion, damage the effectiveness of your paper, and perhaps make you vulnerable to a charge of plagiarism. Proper documentation is more than just good form; it is a powerful indicator of your own commitment to scholarship and the sense of authority that you bring to your writing. Good documentation demonstrates your expertise as a researcher and increases the reader's trust in you and your work; it gives credibility to what you are writing.

Unfortunately, as anybody who has ever written a research paper knows, getting the documentation right can be a frustrating, confusing job, especially for the novice writer. Positioning each element of a single reference citation accurately can require what seems an inordinate amount of time spent thumbing through a style manual. Even before you begin to work on specific citations, there are important questions of style and format to answer.

What to Document

Direct quotes must always be credited, as must certain kinds of paraphrased material. Information that is basic—important dates, and facts or opinions universally acknowledged—need not be cited. Information that is not widely known, whether fact or opinion, should be documented.

What if you are unsure whether a certain fact is widely known? You are, after all, very probably a newcomer to the field in which you are conducting your research. If in doubt, supply the documentation. It is better to overdocument than to fail to do justice to a source.

The Importance of Consistency

The most important rule regarding documentation of your work is to *be consistent*. Sloppy referencing undermines your reader's trust and does a disservice to the writers whose work you are incorporating into your own argument. And from a purely practical standpoint, inconsistent referencing can severely damage your grade.

The Choice of Style

Some instructors may decide the question of which documentation style to use for you; others may allow you to choose. Documentation systems normally recognized by departments of religion include the ones published by the Modern Language Association (MLA) and the American Psychological Association (APA) and the author-date version of the system detailed in chapter 15 of the sixteenth edition of the *Chicago Manual of Style* (*CMS*), which, due to its widespread use in religion, humanities, and social sciences, is presented here.[3] In addition to the author-date system of the *CMS*, this manual also reprints, with permission, the style sheet published online by the *Journal of the American Academy of Religion* (*JAAR*).[4]

---

[3] University of Chicago Press, *The Chicago Manual of Style*, 16th ed. (Chicago: University of Chicago Press, 2010).

[4] "Style Guide," General Instructions, *Journal of the American Academy of Religion*, Oxford Academic, accessed June 10, 2017, https://academic.oup.com/DocumentLibrary/jaar/style guide.docx.

Why does this manual present two systems? The *CMS* is perhaps the most widely used documentation system for papers presented in religion and theology classes within the university community, and, as such, is an important system for students to become proficient in using. The *JAAR* system offers a slightly but significantly different orientation. The *Journal of the American Academy of Religion*, based at Emory University in Atlanta, serves as the front door to a worldwide community of religion scholars and others interested in religion and theology, and it can be argued that the *JAAR* is the most read journal in the discipline. (We will explore the American Academy of Religion in detail in chapter 4.)

Your instructor may feel that formatting your paper in the same way that papers must be presented for publication to the *JAAR* will help acclimate you to the world of professional scholarship in the disciplines of theology and religion. You will notice that many of the differences between the *CMS* and *JAAR* style systems are slight, at least until it comes to the formatting of the list of references at the end of the paper.

Using the Style Manual

Whichever system you use, read through the guidelines given for it before trying to structure your notes. Unpracticed student researchers tend to ignore questions of bibliographic style until the moment the first note must be worked out, and then they skim through the examples in their style manual of choice looking for the one that perfectly corresponds to the immediate case in hand. But most style manuals do not include every possible documentation model, so it is up to the writer to piece together a coherent reference out of elements from several examples. Reading through all the examples before using them can give you a feel for the placement of information in citations for different kinds of sources—such as magazine articles, book chapters, and electronic texts—as well as for how the referencing system works in general.

> **Note:** If, instead of consulting your style manual, you resort to using one of the electronic citation generators available online, be aware that few, if any, of them, produce citations that are 100 percent accurate. So you will still need to check your citations carefully against the style manual approved by your instructor.

The Author-Date Style System of the *Chicago Manual of Style*: Citations

When you use the author-date system of citation, you place a note in parentheses within the text, following the passage where your source material appears. In order to not distract the reader from the argument, make the reference as brief as possible, containing just enough information to refer the reader to the full citation in the reference list following the text. Usually the minimum information necessary is the author's last name, the year of the publication of the source, and, if you are referring to a specific passage instead of the entire work, the page number(s) of the passage you are using. As indicated by the models below, this information can be given in several ways.

Models of full citations that are keyed to these in-text models and would appear in the list of references at the end of the paper are given in the next section of this chapter.

Author, Date, and Page in Parentheses

Several critics found the pastor's remarks to be, in the words of one, "hope-lessly off the mark and dangerously incendiary" (Northrup 2015, 28).

Note that, when it appears at the end of a sentence, the parenthetical reference is placed inside the period.

Page and Chapter in Notes A text citation may refer to an entire work, in which case you need not include page numbers, since they are given in the reference list at the end of the paper. However, you will sometimes need to cite specific page and chapter numbers, which follow the date and are preceded by a comma. Note that you do not use the abbreviation *p.* or *pp.* when referring to page numbers, but in the case of a chapter, you would use the abbreviation *chap.* (but in roman type).

Page Numbers

Randalson (2016, 84–86) provides a brief but coherent description of the proposal's evolution.

Chapter Numbers

Over the centuries there have been few attempts to reform the structure of the College of Cardinals (Collins 2014, chaps. 9, 10).

Author and Date in Text The following example focuses the reader's attention on the author of the article:

For a highly critical review of the pastor's performance, see Northrup 2015 (28).

Author in Text; Date and Page in Parentheses Here, again, the emphasis is on the author, for only Northrup's name appears within the grammar of the sentence:

Northrup (2015, 28) called the pastor's remarks "hopelessly off the mark and dangerously incendiary."

Source with Two Authors

The diocese's efforts at reforming the education system are drawing more praise than condemnation (Younger and Petty 2016).

Notice that the names are not necessarily arranged alphabetically. Use the order that the authors themselves sanctioned on the title page of the book, chapter, or article.

Source with Three Authors

Most of the Wiccan communities in southern Alabama support the prac-tice of water birth (Moore, Macrory, and Traylor 2016, 132).

Source with Four or More Authors Place the Latin phrase *et al.*, meaning "and others," after the name of the first author. Note that the phrase appears in roman type, not italics, and is followed by a period:

According to Herring et al. (2004, 42), five pastors backed out of the celebration due to doubts about available security.

> Several of the respondents admitted to never having attended services at either temple (Blougram et al. 2017, 34).

All the authors' names will appear in the citation in the list of references at the end of the paper.

Note with More Than One Source Note that the references are arranged alphabetically and separated by semicolons:

> Several commentators have supported the church council's decision to expand the ruling (Barrere 2014; Grady 2014; Payne 2014).

Multiple References to a Source within a Paragraph When a paragraph of your text contains two or more references to a single page or range of pages from the same source, place only one parenthetical citation for that source after the final reference or at the end of the paragraph. However, if the paragraph contains references to different pages within a source, place a full parenthetical citation after the first reference and only page numbers, in parentheses, after all subsequent references.

> While the ritual explained in Mycroft's 1889 account differs from the performance filmed by the *National Geographic* crew in 1952, those differences are slight (Hazelton 2017, 79). In the printed description, the male performers wore robes woven of hemp and dyed green; the *National Geographic* film features male dancers wearing multihued silk pajamas (88). But the purposes of the movements described in print and rendered in film leave little doubt that the ritual is meant to celebrate the rebirth of a nature spirit (64–65).

Two Authors with the Same Last Name Use a first initial to differentiate the authors:

> Research suggests that few members will appreciate the new budget cuts (B. Grady 2013; L. Grady 2012).

Two Works by the Same Author If two works by the same author appear in the same note, place a comma between the publication dates:

> George (2014, 2007) argues for sweeping ethics reform on the national level.

If the two works were published in the same year, differentiate them by adding lowercase letters to the publication dates, alphabetically, by title. Be sure to add the letters to the reference list, too:

> The Denominational Finance Commission's last five annual reports pointed out the same weaknesses in the structure of the church organization (Estrada 2009a, 2009b).

Source with No Author Named It is not unusual for Internet sources and even an occasional print source not to name the author. In such a case, the citation in the list of references will begin with the title of the work, either in quotation marks or in italics, depending on the type of work it is. The in-text citation will begin with the title, which, if it is lengthy, may be shortened, so long as the abbreviated version includes the first word that is not an initial article (*a, an, the*). The title is followed by the date of publication with no comma in between and, if known, the page number of the reference:

> The press saw the case very differently from the way the diocese did ("Public Confused by Bishop's Behavior" 2016, 7).

Source with No Date of Publication Given When a printed source gives no indication of its publication date, use the abbreviation *n.d.* (in roman type) in place of the year.

> It was determined that the entire congregation should undergo the ritual (Blankenship n.d., 14).

Reprints It is sometimes significant to note the date when an important text was first published, even if you are using a reprint of that work. In this case, the date of the first printing appears in brackets before the date of the reprint:

> During that period, there were three evangelism strategies that were deemed potentially useful to religious reformers (Adams [1970] 2017, 12).

Classical Texts The *CMS* 16 advises that references to classic texts (Greek, Latin, Medieval, etc.) be given only in the text or notes and not in the list of references, unless you are referring to the work of a modern author, such as a translator or annotator. Refer to classic texts using the systems by which they are subdivided. Since all editions of a classic text employ the same standard subdivisions, this reference method has the advantage of allowing your reader to find the citation in any published version of the text.

> According to the *Annals* of Tacitus (15.44.1), Nero threw suspicion for starting the great fire on local Christians because the civilian population had begun to blame him for it.

Scriptural Texts As with classical texts, *CMS* 16 advises that scriptural texts should be cited within the text of your paper but not necessarily with a corresponding citation in the list of references. You may cite a biblical passage by referring to the particular book, chapter, and verse, all in roman type, with the version given after the verse number. In running text, do not abbreviate books of the Bible:

> The pastor took as his text a passage from Isaiah.

In parenthetical citations, in references, or when several biblical passages are listed together, use abbreviations. It is also appropriate to abbreviate versions and sections of the Bible:

> "But the path of the just is as the shining light, that shineth more and more unto the perfect day" (Prov. 4:18 AV).

> The online concordance I use lists four instances of the word *resort* in the Authorized (King James) version: Neh 4:20, Ps 71:3, Mk 10:1, and Jn 18:20.

The abbreviation used in the first example above, "AV," is for "Authorized (King James) Version." *CMS* 16 stresses the importance of including the version used and suggests that its name be spelled out in full the first time it appears in your paper.

Lists of abbreviations for the books, sections, and versions of the Bible recommended by *CMS* 16 appear in an appendix at the back of this manual.

Reference to the sacred works of other religions are treated much like citations for biblical texts, providing section numbers and, in most cases, citing the name of the work in roman type.

> The Qur'an (10:26–27) states explicitly that good deeds will be rewarded with good, and those who are evil will be rewarded with evil.

While the names of such collective texts as the Vedas or the Upanishads are given in roman type, the names of particular sections within those works are italicized.

> The first part of each of the Vedas is the *Samhitas*, which, in turn, is a collection of *mantras*, or hymns, mostly concerning the elements of nature worshipped, symbolically, as divinities.

Interviews   Unpublished interviews should be identified within the running text or in a note rather than in a parenthetical citation, and they do not need to be included in the list of references at the end of the paper. Include in the text the names of the interviewer and the interviewee, the means of communication (whether by telephone or other electronic device, written correspondence, or a formal, face-to-face interview), the date, and, if relevant, the location.

> In an April 23, 2016, phone conversation with this author, Dr. Kennedy expressed her disappointment with the Vatican's decision.

If the interview you are citing is published, however, it should be given both a text citation and an entry in the reference list at the end of the paper. Here is an in-text model:

> The *Times* interview allowed Simon ample room to criticize the use of private funds to build such parish projects as the coliseum (Simon 2015, 15–16).

A sample entry for the list of references appears in the next section of this chapter.

Electronic Sources   Whenever possible, in-text references to electronic sources should present the same sorts of information given in in-text references to printed sources. In other words, include the author's last name, the year of publication, and the relevant page number from the source, if given. However, some types of information commonly available in print materials, such as the author's name, exact date of publication, and relevant page numbers, are often missing in electronic sources and so cannot appear in the reference. If the author's name is missing, the parenthetical reference can include the title of the document, in quotation marks. If the online article has numbered paragraphs instead of page numbers, you may supply numbers for paragraphs bearing the relevant passages:

> The crisis that confronted the Southern Baptists on the first day of their June convention was one that no one in the executive offices foresaw ("Effects of the Landmark Election," 2017, para. 12–14).

Unpublished Sources
Theses, Dissertations, and Papers Presented at Meetings   In-text citations for such items should, when possible, include the same information found in in-text citations for published books: last name of author, date, and page number of relevant passage.

Suarez's (2015) description of the community's response to the sudden change in doctrine stresses the panic it caused among minorities.

Note: It is possible to add an identifying date of publication, in parentheses, to a proper name with a possessive, as in the above model, because author-date citations refer not to the person of the author but to the author's work.

Personal Communications Phone calls, emails, texting messages, and other such informal correspondence should be identified within the running text or in a note rather than in a parenthetical citation. Like unpublished interviews, they need not be included in the list of references at the end of the paper.

Three days later, on January 17, the imam responded in an email to the author to explain the importance of the ritual and the benefit it would be to the community.

Sources in Private Collections Identifying information for letters, unpublished papers, and memoranda in the author's possession or in a private, unarchived collection can be given in the running text or in parentheses.

Rita Borges's impression of the 1908 campaign along the Rio Grande, given in her unpublished account, was that it succeeded only in alienating the indigenous inhabitants.

One account of the 1908 campaign did not paint a hopeful picture (Borges).

Sources in Archived Collections Include the date, when available, of the individual item you are citing from an archived collection within the running text, and cite the name of the collection in parentheses.

In a letter to Bradford dated April 11, 1651 (Aurelia Collection), Allen described the hardships that attended the founding of the congregation.

The entry in the list of references will begin with the name of the collection. For an example, see the next section of this chapter.

The Author-Date Style System of the *Chicago Manual of Style*: Reference List

In a paper using the author-date bibliographic system, the parenthetical references point the reader to the full citations in the reference list. This list, which always follows the text of the paper, is arranged alphabetically according to the first element in each citation. Usually this element is the last name of the author or editor, but in the absence of such information, the citation is alphabetized according to the title of the work, which is then the first element in the citation.

The bibliography is double-spaced throughout, even between entries. As with most alphabetically arranged bibliographies, a kind of reverse indentation system called a "hanging indent" is used: After the first line of a citation, all subsequent lines are indented five spaces.

Capitalization   The author-date bibliographical system presented in *CMS* 16 uses standard, or headline style, capitalization rules for titles. In this style, all first and last words in a title, and all other words except articles (*a*, *an*, *the*), coordinating words (*and*, *but*, *or*, *for*, *nor*), and all prepositions, are capitalized.

Books
One Author

> Northrup, Alan K. 2015. *Exhausted Spirits: Revival in the Age of the Great Awakening*. Cleveland: Johnstown.

First comes the author's name, inverted, then the date of publication, followed by the title of the book in italics, the place of publication, and the name of the publishing house. For place of publication, do not identify the state unless the city is not well known. In that case, use postal abbreviations to denote the state (e.g., OK, AR).

Periods are used to divide most of the elements in the citation, although a colon is used between the place of publication and publisher. Custom dictates that the main title and subtitle be separated by a colon, even though a colon may not appear in the title as printed on the title page of the book.

Two Authors   The name of only the first author is reversed, since it is the one by which the citation is alphabetized:

> Spence, Michelle, and Kelly Rood. 2005. *Religion and the Law*. Boston: Tildale.

Three Authors

> Moore, J. B., Jeannine Macrory, and Natasha Traylor. 2016. *Down on the Farm: Reviving Folk Religion in the Deep South*. Norman: Univ. of Oklahoma Press.

You may abbreviate the word *University* if it appears in the name of the press, as long as you do it consistently.

Four or More Authors   For a book by more than three authors, do not use *et al*. Instead, include all the authors' names in the reference list entry.

> Herring, Ralph, Allen LePage, Norma Shearer, and Beth Lee Hopkins. 2004. *Funding Parish Projects*. Atlanta: Jessup Institute for Policy Development.

Editor, Compiler, or Translator as Author   When no author is listed on the title page, begin the citation with the name of the editor, compiler, or translator, followed by the appropriate phrase—*ed*., *comp*., or *trans*., in roman type:

> Trakas, Hayley, comp. 2004. *A Comparison of Greek Orthodox and Russian Orthodox Dogma*. El Paso: Del Norte Press.

Editor, Compiler, or Translator with Author   Place the name of the editor, compiler, or translator after the title, prefaced by the appropriate phrase. Do not abbreviate *Edited by* or *Translated by*.

Pound, Ezra. 1953. *Literary Essays*. Edited by T. S. Eliot. New York: New Directions.

Stomper, Jean. 1973. *Grapes and Rain*. Translated and edited by Molly Glenn. New York: Baldock.

Two or More Works by the Same Author   When citing more than one work by the same author or authors, replace the author names in all entries after the first one with a three-em dash (the equivalent of six hyphens). Arrange the works chronologically by publication date rather than alphabetically by title:

Russell, Henry. 1978. *Famous Valedictions: Notable Final Speeches of the Popes*. New Orleans: Liberty Publications.

———, ed. 1988. *Crusades to Remember*. Denver: Axel & Myers.

Chapter in a Multiauthor Collection   *CMS* 16 allows you to designate the position of the chapter in the book either by chapter number or by inclusive page numbers, as the next two models indicate:

Gray, Alexa North. 2015. "Foreign Policy and the Clergy." Chap. 6 in *Current Media Issues*, edited by Barbara Bonnard. New York: Boulanger.

The parenthetical text reference may include the page reference:

(Gray 2015, 191)

If the author and the editor are the same person, you must repeat the name:

Framer, Susan A. 2004. "Salvation on the Front Lines." In *A History of Chaplaincy in the U.S. Armed Forces*, edited by Susan A. Framer, 29–53. New York: Delos and Sprat.

Author of a Foreword or Introduction   There is no need to cite the author of a foreword or introduction in your bibliography unless you have used material from that author's contribution to the volume. In that case, the bibliography entry is listed under the name of the author of the foreword or introduction. Place the name of the author of the work itself after the title of the work, followed by the page range for the part of the book that is the focus of the reference:

Farris, Carla. 2017. Foreword to *Marital Stress and the Clergy: A Case Study*, by Basil Givan, viii–xvi. New York: Galapagos.

The parenthetical text reference cites the name of the author of the foreword or introduction, not the author of the book:

(Farris 2017)

Subsequent Editions   If you are using an edition of a book other than the first, you must cite the number of the edition or the status, such as *Rev. ed.* for *Revised edition*, if there is no edition number:

Hales, Sarah. 2017. *The Coming Holy Wars*. 2nd ed. Pittsburgh: Blue Skies.

Multivolume Work   If you are citing a multivolume work in its entirety, use the following format:

Graybosch, Charles. 1988–89. *The Upanishads in Western Literature*. 3 vols. New York: Starkfield.

If you are citing only one of the volumes in a multivolume work, use the following format:

Ronsard, Madeleine. 2014. *Spirits of the Northern Tribes*. Vol. 2 of *A History of American Religions*, edited by Joseph M. Sayles. Boston: Renfrow.

Book with No Author Named   Begin the reference with the title, followed by the year of publication. If there is an initial article in the title, it is ignored in alphabetizing.

An Account of the Surprising Conversions Taking Place in Fairfax County and the Means by Which Our Lord Accomplished Them. 1824. Boston: Praighter.

Book with No Date of Publication Given

Blankenship, Elize. n.d. *Weird Service: 18th Century Frontier Protestantism.* Houston: Livry.

Note that the abbreviation *n.d.* is not capitalized, even though it appears after a period.

Reprints

Adams, Sterling R. [1964] 1988. *How to Win Souls: Promotional Campaign Strategies.* New York: Starkfield.

Modern Editions of Classics   If the original year of publication is known, include it, in brackets, before the publication date for the edition used:

Burke, Edmond. [1790] 1987. *Reflections on the Revolution in France.* Edited by J. G. A. Pocock. Indianapolis: Hackett.

Remember, if the classic text is divided into short, numbered sections (such as the chapter and verse divisions of the Bible), you do not need to include the work in your bibliography unless you wish to specify a particular edition.

Tacitus. 1937. *Annals.* Edited by J. Jackson. Vol. 5. Loeb Classical Library. Cambridge, MA: Harvard University Press, 1937.

Periodicals

Journal Articles   Journals are periodicals, usually published either monthly or quarterly, that specialize in serious scholarly articles in a particular field. *CMS* 16 stipulates that an author-date reference for a journal article must include the volume and, when available, the issue number (in parentheses) and publication date. While the in-text note gives the page number of the source material within the article, the citation in the list of references includes the range of pages of the whole article.

Galt, McKinley. 2017. "Dance in the Desert: Traditions of the Igbe Religion." *Journal of African Religions* 7 (2): 54–68.

If the month or season is given, you may use it to replace the issue number.

Hunzecker, Joan. 2014. "Teaching the Unteachable: Evangelism in Out-of-the-Way Places." *Front-Line Religions* 4 (June): 250–62.

Note that the name of the journal, which is italicized, is followed without punctuation by the volume number. A colon separates the issue number or month, in parentheses, from the inclusive page numbers. Do not use *p.* or *pp.* to introduce the page numbers.

Magazine Articles   Magazines, which are usually published weekly, bimonthly, or monthly, appeal to the popular audience and generally have a wider circulation than journals. *Newsweek* and *Scientific American* are examples of magazines. According to *CMS* 16, citations for magazine articles need not be included in the list of references as long as the article has been satisfactorily documented within the text:

> In a July 2005 article for *Sunship Magazine*, Ephraim Snodgrass explains two of the ceremonial purposes of the Zuni fetish animals.

If, however, a citation for the list of references is required, note that the month of publication is separated from the italicized name of the magazine by a comma, as are the inclusive page numbers from the month.

> Snodgrass, Ephraim. 2005. "Mystery and Wonder: The Zunis and Their Stone Icons." *Sunship Magazine*, July, 37–49.

A weekly or bimonthly magazine will include the day of the issue's publication.

> Bruck, Connie. 2016. "The Chant in American Forms of Worship." *New Californian*, October 18, 14–21.

Newspaper Articles   As it does with regard to magazine articles, *CMS* 16 states that full citations for newspaper articles are not necessary in a reference list as long as the source is sufficiently documented within the text of the paper. If such a citation is required, here is a possible model:

> Santoni, Elise. 2017. "Local Diocese Happy to Embrace Refugee Population." *New York Times*, April 8, 4.

Note that *The* is omitted from the newspaper's title. If the name of the city in which an American newspaper is published does not appear in the paper's title, it should be appended in parentheses. (If the city is not well known, the postal abbreviation for the name of the state is added to the parentheses).

> Janeway, Arabella. 2014. "'Blest Be the Tie' Sung at Ball Game," *Daily Gazette* (Altus, OK), June 22, 5.

Newspaper Article with No Author Given   Begin the reference with the title of the article, followed by the year.

> "Thousands Cheer the Dalai Lama's Appearance." 2015. *Los Angeles Democrat Chief*, April 7, 1.

Interviews

Unpublished interviews should be identified within the running text or in a note rather than in a parenthetical citation, and left out of the reference list. For a published interview, begin the citation with the name of the person interviewed, followed by the name of the interviewer.

Untitled Interview in a Book

> Jorgenson, Mary. 2004. Interview by Alan McAskill. In *Hospice Pioneers*, edited by Alan McAskill, 62–86. Richmond: Dynasty Press.

Titled Interview in a Periodical

> Simon, Andrew. 2015. "Whose Parish Is It? An Interview with Andrew Si-
> mon." By Selena Fox. *Tri-City Times* (Chapel Hill, NC), March 14, 40–46.

Interview on Television

> Snopes, Edward. 2004. Interview by Klint Gordon. *Oklahoma Politicians.*
> WKY Television, June 4.

Electronic Sources

If a source is available in both print and electronic forms, it is preferable to use the print form. But if you are using an electronic version of a source, the general practice is to make your reference to the electronic source as similar as possible to that of the print version, adding the full retrieval path (the electronic address), whether it is a URL (Uniform Resource Locator) or a DOI (Digital Object Identifier). If given the choice between including a URL or a DOI, choose the DOI, which is a more stable identifier. End the citation with a period.

While some citation formats for electronic sources require the date of access—the date on which you consulted the source online—*CMS* 16 does not, unless the source does not list a date of publication or date of revision. It may be that your instructor will require the date of access to be included in all citations for electronic sources in your list of references.

It is always wise to check with the instructor for any alterations in the format described here.

Electronic Book Begin with the author's name, reversed, followed by the date of publication (if possible), then the title of the work, the retrieval path (again, if possible), and the date of your last access to the work, in parentheses.

> Amshiral, Sretas. 2014. *Avatars throughout History.* New York: Hickham
> Olney. doi: 10.10743/334971.

Do not capitalize the *d* in *doi*.

If the book was accessed from a bookseller or a library, even though there may be a printed version, it is necessary to indicate that the version you accessed was not that version. You may do so by naming the type of source at the end of the citation, which otherwise conforms to the citation for the printed version of the source.

> Eddington, Cora. *Fitness among the Rulers: A Survey of Old-Testament
> Kings.* New York: Anglo, 2017. Kindle edition.

Chapter in an Electronic Book

> Burris, Akasha. 2013. "Experiments in Transubstantiation." In *Surviving
> Spiritual Disaster*, edited by Jessica Ransom, 72–102. Los Angeles: Arc
> of Hope Press. http://www.arcofhope.com/2013/04/12/paleoearth/361spei-
> ghtnw/heightened/1456/78.html.

> **Note:** You may continue a lengthy URL on the next line of the reference. Do not add a hyphen at the end of the first line. Break a line only after a colon or a double slash or before a single slash, period, or other punctuation.

Electronic Journals   Include all the information that you can find that would be appropriate for the citation for a print journal. Order the information thus: name of author, reversed; year of publication; title of article, in quotation marks; title of journal, in italics; any further publication information, such as volume number, issue number, month, day; inclusive page numbers; and full retrieval path. Note that the online source referenced in this model does not provide page numbers for the article:

> Zoheret, Jeanie. 2013. "The Politics of Social Deprivation." *B & N Digest* 3 (February). http://www.b&ndig/zojeh/o2362/13.html.

Material from a Website   The author's name (reversed) and year of publication are followed by the title of the article, in quotation marks; and the title of the site, in roman type. If no date of publication is given, include the date accessed, followed by the URL.

> Laurence, Ishmael R. "A Virtual Tour of the White Temple, circa 1900." *Landmarks of the Faith: Then and Now.* Accessed December 10, 2016. http://www.natlandmk.com/hist.

Material from a Blog   References to blogs are generally relegated to in-text citations. A blog that is frequently cited, however, may have its own citation in the list of references. The citation generally includes the author of the entry; the name of the entry, in quotation marks; the title of the blog, in italics, or a description; and the URL. If the blog's title doesn't include the word *blog*, place it, in parentheses, after the title.

> Peck, Nyla. "Prayer in Schools?" *Nyla's Natterings* (blog), August 1, 2017. http://nylanat.blogspot.com.

A reference for a comment on a blog entry should begin with the name of the commenter and the date of the comment, followed by the phrase "comment on" and the citation for the related entry.

> J the Baptist. August 2, 2017. Comment on Nyla Peck. "Prayer in Schools?" *Nyla's Natterings* (blog), August 1, 2017. http://nylanat.blogspot.com.

Unpublished Sources

Theses and Dissertations   As with other unpublished works, place the title in quotation marks, not italics. Include the URL if you have consulted the document online. If you found the document in a database, include the name of the database and, if available, any identifying number.

> Hoarner, Art. 2016. "Protestantism and the Free Soil Movement." PhD diss. University of Virginia.

> Suarez, Elena. 2015. "Black Women in the Assembly of God Ministry: A Troubled History." Master's thesis. Oregon State University. ProQuest Dissertations & Theses Global (9873543).

Papers Presented at Meetings

> Zelazny, Kimberly, and Ed Gilmore. 2017. "Vision of the Deity in Times of War: Twenty Centuries of Troubled Art." Presented at the Annual Meeting of the Conference of Metropolitan Arts Councils, San Francisco, June.

Personal Communications
According to *CMS* 16, such personal communications as emails are dealt with in running text and do not need entries in reference lists.

> Jack Tester, one of the festival organizers, told the author in an email that such disruptive behavior was actually one of the goals of the event.

An in-text citation may also be used. It must begin with the name of the person concerned, followed by a phrase such as *personal communication* or *unpublished data*, and the person listed must be fully identified in the text.

> One of the festival organizers told the author in an email that such disruptive behavior was actually one of the goals of the event (Jack Tester, personal communication).

Sources in Private Collections
Letters, unpublished papers, and memoranda in the author's possession or in a private, unarchived collection are cited like other unpublished items.

> Borges, Rita V. Notes on Mexican-American Evangelistic Efforts 1825–1930. In the author's possession.

Sources in Archived Collections
If available, dates of individual items from the collection are given in the text and not in the citation for the list of references.

> Aurelia Collection. Billups Holdings. Augustan College of Letters.

> **Note:** Most of the sources used as models in this chapter are not references to actual publications.

The Style System of the *Journal of the American Academy of Religion*

What follows is the online style sheet of the *Journal of the American Academy of Religion* (*JAAR*), reprinted here by permission. The first few paragraphs offer a cogent description of the journal, its publication philosophy, and its readership; the advice it gives to prospective contributors provides a concise and witty primer on how to produce writing that truly contributes to the discipline.

There is also much to learn by studying the grammatical and rhetorical structures listed in the various, wonderfully succinct sections of the style sheet. Most of the rules given here complement those described in the earlier pages of this chapter, but some offer alternative strategies for crafting your writing. As you read, bear in mind what was said in earlier pages about audience consideration and consistency of usage.

The greatest differences between the two systems occur in (1) the models for the in-text citations, which in the *JAAR* style sheet employs alternative punctuation, and (2) the list of references, for which the *JAAR*'s system differs in many respects from that of the *CMS*. No matter which system you use, *be consistent*.

Information for Authors: Articles

The *Journal of the American Academy of Religion* (*JAAR*) publishes scholarly research of exceptional merit, addressing important issues and demonstrating the highest standards of excellence in conceptualization, exposition, and methodology. We use a double-blind review process [so that] . . . authors do not know the identity of reviewers, and reviewers do not know the identity of authors. . . . Because *JAAR* reaches a local audience of members of the American Academy of Religion as well as a much wider academic audience, authors must demonstrate that their analysis illuminates a significant research problem or engages with an important research question of broad and fundamental interest to the study of religion.

The words "broad and fundamental" are key. In writing for us you are writing for the field of religious studies as a whole. We are not asking authors to speak to the lowest common denominator interests of the *JAAR* audience. Articles should—and almost inevitably will—draw on and speak to a particular subfield. However, they also need to offer content and conclusions that will be of interest to people outside that subfield.

We read carefully and take seriously every article that is submitted to us. Given our volume of submissions and our small editorial staff, it may take a month or more for us to do a close reading of your manuscript and determine if it should be sent out for peer review, or alternatively, if it would be better served by a journal other than *JAAR*. External reviewers are given a month to review a submission, but sometimes need more time. Occasionally, external reviewers are unable to follow through, and alternate reviewers must be identified and given time to read a submission and comment on it. All told, it may take up to six months before we come to a decision on a manuscript. If you consider your material especially timely, please draw the Editor's attention to this, and as necessary, the process will be expedited.

Style Sheet, *Journal of the American Academy of Religion*

General

e.g., i.e.,
Use serial comma
Use elided numbers
Use gender-neutral language
Do not generally use contractions
Add space between initials in names
Give the first name(s) of an author the first time you cite them
Set words used as words in italics
Set quotes of five lines or more as extracts (except in book reviews)
Omit ellipses at beginning and end of quotes (possible exception in dialogue)
Silently capitalize or lowercase initial letter of quote
Spell out acronyms once, then use (almost) exclusively

Italicize all foreign words at every instance

Do not italicize punctuation with italicized words

Do not leave two spaces after a period

Do not refer to your article as an "essay"

Numbers

Spell out numbers one to ninety-nine, except with *percent*

Spell out large, round whole numbers

Words

Generally, use "down" style, lowercasing in most cases, particularly official titles standing alone (i.e., the president, *but* President Clinton).

Use American spelling over British. Specifically,

- chapter, chap. (in parens)
- for example, *not* e.g. (*except in parentheses*)
- that is, *not* i.e. (*except in parentheses*)
- lowercase book parts/use numerals for book parts: part 2, chapter 11
- History of Religions, history of religions
- Internet, web, website, e-mail, www.aaanet.org
- the West, Western, Westernization when referring to the Occident; otherwise lowercase
- the "Other" (capped when used in this specific context)

Margins and Block Quotations

Please use 1″ margins (not 1.25″) if at all possible. Block quotations should be inset, left and right, by an extra ½″.

Citations

Use in text citations, not footnotes (footnotes should be used to raise points outside of the body of the article, but do not use them for your citations)

Use parentheses for citations at ends of extracts

For a simple "see Author" citation, do not create a footnote

"See Farago (2006)" should be set in parentheses in the main text and not as a footnote

Cite page number in text at end of quote, or in footnote

Examples

There are many examples of this dichotomy in the literature (Allen and Wortham; Frank; Wolf 1996: 33).

Clarkson notes, "Hinduism is similar to Buddhism" (1995: 45–6). Michael Harris wrote not only for theologians, but also for politicians.[5]

For an extended discussion of how his work was received by the Canadian government, see Clarkson 1995.

(Bell 2008, 88)

In citation with original pub date:
Weber [1905]

The corresponding reference would be:
Weber, Max [1905] 2010. *Musings on Editing*. Oxford, NY: Oxford University Press.

References

Include electronic citations in reference list, not in footnotes.
Do not include personal communication citations in reference list; cite in footnotes.

Examples

Barber, Theodore. 1989. "Phantasmagorical Wonders: The Magic Lantern Ghost Show in Nineteenth-Century America," *Film History* 3 (2): 73–86.

Choi, Mihwa. 2008. "Contesting *Imaginaires* in Death Rituals during the Northern Song Dynasty." PhD diss., University of Chicago.

Choi, Stephen J., and G. Mitu Gulati. 2008. "Bias in Judicial Citations: A Window into the Behavior of Judges?" *Journal of Legal Studies* 37 (January): 87–129. doi:10.1086/588263.

Ellet, Elizabeth F. L. 1968. "By Rail and Stage to Galena." In *Prairie State: Impressions of Illinois, 1673–1967, by Travelers and Other Observers*, edited by Paul M. Angle, 271–79. Chicago: University of Chicago Press.

Fogel, Robert William. 2004a. *The Escape from Hunger and Premature Death, 1700–2100: Europe, America, and the Third World*. New York: Cambridge University Press.

Greyson, Bruce. 2000. "Near-Death Experiences." In *Varieties of Anomalous Experiences*, edited by E. Cardeña, S. J. Lynn, and S. Krippner, 315–52. Washington, DC: American Psychological Association.

Heinrich, Larissa. 2008. *The Afterlife of Images: Translating the Pathological Body between China and the West*. Durham, NC: Duke University Press.

Kaye, Randi and Chelsea J. Carter. 2013. "Stories of Life, Death and Faith: 'To Heaven and Back.'" *CNN*, November 29. Available at http://www.cnn.com/2013/11/29/us/to-heaven-and-back/. Accessed August 21, 2015.

Phibbs, Brendan. 1987. "Herrlisheim: Diary of a Battle." In *The Other Side of Time: A Combat Surgeon in World War II*, 117–63. Boston: Little, Brown.

Strunk, William, Jr., and E. B. White. 2000. *The Elements of Style*. 4th ed. New York: Allyn and Bacon.

Read&Write 3.4 Create a Scholarly Bibliography

Using one of the two formats given here, the author-date format from the *Chicago Manual of Style* (16th ed., 2010) or the format from the style sheet of the *Journal of the American Academy of Religion* (*JAAR*), create a twelve-item scholarly bibliography that includes at least two *actually published* entries from each of the following information types:

- An academic religion journal article
- A recent religion book

- A sacred text
- A religion book review
- A recent article from a popular religion commentary magazine
- A religion-oriented or religion-based news program
- A blog post
- A social media comment (e.g. Twitter, Instagram)

3.5 AVOID PLAGIARISM

Plagiarism is the use of someone else's words or ideas without proper credit. Although some plagiarism is deliberate, produced by writers who understand that they are guilty of a kind of academic thievery, much of it is unconscious, committed by writers who are not aware of the varieties of plagiarism or who are careless in recording their borrowings from sources. Plagiarism includes:

- Quoting directly without acknowledging the source
- Paraphrasing without acknowledging the source
- Constructing a paraphrase that closely resembles the original in language and syntax

You want to use your source material as effectively as possible. This will mean that sometimes you should quote from a source directly, whereas at other times you will want to express such information in your own words. At all times, you should work to integrate the source material skillfully into the flow of your written argument.

When to Quote

You should quote directly from a source when the original language is distinctive enough to enhance your argument, or when rewording the passage would lessen its impact. In the interest of fairness, you should also directly quote a passage to which you will take exception. Rarely, however, should you quote a source at great length (longer than two or three paragraphs). Nor should your paper, or any substantial section of it, be merely a string of quoted passages. The more language you take from the writings of others, the more the quotations will disrupt the rhetorical flow of your own words. Too much quoting creates a choppy patchwork of varying styles and borrowed purposes in which your own sense of control over your material is lost.

Quotations in Relation to Your Writing

When you do use a quotation, make sure that you insert it skillfully. According to *CMS* 16 (13.9–10), quotations of fewer than one hundred words (approximately eight typed lines) should generally be integrated into the text and set off with quotation marks:

"In the last analysis," Alice Thornton argued, "the denomination cannot afford not to embark on a radical program of education reform" (2006, 12).

A quotation of one hundred words or longer (eight typed lines or longer) should be formatted as a *block quotation*; it should begin on a new line, be indented from the left margin, and not be enclosed in quotation marks.

Blake's outlook for the solution to the diocese's problem of recruiting priests is anything but optimistic:

> If the trend in priest recruitment due to lack of community support continues, the cost of doing nothing may be too high. The five-year period from 2012 to 2017 shows an annual decrease in applications to seminary of roughly twenty percent. Such a downward trend for a sustained period of time would eventually place a disastrous hardship on the diocese's resources. And yet the bishop seems bent on following the tactic of inaction, one result of which may well be the very downturn in community support that has occasioned this report. In other words, the diocese is caught in a vicious spiral: the fewer viable candidates for the priesthood recorded, the more precipitous the decline in community support; the faster the decline in support, the fewer the viable candidates for the priesthood. (2017, 8)

Acknowledge Quotations Carefully

Failing to signal the presence of a quotation skillfully can lead to confusion or choppiness:

> Cardinal Frassbender believes that lay person training programs have succeeded because of additional of resources within the church culture. "The American Catholic community has come to visualize the need to invest in its lay leadership" (Winn 2016, 11).

The first sentence in the above passage seems to suggest that the quote that follows comes from Cardinal Frassbender. Note how this revision clarifies the attribution:

> According to reporter Fred Winn, Cardinal Frassbender believes that lay person training programs have succeeded because of additional of resources within the church culture. Summarizing the cardinal's view, Winn writes, "The American Catholic community has come to visualize the need to invest in its lay leadership" (2016, 11).

The origin of each quote must be indicated within your text at the point where the quote occurs as well as in the list of works cited, which follows the text.

Quote Accurately

If your transcription of a quotation introduces careless variants of any kind, you are misrepresenting your source. Proofread your quotations very carefully, paying close attention to such surface features as spelling, capitalization, italics, and the use of numerals.

Occasionally, to make a quotation fit smoothly into a passage, to clarify a reference, or to delete unnecessary material, you may need to change the original wording slightly. You must, however, signal any such change to your reader. Some alterations may be noted by brackets:

> "Several times in the course of his speech, the attorney general said that his stand [on gun control] remains unchanged" (Caffey 2016, 2).

Ellipses indicate that words have been left out of a quote:

> "The last time members refused to endorse one of the cardinal's policies . . . was back in 1982" (Laws 2005, 143).

When you integrate quoted material with your own prose, it is unnecessary to begin the quote with ellipses:

> Benton raised eyebrows with his claim that "nobody in the bishop's office knows how to tie a shoe, let alone balance a budget" (Williams 2006, 12).

Paraphrasing

Your writing has its own rhetorical attributes, its own rhythms and structural coherence. Inserting several quotations into one section of your paper can disrupt the patterns of your prose and diminish its effectiveness. *Paraphrasing*, or recasting source material in your own words, is one way to avoid the choppiness that can result from a series of quotations.

Remember that a paraphrase is to be written in your language; it is not to be a near-copy of the source writer's language. Merely changing a few words of the original does justice to no one's prose and frequently produces stilted passages. This sort of borrowing is actually a form of plagiarism. To fully integrate another's material into your own writing, use your own language.

Paraphrasing may increase your comprehension of source material, because in recasting a passage you will have to think very carefully about its meaning—more carefully, perhaps, than if you had merely copied it word for word.

Avoiding Plagiarism When Paraphrasing   Paraphrases require the same sort of documentation as direct quotes. The words of a paraphrase may be yours, but the idea belongs to someone else. Failure to give that person credit, in the form of references within the text and in the bibliography, may make you vulnerable to a charge of plagiarism.

One way to guard against plagiarism is to keep careful notes of when you have directly quoted source material and when you have paraphrased—making sure that the wording of the paraphrases is your own. Be sure that all direct quotes in your final draft are properly set off from your own prose, either with quotation marks or in indented blocks.

What kind of paraphrased material must be acknowledged? Basic material that you find in several sources need not be documented by a reference. For example, it is unnecessary to cite a source for the information that Mohandas Gandhi was assassinated on January 30, 1948, because this is a commonly known fact. However, Professor Smith's opinion, published in a recent article, that Gandhi's kindness to Muslims hastened his death is not a fact, but a theory based on Smith's research and defended by her. If you wish to use Smith's opinion in a paraphrase, you need to credit her, as you should all judgments and claims from any other source. Any information that is not widely known, whether factual or open to dispute, should be documented. This includes statistics, graphs, tables, and charts taken from sources other than your own primary research.

Read&Write 3.5   Summarize an Article from *Shambhala Sun, Moment,* or *Guideposts*

Select an article from a recent copy of *Shambhala Sun, Moment,* or *Guideposts,* and summarize it properly in your own words, without plagiarizing, in approximately five hundred words. Attach a copy of the article itself to your summary.

4

BECOME FAMILIAR WITH
QUALITY INFORMATION
SOURCES

4.1   WELCOME TO THE AMERICAN
ACADEMY OF RELIGION (AAR)

The American Academy of Religion is an excellent first stop for many different sorts of religion research and writing projects. According to the AAR's website (aarweb .org), the discipline of religion as we know it today began in 1909, when Syracuse University Professor Ismar J. Peritz and some colleagues organized the Association of Biblical Instructors in American Colleges and Secondary Schools, which first met in 1910. In 1922 the organization became the National Association of Biblical Instructors. Its new acronym (NABI) conveniently means prophet in Arabic. In 1963 NABI was given its present name. In 1969 the AAR and the Society of Biblical Literature (SBL) began holding concurrent (and, since 2011, same-city) annual meetings. Based at Emory University's Luce Center, the AAR now serves nine thousand members based in universities around the world.

If you visit AAR's website you will find a vast array of sources of information about the discipline and study of religion, and about religions around the world. You will find lists of journals, associated religion organizations, and many other interesting sources of information, such as Reading Religion, described here in a passage taken from the AAR website:

> Reading Religion (RR) is an open book review website published by the American Academy of Religion. Launched in 2016, the site provides up-to-date coverage of scholarly publishing in religious studies, reviewed by scholars with special interest and/or expertise in the relevant subfields. Reviews are concise, comprehensive, and timely. RR reviews scholarly books about religion. Reviewers do not need to be members of the AAR, or be professional religious studies scholars. We welcome reviewers from diverse fields and viewpoints who engage with the topic of religion.[1]

---

[1]   "Reading Religion," AAR: American Academy of Religion, accessed December 13, 2016, https:// www.aarweb.org/publications/reading-religion.

Like most other major academic disciplines, AAR hosts a wide variety of groups who focus studies on subjects within the discipline. Just to give you an idea of how richly diverse and active AAR and religion scholars are today, here is the list of sections (major, inclusive units) and groups (specialized units) from the Session Index of the 2016 AAR Annual Meeting, held in San Antonio, Texas, November 19 through 22.[2]

AAR Sections

Arts, Literature, and Religion
  Buddhism
Christian Systematic Theology
Comparative Studies in Religion
  Ethics
History of Christianity
North American Religions
Philosophy of Religion

Religion and Politics
Religion and the Social Sciences
Religion in South Asia
Study of Islam
Study of Judaism
Teaching Religion
Theology and Religious Reflection
Women and Religion

AAR Groups

African Diaspora Religions
African Religions
Afro-American Religious History
Animals and Religion
Anthropology of Religion
Asian North American Religion,
  Culture, and Society
Augustine and Augustinianisms
Baha'i Studies
Bible in Racial, Ethnic, and Indigenous
  Communities
Bioethics and Religion
Black Theology
Body and Religion
Bonhoeffer: Theology and Social
  Analysis
Buddhism in the West
Buddhist Critical–Constructive
  Reflection
Buddhist Philosophy
Childhood Studies and Religion
Chinese Religions
Christian Spirituality
Class, Religion, and Theology
Cognitive Science of Religion
Comparative Approaches to Religion
  and Violence

Comparative Religious Ethics
Comparative Theology
Confucian Traditions
Contemplative Studies
Contemporary Islam
Contemporary Pagan Studies
Critical Approaches to Hip-Hop and
  Religion
Critical Theory and Discourses on
  Religion
Cultural History of the Study of
  Religion
Daoist Studies
Death, Dying, and Beyond
Eastern Orthodox Studies
Ecclesial Practices
Ecclesiological Investigations
Evangelical Studies
Feminist Theory and Religious Reflection
Gay Men and Religion
Hinduism
Human Enhancement and
  Transhumanism
Indigenous Religious Traditions
International Development and
  Religion
Interreligious and Interfaith Studies

2   "AAR Session Index," AAR: American Academy of Religion, accessed December 13, 2016, https://papers.aarweb.org/Session_Index.pdf.

Islam, Gender, Women
Islamic Mysticism
Jain Studies
Japanese Religions
Kierkegaard, Religion, and Culture
Korean Religions
Latina/o Critical and Comparative Studies
Latina/o Religion, Culture, and Society
Law, Religion, and Culture
Lesbian-Feminisms and Religion
Liberal Theologies
Liberation Theologies
Martin Luther and Global Lutheran Traditions
Men, Masculinities, and Religions
Middle Eastern Christianity
Moral Injury and Recovery in Religion, Society, and Culture
Mormon Studies
Music and Religion
Mysticism
Native Traditions in the Americas
New Religious Movements
Nineteenth Century Theology
North American Hinduism
Open and Relational Theologies
Pentecostal—Charismatic Movements
Platonism and Neoplatonism
Practical Theology
Pragmatism and Empiricism in American Religious Thought
Psychology, Culture, and Religion
Quaker Studies
Queer Studies in Religion
Qur'an
Reformed Theology and History
Religion and Cities
Religion and Disability Studies
Religion and Ecology
Religion and Economy
Religion and Food
Religion and Humanism
Religion and Migration
Religion and Popular Culture
Religion and Public Schools: International Perspectives
Religion and Science Fiction
Religion and Sexuality
Religion in Europe

Religion in Latin America and the Caribbean
Religion in Premodern Europe and the Mediterranean World
Religion in Southeast Asia
Religion in the American West
Religion, Affect, and Emotion
Religion, Colonialism, and Postcolonialism
Religion, Film, and Visual Culture
Religion, Holocaust, and Genocide
Religion, Media, and Culture
Religion, Memory, History
Religion, Sport, and Play
Religions in Chinese and Indian Cultures: A Comparative Perspective
Religions, Medicines, and Healing
Religions, Social Conflict, and Peace
Religious Conversions
Ricoeur
Ritual Studies
Roman Catholic Studies
Sacred Texts and Ethics
Sacred Texts, Theory, and Theological Construction
Schleiermacher
Science, Technology, and Religion
Scriptural Reasoning
Secularism and Secularity
Sikh Studies
Sociology of Religion
Space, Place, and Religion
Tantric Studies
Theology and Continental Philosophy
Theology of Martin Luther King Jr.
Tibetan and Himalayan Religions
Tillich: Issues in Theology, Religion, and Culture
Traditions of Eastern Late Antiquity
Transformative Scholarship and Pedagogy
Vatican II Studies
Wesleyan Studies
Western Esotericism
Womanist Approaches to Religion and Society
Women of Color Scholarship, Teaching, and Activism
World Christianity
Yoga in Theory and Practice
Yogācāra Studies

Read&Write 4.1 Write an Email to an AAR Section Chair

Begin this task by identifying a topic in religion in which you are interested. If you need an idea of where to start, browse the names of the AAR sections. Once you identify a topic, clearly explain in several sentences exactly what you are interested in researching. Next, on AAR's website, locate the section that covers your topic, and go to that section's own website to find the chair of that section. Compose an email to that person. Ask him or her to provide you with: (1) guidance on researching the topic, (2) names of scholars in the United States (and abroad) who are knowledgeable in this subject, and (3) the names of journals, research institutes, university departments, and other resources of information on your topic. Be sure to thank the chair for any information he or she may be able to provide. You may then present both the email you wrote and the chair's response to your course professor.

For example, let's suppose you are interested in Buddhism. You decide that you want to know more about the extent to which mystical experiences are important in Buddhists' lives. On AAR's Buddhism section website (as of June 2017) you find the following information about the current section chairs:

James Robson, jrobson@fas.harvard.edu

Reiko Ohnuma, reiko.ohnuma@dartmouth.edu

Write to either chair an email as described above.

Now find your section chair and write a summary of the information that person provides for you.

4.2   WELCOME TO THE SOCIETY OF BIBLICAL LITERATURE (SBL)

As mentioned in the preceding section, the Society of Biblical Literature holds its annual meeting in conjunction with the AAR. Founded in 1880 to promote biblical scholarship, today it has more than 8,000 members, more than 2,500 of whom are from countries other than the United States. Among the many benefits to be gained from visiting its website (sbl-site.org) are the vast numbers of resources for biblical studies that can be found there. One example is its lists of program affiliates and peer organizations.[3] Here are the organizations on these lists:

Program Affiliates

Academy of Homiletics

African Association for the Study of Religions

Anglican Association of Biblical Scholars

Ethnic Chinese Biblical Colloquium

GOCN Forum on Missional Hermeneutics

Institute for Biblical Research

International Organization for Septuagint and Cognate Studies

---

[3] "Associations," SBL: Society of Biblical Literature, accessed December 15, 2016, http://www.sbl-site .org/aboutus/associations.aspx.

International Qur'anic Studies Association
Journal of Feminist Studies in Religion
Karl Barth Society of North America
Korean Biblical Colloquium
National Association of Professors of Hebrew
Nida Institute for Biblical Scholarship at the American Bible Society
North American Association for the Study of Religion
Society for Ancient Mediterranean Religions
Society for Comparative Research on Iconographic and Performative Texts
Society for Pentecostal Studies
Søren Kierkegaard Society
Wabash Center for Teaching and Learning in Theology and Religion
Westar

Peer Organizations

American Academy of Religion (AAR)
American Council of Learned Societies (ACLS)
American Schools of Oriental Research (ASOR)
Association of American University Presses (AAUP)
Catholic Biblical Association of America (CBA)
Coalition on the Academic Workforce (CAW)
Council of Independent Colleges (CIC)
International Association for the History of Religions (IAHR)
International Organization for Masoretic Studies (IOMS)
International Organization for Septuagint & Cognate Studies (IOSCS)
International Qur'anic Studies Association (IQSA)
National Association of Professors of Hebrew
National Humanities Alliance (NHA)
Nida Institute for Biblical Scholarship at the American Bible Society
Pontifical Biblical Institute (PIB)
The Fund for Theological Education (FTE)
Wabash Center for Teaching and Learning in Theology and Religion

The Society's annual meeting, details of which are provided at sbl-site.org/meetings/AnnualMeeting.aspx, presents an exceptional opportunity to engage current biblical scholarship. The web page announcing the 2016 meeting included this description:

> With more than 1,200 academic sessions, and workshops, along with one of the world's largest exhibits of books and digital resources for biblical studies, the Annual Meeting is one of the largest events of the year in the fields of biblical scholarship, religious studies and theology.[4]

---

[4] "SBL Annual Meeting [2016]," SBL: Society of Biblical Literature, accessed December 15, 2016, https://www.sbl-site.org/meetings/AnnualMeeting.aspx.

Read&Write 4.2 Write an Email to an SBL Section Author

Your task here is similar to the one in the previous section. Begin by identifying a topic in biblical studies in which you are interested. If you need an idea of where to start, locate the search engine for the most recent past SBL Annual Meeting program book. Once you find an interesting topic (e.g., diaspora or Moses), enter the topic in the search engine and find a list of papers presented at the meeting that deal with that topic. Select a paper of interest and identify its author and his or her academic affiliation. At the author's university or other organization website, locate the author's email address. Then compose an email to that person. Ask the author to provide you with (1) guidance on researching the topic, (2) names of scholars in the United States (and abroad) who are knowledgeable in this subject, and (3) the names of journals, research institutes, university departments, and other resources of information on your topic. Be sure to thank the author for any information he or she may be able to provide. Present both the email you wrote and the author's response to your course professor.

For example, let's suppose you are interested in the New Testament book of Luke. In the 2015 Annual Meeting Program you will find this panel:

Formation of Luke and Acts
11/21/2015
4:00 pm to 6:30 pm
Room: Spring (Atlanta Conference Level)—Hyatt
Theme: *New Research on the Synoptic Problem and Other Conundra*
The session aims to clarify issues in the formation of Luke as it relates to the Synoptic Problem, including work on the minor agreements and other features of demonstrable formative influence.
Patricia Walters, Rockford University, Presiding
Jeffrey Peterson, Austin Graduate School of Theology
Luke's Transformation of Matthaean Motifs (25 min)
Discussion (5 min)
Jordash Kiffiak, University of Zurich
"And it came to pass, when Jesus had finished these words . . .": Evaluating the Case for Luke's Direct Use of Matthew (25 min)
Discussion (5 min)
Hugo Mendez, Yale University
Did God "Speak Forever"? Reconsidering the Sources and Formation of the Lukan Infancy Hymns (25 min)
Discussion (5 min)
Chang Wook Jung, Chongshin University
Minor Agreements in Luke 8:9–10 and Luke's Source for the Verses (25 min)
Discussion (5 min)
Discussion (30 min)[5]

You would then email the author of one of the four studies listed here and, once he or she has responded to your questions, write a summary of the information that person has provided you.

---

[5] "Program Book [2015]," SBL: Society of Biblical Literature, accessed December 15, 2016, https://www.sbl-site .org/meetings/Congresses_ProgramBook.aspx?MeetingId=27.

4.3   HOW TO LOCATE RELIGION AND THEOLOGY DISSERTATIONS AND THESES

Dissertations and theses are papers written to fulfill requirements for master's and doctoral degrees. To be accepted by universities that issue graduate degrees, dissertations and theses normally must (1) exhibit a demonstrated ability to meet widely recognized standards of scholarship, and (2) make an original contribution to knowledge. In the United States the word *dissertation* normally refers to papers written to achieve the doctor of philosophy and other doctoral degrees, while the term *thesis* is most often attached to a paper written for a master's degree. In Europe and elsewhere, however, this distinction is less common. Dissertations are often published after graduation as monographs, articles, or books. While quantitative dissertations—papers dealing largely with statistics and statistical analyses—are often fewer than fifty pages in length, qualitative dissertations, which tend to use descriptive language to argue specific viewpoints, may run to several hundred pages.

A good place to start your search for dissertations is the search engine for the online catalog of the Global Resources Network's Center for Research Libraries (CRL). On the "About CRL" page, the center makes the following statement:

> The Center for Research Libraries (CRL) is an international consortium of university, college, and independent research libraries. Founded in 1949, CRL supports original research and inspired teaching in the humanities, sciences, and social sciences by preserving and making available to scholars a wealth of rare and uncommon primary source materials from all world regions.
>
> CRL's deep and diverse collections are built by specialists and experts at the major U.S. and Canadian research universities, who work together to identify and preserve unique and uncommon documentation and evidence, and to ensure its long-term integrity and accessibility to researchers in the CRL community.
>
> CRL is based in Chicago, Illinois, and is governed by a Board of Directors drawn from the library, research and higher education communities.[6]

Dissertations links that are typically found on college libraries' web pages will also provide databases of varied strengths depending upon the library's research capabilities.

Read&Write 4.3   Collect Six Dissertation Abstracts on a Topic of Interest

Using the dissertation location services described above, (1) locate six dissertations of importance to a research topic of your choice, and (2) write a brief (one- to two-paragraph) abstract of each one that describes the value of the dissertation to the topic at hand.

---

[6]   "About CRL," Center for Research Libraries Global Resources Network, accessed December 1, 2016, http://www.crl.edu/about.

4.4   HOW TO LOCATE STUDIES BY THINK TANKS

Private research institutes, popularly known as think tanks, provide a wealth of information on virtually any topic you can imagine. A Google search on "think tanks" will provide many lists of them, but an excellent place to start is the Harvard Kennedy School's Library and Knowledge Services page available here: guides.library. harvard.edu/hks/think_tank_search. In this search engine, you can enter specific topics (e.g., family) or specific institutes (e.g., the Hoover Institution).

Read&Write 4.4   Collect Six Think Tank Studies on a Topic of Interest

Using the Harvard Kennedy School's search engine, (1) locate six studies of importance to a research topic of your choice, and (2) write a summary of each one that describes the value of the study to the topic at hand.

4.5   WELCOME TO THE LIBRARY OF CONGRESS (LOC)

Expect to be amazed at the phenomenal collections of the Library of Congress (loc.gov). Here you will find access to millions of documents of every conceivable source.

The manuscripts section alone declares: "The Library of Congress holds approximately sixty million manuscript items in eleven thousand separate collections, including some of the greatest manuscript treasures of American history and culture."[7]

Though massive today, the library's collections had a more modest beginning, as the website's history link describes:

> The Library of Congress was established by an act of Congress in 1800 when President John Adams signed a bill providing for the transfer of the seat of government from Philadelphia to the new capital city of Washington. The legislation described a reference library for Congress only, containing "such books as may be necessary for the use of Congress—and for putting up a suitable apartment for containing them therein."
>
> Established with $5,000 appropriated by the legislation, the original library was housed in the new Capitol until August 1814, when invading British troops set fire to the Capitol Building, burning and pillaging the contents of the small library.
>
> Within a month, retired President Thomas Jefferson offered his personal library as a replacement. Jefferson had spent 50 years accumulating books, "putting by everything which related to America, and indeed whatever was rare and valuable in every science"; his library was considered to be one of the finest in the United States. In offering his collection to Congress, Jefferson anticipated controversy over the nature of his collection, which included books in foreign languages and volumes of philosophy,

---

[7] "Collections with Manuscripts," Library of Congress, accessed March 7, 2016, https://www.loc.gov /manuscripts/collections.

science, literature, and other topics not normally viewed as part of a legislative library. He wrote, "I do not know that it contains any branch of science which Congress would wish to exclude from their collection; there is, in fact, no subject to which a Member of Congress may not have occasion to refer."

In January 1815, Congress accepted Jefferson's offer, appropriating $23,950 for his 6,487 books, and the foundation was laid for a great national library. The Jeffersonian concept of universality, the belief that all subjects are important to the library of the American legislature, is the philosophy and rationale behind the comprehensive collecting policies of today's Library of Congress.[8]

Read&Write 4.5 Examine Some Religion Items from the Library of Congress Collections

One of the subjects in "Digital Collections" on loc.gov is Religion & Philosophy. Following this link for that subject, you will find a page of links to special collections. For example, one current collection is "Sikkim Photos, Kandell Collection." The Library's description of this collection includes the following:

> This selection of 300 images portrays the people and landscape of a kingdom high in the Himalaya Mountains. Sikkim, now part of India, borders on Tibet, Nepal, and Bhutan. Dr. Kandell captured these vivid scenes in order to document a vanishing culture. During visits between 1965 and 1979 (primarily 1965–1971), Dr. Kandell received special permission to photograph Buddhist monks and lamas, ceremonial dances, and monasteries; people working on farms, in canning factories, and at special crafts; and the royal palace and chapel at Gangtok, including the last king, Chogyal Palden Thondup Namgyal, his American wife Queen Hope Cooke (Dr. Kandell's college friend), and their family.[9]

Your task in this exercise is to peruse the Library of Congress collections, select a particular collection, and write a brief paper describing and evaluating the content and importance of the information it contains.

8   "History of the Library," Library of Congress, accessed March 7, 2016, http://www.loc.gov/about/history-of-the-library.

9   "Sikkim Photos (Kandell Collection)," Library of Congress, accessed December 13, 2016, https://www.loc.gov/collections/sikkim-photos/about-this-collection.

5

LEARNING OBSERVATION

SKILLS

5.1   CONDUCT AN INTERVIEW

The phrase *spiritual life* can have different meanings. It can refer to the time one spends enjoying fellowship and participating in service activities in a church, temple, or mosque. It can also suggest that part of life devoted to prayer and meditation, activities aimed at promoting transcendent contentment. Notions of what constitutes spiritual life and strategies that people adopt in order to achieve their spiritual goals are among the most important and fruitful topics of study for scholars of religion and theology. And, as for any scientist, one of the most effective tools available to the scholar of religion working to gain insight into the nature and processes of the spiritual life is the act of direct observation.

One time-honored, specialized form of direct observation is the *interview*. Many of the world's great religious and philosophical texts are phrased as conversations, question-and-answer sessions in which seekers of wisdom, in effect, interview people believed to have answers to important spiritual questions. The Upanishads are basically question-and-answer sessions between students and sages. Nicodemus interviews Jesus about spiritual rebirth. Fan Chi interviews Confucius about wisdom and goodness.

The field of potentially useful interview subjects concerning the topic of the spiritual life is limitless. Anyone may have a useful comment to make, and students of religion and theology will find real profit in sharpening their interview skills. A good way—a congenial way—to start would be to approach one of your community's religious leaders and ask for an interview. Whatever paper topic your religion or theology instructor has assigned to you will very probably benefit from such an interview.

If you want to gain some valuable information from a local religious leader, go prepared. Request an interview time at that person's convenience. Dress appropriately for the occasion. After asking for and being granted permission to do so, take lots of notes.

Prepare some open-ended questions ahead of time. The person you interview may take off in a rich spate of insights and observations that leave you struggling to keep up. Or you may get short, nondescript answers and little else. Most likely you will experience something in between these extremes.

Most important, your list of thoughtfully prepared questions will help you hear what you really want to know. No matter what the specific topic of your interview is, you can approach it through a range of perspectives. There are a lot of possibilities for focusing your interview, as this short list indicates:

- *Spirituality:* How does one pursue genuine spiritual experiences? Does the person being interviewed have any he or she would like to share?
- *Doctrine:* What does the interviewee think about the role of women in his or her church? How does he or she approach teachings about family, community, duty, divorce?
- *Ethics:* How should a person conduct his or her business and professional relationships? Should leadership take political stands?
- *Leadership:* How are people effectively motivated, consoled, inspired, included?
- *Ritual:* What rituals are the most important for spiritual life? What makes them important?
- *Service:* What are some effective and needed services that members can provide their parishes and congregations?

Read&Write 5.1   Interview a Local Religious Leader

Select a local religious leader and set up an interview. Be sure to let that person know that you are writing a paper for a class exercise. Construct a list of five or six open-ended questions from topics like the ones above. They should be designed to allow the person interviewed some latitude in response. You want to allow that person to share his or her enthusiasms while gaining insight into your own areas of interest. You may want to begin by asking about that person's personal journey. What led him to his current career? What have been her greatest challenges and satisfactions?

Immediately after the interview, rewrite your notes, adding ideas and insights you have gained. Then write an essay in which you describe the content of your conversation, the insights you gained in the process, your evaluation of the experience, and ideas to improve your skills for your next interview.

5.2   CONDUCT A FOCUS GROUP

In Nikos Kazantzakis's popular novel *Zorba the Greek* (1946), the colorful title character, facing difficulties in establishing a mining operation, exclaims, "Trouble? Life is trouble. Only death is not."[1] Let's revise this phrase to say, "Religion? Religion is controversy. Only life without thinking is not." For example, many Christians would agree that the Bible is wholly and unequivocally the word of God. But Christians seem to disagree about many of God's directives as formulated in the Bible. A recent Internet search of varieties of American Baptists alone yielded more than four hundred distinct associations. Under the broader umbrella of Christianity, one need look no further than gender and sexuality to find a panoply of controversies—abortion, birth control, homosexuality, celibacy, women in ecclesiastical roles, and so forth.

A productive method of initiating research on any religious controversy is to conduct a *focus group*, normally composed of five to ten people who discuss a specific topic,

---

[1]   Nikos Kazantzakis, *Zorba the Greek*, trans. Carl Wildman (London: Faber and Faber, 1974), 105.

most often a controversial one. A group coordinator guides the discussion, takes notes, and summarizes agreements, disagreements, and insights generated in the discourse.

Focus groups make for excellent in-class exercises, when the class is formed into four- to six-member units, each discussing either the same topic or different issues.

Read&Write 5.2   Conduct a Focus Group on a Topic of Interest

For this exercise, the instructor may divide the class into groups and assign each group a topic. Or the instructor may invite students to propose topics, listing them on the board, and then form groups based on student interest. Each topic should be formulated as a question. Instead of stating a topic such as "Clergy and Politics," the instructor might write, "What limits, if any, should clerics place upon raising political issues in their sermons?" Each group then attempts to arrive at an answer to its question, and time is reserved near the end of the class period for each group to present its answer to the class for further discussion.

5.3   CONDUCT A CASE STUDY

A *case study* is an in-depth investigation of a social unit, undertaken to identify the factors that influence the way the unit functions and how it affects its community. The unit under study can be a single individual or a group, and the group may be large or small. Psychologists have used case studies of mental patients for many years to support or refute behavioral theories. Sociologists use the case-study approach to describe and draw conclusions about a wide variety of subjects, such as labor unions, police departments, medical schools, gangs, public and private bureaucracies, religious groups, cities, and social classes. Political scientists use case studies to examine such things as leadership styles in government agencies and group dynamics in political parties. Typical religion case studies include:

- An evaluation of the internal cohesion achieved by the parish council, and the effects of this cohesion on the church membership as a whole
- A study of the effectiveness of a diocese's charity programs
- A study of the strategies of a temple's outreach program
- A study of a mosque's community relations
- A study of a congregation's approach to divorce within its membership

The success of a case study depends heavily on the open-mindedness, sensitivity, insightfulness, and integrative abilities of its investigator. Case studies fulfill many educational objectives. As a student in a religion course, you may write a case study in order to improve your ability to do the following:

- Carefully and objectively analyze information
- Solve problems effectively
- Present your ideas in clear written form to a specific audience

In addition, writing a case study allows you to discover some of the problems you will face if you become involved in an actual situation that parallels your case study. For example, writing a case study can help you to understand the following:

- Some of the potentials and problems of religious life in general
- The operation of a particular parish, denomination, or new religious movement

- The development of a particular problem, such as interdenominational disagreements, policies for dealing with sexual abuse, or strategies to increase membership of a congregation
- The interrelationships—within a particular setting—of people, structures, doctrines, politics, evangelism, and many other factors

Before writing a case study, you should be aware of the limitations of the methods you will be using, in order to avoid drawing conclusions that are not justified by the knowledge you acquire. First, case studies are relatively subjective exercises. When you write a case study, you select the facts and arrange them into patterns from which you may draw conclusions. The quality of the case study will depend largely upon the quality of the facts you select and the way in which you interpret those facts.

A second potential liability to the case-study method is that every case study, no matter how well written, is in some sense an oversimplification of both the events that are described and the environment within which those events take place. To simplify an event or series of events makes a situation easier to understand but at the same time distorts its effects and importance. It can always be argued that the results of any case study are peculiar to that one case and, therefore, offer little as a rationale for a general explanation or prediction.

A third caution about case studies pertains strictly to their use as a learning tool in the classroom. Remember that no matter how astute or sincere they may be, any interpretations you come up with for a case study in your class are essentially parts of an academic exercise and therefore may not be applicable in an actual situation.

The following list presents a sample of recently published religion case studies:

- *Islam and the Métropole: A Case Study of Religion and Rhetoric in Algeria*[2]
- *Variations on the Messianic Theme: A Case Study of Interfaith Dialogue*[3]
- *Introducing Ordinary African Readers' Hermeneutics: A Case Study of the Agikuyu Encounter with the Bible*[4]
- "Religious Differences in Female Genital Cutting: A Case Study from Burkina Faso"[5]
- "Religious Networking Organizations and Social Justice: An Ethnographic Case Study"[6]
- "Unlocking the Spiritual with Club Drugs: A Case Study of Two Youth Cultures"[7]

---

[2] Ben Hardman, *Islam and the Métropole: A Case Study of Religion and Rhetoric in Algeria*, American University Studies (New York: Peter Lang, 2009).

[3] Marion Wyse, *Variations on the Messianic Theme: A Case Study of Interfaith Dialogue*, Judaism and Jewish Life (Brighton, MA: Academic Studies Press, 2009).

[4] Johnson Kinyua, *Introducing Ordinary African Readers' Hermeneutics: A Case Study of the Agikuyu Encounter with the Bible*, Religions and Discourse 54 (New York: Peter Lang, 2011).

[5] Sarah R. Hayford and Jenny Trinitapoli, "Religious Differences in Female Genital Cutting: A Case Study from Burkina Faso," *Journal for the Scientific Study of Religion* 50, no. 2 (2011): 252–71.

[6] N. R. Todd, "Religious Networking Organizations and Social Justice: An Ethnographic Case Study," *American Journal of Community Psychology* 50 (September 2012): 229–45.

[7] K. Joe-Laidler and G. Hunt, "Unlocking the Spiritual with Club Drugs: A Case Study of Two Youth Cultures," *Substance Use & Misuse* 48, no. 12 (September 2013): 1099–1108, doi:10.3109/10826084 .2013.808067.

- "The Influence of Culture on Home-Based Family Caregiving at End-of-Life: A Case Study of Dutch Reformed Family Care Givers in Ontario, Canada"[8]
- "Gender, Religion, and the Experience of Suffering: A Case Study"[9]
- "Case Study. Faith and Futility in the ICU. Commentary"[10]
- "Religiosity and Its Relation to Quality of Life in Primary Caregivers of Patients with Multiple Sclerosis: A Case Study in Greece"[11]
- "Developing Religious Identities of Muslim Students in the Classroom: A Case Study from Finland"[12]

Read&Write 5.3   Conduct a Case Study on a Local Religious Group

Your mission in this exercise is to conduct and write a case study of a local religious group. To accomplish this task, you must:

- Conduct at least one interview with clergy of this religious group (see section 5.1 of this chapter)
- Conduct at least one interview with a layperson of this religious group
- Practice participant observation skills by attending a minimum of two meetings of this religious group and taking notes on what transpires; these meetings could be two formal services or one formal service and one less formal service, such as a Bible study or prayer meeting
- Collect information from this organization's official publications

Your paper will comprise an in-depth description of this organization. Your narrative should include:

- A general description of the religion represented (introduction)
- A summary of the group's belief structure
- A description of the physical settings of the religious meetings
- A description of the worship or other services or meetings you attended

Your paper's conclusions section will include:

- Your observations about the roles of men and women in this religious group
- Your observations about the roles of clergy and laypeople in this religious group
- Your personal observations and feelings: What did you learn? (conclusions)

---

8   R. Donovan, A. Williams, K. Stajduhar, K. Brazil, and D. Marshall, "The Influence of Culture on Home-Based Family Caregiving at End-of-Life: A Case Study of Dutch Reformed Family Care Givers in Ontario, Canada," *Social Science & Medicine* 72, no. 3 (February 2011): 338–46, doi:10.1016/j.socscimed.2010.10.010.

9   H. K. Black, "Gender, Religion, and the Experience of Suffering: A Case Study," *Journal of Religion and Health* 52, no. 4 (December 2013): 1108-19, doi:10.1007/s10943-011-9544-y.

10   A. Mendola, "Case Study. Faith and Futility in the ICU. Commentary," *Hastings Center Report* 45, no. 1 (January–February 2015): 9–10, doi:10.1002/hast.409.

11   A. A. Argyriou, G. Iconomou, A. A. Ifanti, P. Karanasios, K. Assimakopoulos, A. Makridou, F. Giannakopoulou, and N. Makris, "Religiosity and Its Relation to Quality of Life in Primary Caregivers of Patients with Multiple Sclerosis: A Case Study in Greece," *Journal of Neurology* 258, no. 6 (June 2011): 1114–19, doi:10.1007/s00415-010-5894-8.

12   Inkeri Rissanen, "Developing Religious Identities of Muslim Students in the Classroom: A Case Study from Finland," *British Journal of Religious Education* 36, no. 2 (2014): 123–38, http://dx.doi.org/10.1080/01416200.2013.773194.

5.4 CONDUCT A SURVEY

The Skill of Conducting Accurate Surveys and Polls

A *survey* is a series of statements or questions that define a set of preferences to be polled. A *poll* is a device for counting preferences, practices, and affiliations. If a poll is conducted on the subject of religious-service attendance, for example, a survey will be constructed that will consist of a series of questions, such as "How frequently do you attend religious services?" or "What types of religious occasions do you attend?"

Writing your own survey paper will serve two purposes. First, you will learn how to construct, conduct, and interpret a poll, the means by which much research is done by most religious organizations and by other institutions that study religion (see the Pew Trust surveys in section 9.1 of this manual). You will thus begin to learn a skill that you may use in your professional life. Second, by writing a survey paper, you will gain firsthand experience of the strengths and weaknesses of the polling process and discover how to evaluate polls thoughtfully and critically. Although it is much easier to use an online polling device such as surveymonkey, if you do so you will lose the opportunity to genuinely understand how the polling process works.

In this chapter, you will learn how to construct and conduct a simple poll and how to apply some elementary data analysis and evaluation techniques to your poll results. Your instructor may want to add supplemental tasks, such as other statistical procedures, and texts in statistics will tell you much more about the process of research. The following set of directions, however, will provide the basics needed to create and interpret a poll.

Focus on a Specific Topic

The first step in writing a religion survey paper is to select a topic that is focused on one specific issue. Although nationally conducted polls sometimes cover a broad variety of topics, confining your inquiry to one narrowly defined issue will allow you to gain an appreciation for even a single topic's complexity and the difficulties inherent in clearly identifying opinions. Precision is important in clearly understanding public opinion.

Perhaps you wish to identify opinions and attitudes within your own or another parish, temple, or congregation. You may, for example, want to discover priorities in people's lives to better meet their needs. Some initial conversations with members of the group you wish to study can help you narrow the list of potential research items.

Formulate a Research Question and a Research Hypothesis

Once you have selected a topic, your task is to determine what you want to know about people's attitudes or behaviors concerning that topic. If you choose church programs for the homeless, for example, you may want to know the extent to which people are concerned about homeless people and what changes in current church programs they will support. You need to phrase your questions carefully. If you ask simply, "Are you concerned about the homeless?" you will probably receive a positive reply from a substantial majority of your respondents. But what does this actually tell you? Does it reveal the depth and strength of people's concern about the homeless? Do you know how the respondents will vote on any particular program or project proposal? Do people have different attitudes toward mental illness, drug use, or children's nutrition? To find out, you will need to design more specific questions. The following sections of this chapter will help you to do this.

Select a Sample

Large-scale surveys of opinion are usually conducted to find out what sizable groups of people, such as evangelicals, fundamentalists, Presbyterians, or Orthodox Jews, think about a particular issue. It is normally unnecessary and too costly to obtain the views of everyone in these groups. Most surveys, therefore, question a small but representative percentage of the group being studied. The *elements* of surveys are the individual units being studied. Elements might be interest groups, corporations, or church denominations, but they are most often individuals. The *population* is the total number of elements covered by the research question. If the research question is "Are Methodists in Calaveras County in favor of increasing child-care assistance to immigrants?" then the population is the Methodists of Calaveras County. The *sample* is the part of the population that is selected to respond to the survey. A *representative sample* includes numbers of elements in the same proportions as they occur in the general population. In other words, if the population of Methodists of Calaveras County is 14 percent Latino and 57 percent female, a representative sample will also be 14 percent Latino and 57 percent female. A *nonrepresentative sample* does not include numbers of elements in the same proportions as they occur in the general population.

All samples are drawn from a *sampling frame*, which is the part of the population being surveyed. To represent the population accurately, a sampling frame should include all types of elements (e.g., youth, women, Latinos) of interest to the research question. If the population is the Methodists of Calaveras County, a sampling frame might be the parents of children in several selected Methodist congregations. *Strata* are groups of similar elements within a population. Strata of the Methodists of Calaveras County may include members under the age of thirty, women, college-educated people, or Latinos. *Stratified samples* include numbers of respondents in different strata that are not in proportion to the general population. For example, a stratified sample of Methodists of Calaveras County might purposely include only Latino women if the purpose of the survey is to determine the views of this group.

A survey research design of the Calaveras County issue would thus be constructed as follows:

Research question: "Are Methodists in Calaveras County in favor of increasing child-care assistance to immigrants?"

Research hypothesis: 55 percent of the Methodists in Calaveras County will favor a special, dedicated contribution to increase child-care assistance to immigrants.

Elements: Individual Methodist church members

Population: Methodist church members in Calaveras County

Sampling frame: Five hundred Methodist church members in Calaveras County selected at random from church membership lists

Sample: Of the five hundred Methodist church members in Calaveras County selected at random from voter registration lists, those who answer the survey questions when called on the telephone

How large must a sample be in order to represent the population accurately? This question is difficult to answer, but two general principles apply. First, a large sample is more likely, simply by chance, to be more representative of a population than a small sample. Second, the goal is to obtain a sample that includes representatives of all the strata within the whole population.

You will find it convenient if you use as your sample the class for which you are writing your survey paper. In this case, you would most likely want to conduct a poll of religious affiliations or attendance. The disadvantage of this sample selection is that your class may not be representative of the people of the city, county, or state in which your survey is conducted. Even if this is the case, however, you will still be learning the procedures for conducting a survey, which is the primary objective of this exercise.

Note: Surveys ask people for their opinions, affiliations, or behaviors. The people whose information is sought are known as human subjects of the research. Most colleges and universities have policies concerning research with human subjects. Sometimes administrative offices known as institutional review boards are established to review research proposals, to ensure that the rights of human subjects are protected. It may be necessary for you to obtain permission from such a board, or other department in your institution, to conduct your survey. Be sure to comply with all policies of your institution with respect to research with human subjects.

Construct the Survey Questionnaire

Your research question will be your primary guide for constructing your survey questions. As you begin to write your questions, ask yourself what it is that you really want to know about the topic. Suppose that your research question is, "What are the views of religion students regarding the role of the government in regulating abortions?" If you ask, for example, "Are you for abortion?" you may get a negative answer from 80 percent of the respondents. If you then ask, "Are you for making abortion *illegal?*" you may get a negative answer from 80 percent of your respondents. These answers seem to contradict each other. By asking additional questions you may determine that, whereas a majority of the respondents may view abortion negatively, only a minority may want to make it illegal. But even this may not be enough information to get a clear picture of people's opinions. The portion of the population that wants to make abortion illegal may be greater or smaller according to the strength of the legal penalty to be applied. In addition, some of the students who want no legal penalty for having an abortion may want strict medical requirements imposed on abortion clinics, while others may not. You will need to design additional specific questions to accurately determine respondents' views on these issues.

The number of questions to include in your questionnaire is a matter to be carefully considered. The first general rule, as mentioned earlier, is to ask a sufficient number of questions to find out precisely what it is you want to know. A second principle, however, conflicts with this first rule. This principle, which may not be a problem in your religion class, is that people in general do not like to fill out surveys. Survey information can be very valuable, and pollsters are found on street corners, in airports, and on the telephone. Short surveys with a small number of questions are more likely to be answered completely than long questionnaires. The questionnaire for your paper in survey research methods should normally contain between ten and twenty-five questions.

Surveys consist of two types of questions: closed and open. Closed questions restrict the response of the respondent to a specific set of answers. Many types of closed questions are used in public opinion surveys, but they may be grouped into two categories:

- Two-choice questions
- Multiple-choice questions

Two-choice questions may ask for a simple preference between public policies, such as:

> If you were a member of Congress, would you vote to continue funding for Planned Parenthood?

Issue-centered two-choice questions most often offer respondents a choice between "yes" and "no" or "agree" and "disagree," as shown below:

> Is a mandatory parental consent form to get an abortion for women under the age of eighteen desirable?
>
> ☐ Yes
> ☐ No
>
> Legislation to allow churches to reject providing services contrary to their beliefs should be passed.
>
> ☐ Agree
> ☐ Disagree

Two-choice questions ask respondents to choose between two statements, neither of which they may entirely support. To find out how many people are ambivalent on these issues, multiple-choice questions are often asked, giving respondents a third selection, which is most often "undecided," "no opinion," "uncertain," "do not know," "does not apply," or "not sure":

> I am affiliated with the following religious tradition:
>
> ☐ Catholic
> ☐ Protestant
> ☐ Jewish
> ☐ Other
> ☐ None

Just as often, however, multiple-choice questions are constructed to discriminate more clearly among positions in a range of attitudes. For example, Likert-scale multiple-choice questions are used to distinguish among degrees of agreement on a range of possible views on an issue. A Likert-scale question might be stated like this:

> "American churches should be more open to change in response to social trends." Select one of the following responses to this statement:
>
> ☐ Strongly agree
> ☐ Agree
> ☐ Not sure
> ☐ Disagree
> ☐ Strongly disagree

Guttmann-scale multiple-choice questions allow discrimination among a range of answers by creating a series of statements with which it is increasingly difficult to agree or disagree. A respondent who selects one item on the scale of questions is also likely to agree with the items higher on the scale. Consider the following example.

Select the last answer with which you agree:

1. When Jesus talked about a farmer sowing seed, he was *not* reporting a historical fact.
2. The Bible story of Jesus raising Lazarus from the dead is historical fact.
3. The Bible story of Cain and Abel reports historical fact.
4. The Bible story of Noah and his ark reports historical fact.
5. The Bible story of Jonah and the whale reports historical fact.

Closed questions such as the one above have the advantage of being easy to quantify. A number value can be assigned to each answer, and totals can be made of answers of different types.

By contrast, open questions, or open-ended questions, are not easy to quantify. In open questions, respondents are not provided a fixed list of choices but may answer in any way they want. The advantage of using open questions is that your survey may discover ideas or attitudes of which you were unaware. Suppose, for example, that you ask the following question and give space for respondents to write their answers:

How much money should the church spend on Christmas decorations?

You might get a response like the following:

Enough money to make the church appear to be a magical wonderland to children.

Open questions call for a more active and thoughtful response than do closed questions. The fact that more time and effort are required may be a disadvantage because, in general, the more time and effort a survey demands, the fewer responses it is likely to get. Despite this disadvantage, open questions are to be preferred to closed questions when you want to expand the range of possible answers to find out how much diversity there is among opinions on an issue. For practice, you should include at least one open question in your survey questionnaire.

Perhaps the greatest difficulty with open questions is that of quantifying the results. The researcher must examine each answer and then group the responses according to content. For example, responses clearly in favor of, clearly opposed to, and ambivalent about abortion might be differentiated. Open questions are of particular value to researchers who are doing continuing research over time. The responses they obtain help them to create better questions for their next survey.

In addition to the regular open and closed questions on your survey questionnaire, you will want to add identifiers, which ask for personal information about the respondents, such as gender, age, political party, religion, income level, or other items that may be relevant to the topic of your survey. If you ask questions about women's roles in church, for example, you may want to know if men respond differently than women, if Democrats respond differently than Republicans, or if young people respond differently than older people.

Once you have written the survey questionnaire, you need to conduct the survey. You will need to distribute it to the class or other group of respondents. Be sure to provide clear directions for filling out the questionnaire on the survey form. If the students are to complete the survey in class, read out the directions clearly and ask if there are any questions before they begin.

Collect the Data

If your sample is only the size of a small religion or theology class, you will be able to tabulate the answers to the questions directly from the survey form. If you have a larger sample, however, you may want to use data collection forms or computers.

Analyze the Data

Once you have collected the completed survey forms, you will need to analyze the data that they provide. Statistical procedures are helpful here to perform three tasks:

1. Describe the data
2. Compare components of the data
3. Evaluate the data

There are many statistical procedures specially designed to carry out each of these tasks. This chapter provides only a few examples of the methods that may be used in each category. Consult your instructor or a survey research methods textbook to learn about other types of statistical measurement tools.

Statistics designed to describe data may be very simple. We will start our discussion with two example questions, both employing the Likert scale:

Question 1

"Christians have a moral duty to participate in politics."

Select one of the following responses to this statement:

☐ Strongly agree
☐ Agree
☐ Not sure
☐ Disagree
☐ Strongly disagree

Question 2

"Christians should avoid politics and focus on spiritual practices."

Select one of the following responses to this statement:

☐ Strongly agree
☐ Agree
☐ Not sure
☐ Disagree
☐ Strongly disagree

Our objective in describing the data is to see how our hypothetical respondent sample of forty-two students, as a group, answered these questions. The first step is to assign a numerical value to each answer, as follows:

Answer	Points
Strongly agree	1
Agree	2
Not sure	3
Disagree	4
Strongly disagree	5

Our next step is to count our survey totals to see how many respondents in our hypothetical sample marked each answer to each question:

Answer	Points	Q1 responses	Q2 responses
Strongly agree	1	8	13
Agree	2	16	10
Not sure	3	12	1
Disagree	4	4	12
Strongly disagree	5	2	6

We may now calculate the mean (numerical average) of responses by performing the following operations for each question:

1. Multiply the point value by the number of responses to determine the number of value points.
2. Add up the total value points of all answers.
3. Divide the total value points by the number of respondents (forty-two in this case).

To see how this procedure is done, examine the chart below, which analyzes the responses to question 1. Notice that column 1 contains the answer choices provided to the respondents; column 2 contains the point value assigned to each choice; column 3 contains the number of respondents who selected each answer; and column 4 contains the value points assigned for each answer choice, multiplied by the number of responses.

Value Points

Answer Choices	Assigned Point Values	Number of Responses	Point Values × Number of Responses
Strongly agree	1	8	8
Agree	2	16	32
Not sure	3	12	36
Disagree	4	4	16
Strongly disagree	5	2	10
Total		42	102
Mean			2.43

We can see that there are 42 total responses and 102 total value points. Dividing the number of value points (102) by the total number of responses (42), we get a mean of 2.43.

If we conduct the same operation for the responses to question 2 in our survey, we get the following results:

Value Points

Answer Choices	Assigned Point Values	Number of Responses	Point Values × Number of Responses
Strongly agree	1	13	13
Agree	2	10	20
Not sure	3	1	3
Disagree	4	12	48
Strongly disagree	5	6	30
Total		42	114
Mean			2.71

We see from the above table that the mean of the responses for question 2 is 2.71. Comparing the means of the two questions, we find that the mean for question 1 (2.43) is lower than the mean for question 2. Because the lowest value (1 point) is assigned to a response of "strongly agree," and the highest value (5 points) is assigned for a response of "strongly disagree," we know that a high mean score indicates that the sample surveyed tends to disagree with the statement made in the survey question. It is possible to conclude, therefore, that there is slightly more agreement with the statement in question 1 than with the statement in question 2. Comparing the mean values in this fashion allows us to compare the amount of agreement and disagreement on different questions among the people surveyed.

Standard Deviation Another frequently used statistical measure is the standard deviation, which provides a single number indicating how dispersed the responses to the question are. It tells you, in other words, the extent to which the answers are grouped together at the middle ("agree," "not sure," and "disagree") or are dispersed to the extreme answers ("strongly agree" and "strongly disagree"). To calculate the standard deviation (S) for question 1, we will follow these steps:

1. Assign a value to each response and the frequency of each response.
2. Find the mean for the question.
3. Subtract the value from the mean.
4. Square the results of step 3.
5. Multiply the results of step 4 by the frequency of each value.
6. Sum the values in step 5.
7. Divide the values in step 6 by the number of respondents.
8. Find the square root of the value in step 7, which is the standard deviation.

Our calculation of the standard deviation of question 1 looks like this:

Step 1 Value (V) and frequency (F)	Step 2 Mean	Step 3 Mean minus value	Step 4 Step 3 squared	Step 5 Step 4 times the frequency	Step 6 Sum of values in Step 5	Step 7 Step 6 divided by number of respondents	Step 8 Square root of step 7: standard deviation
V = 1, F = 8	2.43	1.43	2.04	16.32			
V = 2, F = 16	2.43	0.43	0.18	2.88			
V = 3, F = 12	2.43	−.57	0.32	3.84			
V = 4, F = 4	2.43	−1.57	2.46	9.84			
V = 5, F = 2	2.43	−2.57	6.6	13.2			
					46.08	1.10	1.05

The standard deviation of question 1 is 1.05. To understand its significance, we need to know that public opinion samples usually correspond to what is known as a *normal distribution*. In a normal distribution, 68.26 percent of the responses will fall between (1) the mean minus one standard deviation (2.43 − 1.05, or 1.38, in question 1) and (2) the mean plus one standard deviation (2.43 + 1.05, or 3.48, in question 1). In other words, in a normal distribution, about two-thirds of the respondents to question 1 will express an opinion that is between 1.38 and 3.48 on the scale of assigned point values. Another one-third of the respondents will score less than 1.38 or more than 3.48.

For convenience, we will call the responses "strongly agree" and "strongly disagree" as extreme responses, and we will designate "agree," "not sure," and "disagree" as moderate responses. We see that a score of 1.38 is closest to our first extreme, "strongly agree." A score of 3.48 inclines to "disagree," but is close to "not sure." We may conclude that a substantial portion of the respondents (about one-third) tend to give extreme answers to question 1. We may also notice that the score 1.38, which indicates strong agreement, is closer to its absolute extreme (1.38 is only 0.38 away from its absolute extreme of 1.0) than is the score 3.48 (which is 1.52 points from its absolute extreme of 5). This means that the responses are slightly more tightly packed toward the extreme of strong agreement. We may conclude that extreme respondents are more likely to strongly agree than to strongly disagree with the statement in question 1. We can now see more completely the degree of extremism in the population of respondents. Standard deviations become more helpful as the number of the questions in a survey increases, because they allow us to compare quickly and easily the extent of extremism in answers. You will find other measures of dispersion in addition to the standard deviation in your statistical methods textbooks.

After finding the amount of dispersion in responses to a question, you may want to see if different types of respondents answered the question in different ways—that is, you may want to measure relationships in the data. For example, from examining our political party identifier, we find, among our respondents to question 1, fifteen young people (age below thirty), fourteen middle-aged people (ages thirty to fifty-nine), and thirteen seniors (ages sixty and above). To compare their responses, we need to construct a correlation matrix that groups responses by identifier:

Answer	Youth Responses	Middle-Aged Responses	Senior Responses	Total (frequency)
Strongly agree	4	2	2	8
Agree	8	4	4	16
Not sure	3	5	4	12
Disagree	0	2	2	4
Strongly disagree	0	1	1	2

Each number of responses in the matrix is found in a location known as a response cell. The numbers in the total (frequency) column are known as response total cells. From this matrix, it appears that young people are more likely to agree with the question 1 statement than are either middle-aged people or seniors. If this is true for the sample population, there is a correlation between age and opinion on the issue.

Read&Write 5.4   Conduct a Survey on a Topic in Religion

A survey paper is composed of five essential parts:

1. Title page
2. Abstract
3. Text
4. Reference page
5. Appendices

Title Page   The title page should follow the format directions in chapter 3. The title of a public opinion survey paper should provide the reader with two types of information: (1) the subject of the survey and (2) the population being polled. Examples of titles for papers based on in-class surveys are "Baylor University Student Opinions on Same-Sex Marriage," "Ohio Wesleyan University Student Religious Participation," and "Religious Affiliation and Attitudes toward Alcohol Consumption among University of Virginia Students."

Abstract   Abstracts for survey papers should follow the general format directions given in chapter 3. In approximately one hundred words, the abstract should summarize the subject, methodology, and results of the survey. An abstract for the example used in this chapter might appear something like this:

A survey of attitudes of college students toward alcohol consumption was undertaken in January 2017 at the University of South Carolina. The sample was composed of forty-two students in a religion in society class. The purpose of the survey was to determine the extent to which students' religious affiliations and beliefs coincide with their attitudes toward alcohol consumption on campus. The results indicate a moderate correlation between religious affiliation and attitudes toward alcohol, with unaffiliated students favoring fewer restrictions than those who attended religious activities one or more times per week.

Text   The text of the paper should include five sections:

1. Introduction
2. Literature review
3. Methodology
4. Results
5. Discussion

Introduction   The introduction should explain the purpose of your paper, define the research question hypothesis, and describe the circumstances under which the research was conducted. Your purpose statement will normally be a paragraph in which you explain your reasons for conducting your research. You may want to say something like the following:

> The purpose of this paper is to define Calvin College student attitudes toward religion and its role on campus. In particular, this study seeks to understand the extent and vitality and types of religious participation. Further, the survey is expected to indicate the amount of knowledge students have about major religions. The primary reason for conducting this study is to help provide a basis for understanding the role religion plays in campus life today.

Next, the introduction should state the research question and the research hypotheses. The research question in the above example might be "What role does religion play in campus life?" A hypothesis might be "Students will report substantial and sustained religious activity that influences their social and academic lives."

Literature Review   A literature review is written to demonstrate that you are familiar with the professional literature relevant to the survey and to summarize that literature for the reader. Your literature review for a public opinion survey paper should address two types of information: (1) the subject and (2) the methodology of the survey.

The subject of the survey, for example, may be a college's proposed reforms in its religious instruction curriculum. In this case, the purpose of the subject section of your literature review would be to inform your readers about (1) the history and content of the proposed reforms, and (2) the current status of the proposed reforms. In providing this information, you will cite appropriate documents, such as published copies of the proposed reforms and Curriculum Reform Committee meeting minutes.

The purpose of the methodology section of your literature review will be to cite the literature that supports the methodology of your study. Whether you follow the directions in this manual or your course textbook to write your paper, briefly state the procedures and statistical calculations you use in the study, and the source of your information (this manual or your text) about them.

Methodology   The methodology section of your paper describes how you conducted your study. It should first briefly describe the format and content of the questionnaire. For example, how many questions were asked? What kinds of questions (open, closed, Likert-scale, Guttmann-scale) were used, and why were these formats selected? What identifiers were selected? Why? What topics within the subject matter were given emphasis? Why? Here you should also briefly address the statistical procedures used in data analysis. Why were they selected? What information are they intended to provide?

Results   The results section of your paper should list the findings of your study. Here you report the results of your statistical calculations. You may want to construct a table that summarizes the numbers of responses to each question on the questionnaire. Next, using your statistical results, answer your research question; that is, tell your reader if your research question was answered by your results and, if so, what the answer is.

Discussion   In your discussion section, draw out the implications of your findings. What is the meaning of the results of your study? What conclusions can you draw? What questions remain unanswered? At the end of this section, provide the reader with suggestions for further research derived from your research findings.

Reference Page   Your reference page and source citations in the text should be completed according to the directions in chapter 3.

Appendices   See chapter 3 for further directions on placing appendices at the end of your text. Appendices for a public opinion survey paper should include the following:

- A copy of the questionnaire used in the study
- Tables of survey data not sufficiently important to be included in the text but helpful for reference
- Summaries of survey data from national polls on the same subject, if such polls are available and discussed in your text

Note: The applications of the mean and standard deviation suggested in this chapter are controversial because they are applied to ordinal data. In practice, however, such applications are common.

6

LEARNING SCHOLARSHIP
SKILLS

6.1 HOW TO READ RELIGION AND
THEOLOGY SCHOLARSHIP

When you read anything, especially scholarship, you will get more out of it if you ask yourself some questions as you begin: *What am I reading? Why am I reading it? What, exactly, do I expect to get out of it?*

First of all, when you read an academic article, you are reading scholarship. Scholars are people on a quest for knowledge. They want to know *what* exists (detecting, identifying, and categorizing phenomena), *how* it came to be or does what it does, and *why* it acts or reacts in a certain way. To qualify as scholarship accepted by the academic community, the article must make an original contribution to knowledge. When scholars achieve this goal, they participate in an ongoing discussion, becoming members of a community of people contributing to the ever-expanding universal storehouse of knowledge. Scholarship is rarely easy reading. Since its audience is scholars, it assumes basic and sometimes advanced knowledge of languages and practices employed in a discipline.

So what is the best approach to reading scholarship? At this point it might be a good idea to revisit the reading tips given in chapter 1 of this manual. Here is a brief summary of those points, with new emphases geared specifically to the reading of scholarship:

- Before reading, check out the author. Find his or her web page and identify his or her specialty and credentials.
- Read slowly, carefully, deeply, and repeatedly.
- Read everything one section at a time.
- Reread everything one section at a time.
- Refuse to not understand anything you encounter:
  Understand the article.
  Understand the article's implications.
- Imagine applications of the article's insights and discoveries.

- Question everything. Scholars are by no means infallible.
- Take lots of notes.
- Be sure to include in your notes important points, questions you can't answer, and interesting insights the article provides.
- Create outlines as you go along that include the structure of the argument (logic) and the process by which information in the article unfolds.

You will find that most if not all scholarly articles you read include the following elements:

- An *abstract* summarizing what the article purports to have accomplished
- An *introduction* providing reasons for conducting the research
- A *research question* revealing what the article intends to discover
- A discussion of the *methods* used to produce knowledge findings
- A statement of the *outcomes* of applying the methods
- A discussion of the *implications* of the findings
- A *conclusion* explaining the *significance* of the findings
- A list of *references*: sources of information used in the study

Scholarship always has an agenda, something the scholar or scholars who have written the paper are trying to prove. Precisely identify the agenda. Then identify the sequence of points in the argument employed to support the agenda. Is the pattern of points logical? Is it biased?

Read&Write 6.1 Explain the Content of a Recent Article from a Religion or Theology Journal

Your college or university library will most likely hold both paper copies of and online subscriptions to a variety of religion journals. The easiest and perhaps most satisfying way for you to select an article of interest is to peruse the shelved copies in the library. Unless your instructor specifies otherwise, select an article from a scholarly journal (such as the *Journal of the American Academy of Religion*, or the *Journal for the Scientific Study of Religion*), not a popular or journalistic publication (such as *Sojourners* or *Guideposts*). Your instructor may also accept appropriate articles from academic journals in other disciplines, such as anthropology, psychology, history, or sociology.

Having selected an article, first read it slowly, attempting to understand what it is all about. Then reread the article and take notes as described above. Using your notes, write an essay that includes a description in your own words of:

- What the author(s) have attempted to do
- Why the author(s) wanted to do it
- How the author(s) have gone about doing it
- What the author(s) claim to have discovered
- What the author(s) conclude about the importance and the benefits of knowing the discovery

6.2   HOW TO CRITIQUE AN ACADEMIC ARTICLE

The previous section of the chapter explains how to effectively *read* and *describe* an academic article. This section takes that process a step further. An *article critique* is a paper that *evaluates* an article published in an academic journal. A good critique tells the reader what point the article is trying to make and how convincingly it makes that point. Writing an article critique achieves three purposes. First, it provides you with an understanding of the information contained in a scholarly article and a familiarity with other information written on the same topic. Second, it provides you with an opportunity to apply and develop your critical thinking skills as you attempt to evaluate a religion scholar's work. Third, it helps you improve your own writing skills as you attempt to describe the selected article's strengths and weaknesses so that your readers can clearly understand them.

The first step in writing an article critique is to select an appropriate article. Again, as instructed in section 6.1, select an academic journal article (such as the *Journal of the American Academy of Religion* or the *Journal for the Scientific Study of Religion*) and not a popular or journalistic publication (such as *Sojourners* or *Guideposts*).

Choosing an Article

Three other considerations should guide your choice of an article. First, having an interest in a topic will make writing a critique much more satisfying. Hundreds of interesting journal articles are published every year; browse article titles until you find a topic that interests you. The second consideration in selecting an article is your current level of knowledge. Many religion studies employ, for example, sophisticated statistical techniques. You may be better prepared to evaluate them if you have studied statistics.

The third consideration is to select a current article, one written within the last twelve months. Most material in religion is quickly superseded by new studies. Selecting a recent study will help ensure that you will be engaged in an up-to-date discussion of your topic.

Read&Write 6.2   Critique a Recent Article from a Religion or Theology Journal

Once you have selected and carefully read your article, you may begin to write your critique, which will cover five areas:

1. Thesis
2. Methods
3. Evidence of thesis support
4. Contribution to the literature
5. Recommendation

Thesis   Your first task is to find and clearly state the thesis of the article. Please see chapter 2, section 1 of this manual for information about a thesis.

Methods   In your critique, carefully answer the following questions:

1. What methods did the author use to investigate the topic? In other words, how did the author go about supporting the thesis?
2. Were the appropriate methods used?
3. Did the author's approach to supporting the thesis make sense?
4. Did the author employ the selected methods correctly?
5. Did you discover any errors in the way he or she conducted the research?

Evidence of Thesis Support   In your critique, answer the following questions:

1. What evidence did the author present in support of the thesis?
2. What are the strengths of the evidence presented?
3. What are the weaknesses of the evidence?
4. On balance, how well did the author support the thesis?

Contribution to the Literature   This step will probably require you to undertake some research of your own. Identify articles and books published within the past five years on the subject of your selected article. Browse the titles and read perhaps half a dozen of the publications that appear to provide the best discussion of the topic. In your critique, list the most important other articles or books that have been published on your topic and then, in view of these publications, evaluate the contribution that your selected article makes to a better understanding of the subject.

Recommendation   In this section of your critique, summarize your evaluation of the article. Tell your readers several things: Who will benefit from reading this article? What will the benefit be? How important and extensive is that benefit? Clearly state your evaluation of the article in the form of a thesis for your own critique. Your thesis might be something like the following:

> In a 2014 article published in *Evangelical Studies* entitled "Social Media and the New Evangelism," Bartleby Givens of Canon University provides the most concise and comprehensive discussion of the applications of social media to evangelism in recent years. Evangelists should adopt his recommended methods because Givens demonstrates their effectiveness in increasing conversions and church membership.

When writing this assignment, follow the directions for paper formats in chapter 3 of this manual. Ask your instructor for directions concerning the length of the critique, but in the absence of further guidelines, your paper should not exceed five typed, double-spaced pages.

6.3   HOW TO WRITE A BOOK REVIEW

Successful book reviews answer three questions:

1. What did the writer of the book try to communicate?
2. How clearly and convincingly did he or she get this message across to the reader?
3. Was the message worth reading?

Capable book reviewers of several centuries have answered these three questions well. People who read a book review want to know if a particular book is worth reading, for their own particular purposes, before buying or reading it. These potential readers want to know the book's subject and its strengths and weaknesses, and they want to gain this information as easily and quickly as possible. Your goal in writing a book review, therefore, is to help people efficiently decide whether to buy or read a book. Your immediate objectives may be to please your instructor and get a good grade, but these objectives are most likely to be met if you focus on a book review's audience: people who want help in selecting books to buy or read. In the process of writing a book review that reaches this primary goal, you will also

- Learn about the book you are reviewing
- Learn about professional standards for book reviews in religion
- Learn the essential steps of book reviewing that apply to any academic discipline

This final objective, learning to review a book properly, has more applications than you may at first imagine. First, it helps you focus quickly on the essential elements of a book and draw from a book its informational value for yourself and others. Some of the most successful people in government, business, and the professions speed-read several books a week, more for the knowledge they contain than for enjoyment. These readers then apply this knowledge to substantial advantage in their professions. It is normally not wise to speed-read a book you are reviewing because you are unlikely to gain enough information to evaluate it fairly from such a fast reading. Writing book reviews, however, helps you become proficient in quickly sorting out valuable material from material that is not. The ability to make such discriminations is a fundamental ingredient in management and professional success.

In addition, writing book reviews for publication allows you to participate in the discussions of the broader intellectual and professional community of which you are a part. People in law, medicine, teaching, engineering, administration, and other fields are frequently asked to write book reviews to help others assess newly released publications.

Before beginning your book review, read the following sample. It is Gregory M. Scott's review of *Political Islam: Revolution, Radicalism, or Reform?* edited by John L. Esposito. The review appeared in volume 26 of the *Southeastern Religion Review* (June 1998) and is reprinted here by permission:

> Behold an epitaph for the specter of monolithically autocratic Islam. In its survey of Islamic political movements from Pakistan to Algeria, *Political Islam: Revolution, Radicalism, or Reform?* effectively lays to rest the popular notion that political expressions of Islam are inherently violent and authoritarian. For this accomplishment alone John L. Esposito and company's scholarly anthology merits the attention of serious students of politics and religion, and justifies the book's own claim to making a "seminal contribution." Although it fails to identify how Islam as religious faith and cultural tradition lends Muslim politics a distinctively Islamic flavor, this volume clearly answers the question posed by its title: yes, political Islam encompasses not only revolution and radicalism, but moderation and reform as well.
>
> Although two of the eleven contributors are historians, *Political Islam* exhibits both the strengths and weaknesses of contemporary political science with respect to religion. It identifies connections between economics and religion, and between culture and religion, much better than it deciphers the nuances of the relationships

between politics and religious belief. After a general introduction, the first three articles explore political Islam as illegal opposition, first with a summary of major movements and then with studies of Algeria and the Gulf states. In her chapter titled
"Fulfilling Prophecies: State Policy and Islamist Radicalism," Lisa Anderson sets a
methodological guideline for the entire volume when she writes:

> Rather than look to the substance of Islam or the content of putatively Islamic
> political doctrines for a willingness to embrace violent means to desired ends, we
> might explore a different perspective and examine the political circumstances, or
> institutional environment, that breeds political radicalism, extremism, or violence
> independent of the content of the doctrine (18).

Therefore, rather than assessing how Islam as religion affects Muslim politics,
all the subsequent chapters proceed to examine politics, economics, and culture in a
variety of Muslim nations. This means that the title of the book is slightly misleading:
it discusses Muslim politics rather than political Islam. Esposito provides the book's
conclusion about the effects of Islamic belief on the political process when he maintains that "the appeal to religion is a two-edged sword. . . . It can provide or enhance
self-legitimation, but it can also be used as a yardstick for judgment by opposition
forces and delegitimation" (70).

The second part of the volume features analyses of the varieties of political processes in Iran, Sudan, Egypt, and Pakistan. These chapters clearly demonstrate not
only that Islamic groups may be found in varied positions on normal economic and
ideological spectrums, but that Islam is not necessarily opposed to moderate, plural-
ist politics. The third section of the anthology examines the international relations
of Hamas, Afghani Islamists, and Islamic groups involved in the Middle East peace
process. These chapters are especially important for American students because they
present impressive documentation for the conclusions that the motives and demands
of many Islamic groups are considerably more moderate and reasonable than much
Western political commentary would suggest.

The volume is essentially well written. All the articles with the exception of chapter two avoid unnecessarily dense religion jargon. As a collection of methodologically
sound and analytically astute treatments of Muslim religion, *Political Islam: Revolution,
Radicalism, or Reform?* is certainly appropriate for adoption as a supplemental text for
courses in religion and politics. By way of noting what it does not cover, readers may
consider that although it is sufficient for its purposes as it stands, the volume could be
a primary text in a course on Islamic religion if it included four additional chapters:

1. An historical overview of the origins and varieties of Islam as religion
2. A summary of the global Islamic political-ideological spectrum (from liberal to
   fundamentalist)
3. An overview of the varieties of global Islamic cultures
4. An attempt to describe in what manner, if any, Islam, in all its varieties, gives
   politics a different flavor from the politics of other major religions.[1]

Elements of a Book Review

Your first sentence should entice people to read your review. A crisp summary of
what the book is about is inviting to your readers, because it lets them know that

---

[1]   Gregory M. Scott, review of *Political Islam: Revolution, Radicalism, or Reform?* ed. John L. Esposito,
   Southeastern Political Review 26, no. 2 (1998): 512–24.

you can quickly and clearly come to the point. They know that their time and efforts will not be wasted in an attempt to wade through your vague prose in hopes of finding out something about the book. Notice Scott's opening line: "Behold an epitaph for the specter of monolithically autocratic Islam." It is a bit overburdened with large words, but it is engaging and precisely sums up the essence of the review. Your opening statement can be engaging and "catchy," but be sure that it provides an accurate portrayal of the book in one crisp statement.

Your book review should allow the reader to join you in examining the book. Tell the reader what the book is about. One of the greatest strengths of Scott's review is that his first paragraph immediately tells you exactly what he thinks the book accomplishes.

When you review a book, write about what is actually in the book, not what you think is probably there or ought to be there. Do not explain how you would have written the book, but instead how the author wrote it. Describe the book in clear, objective terms. Tell enough about the content to identify the author's major points.

Clarify the book's value and contribution to religion by defining (1) what the author is attempting to do and (2) how the author's work fits within current similar efforts in the discipline of religion or scholarly inquiry in general. Notice how Scott immediately describes what Esposito is trying to do: "This volume clearly answers the question posed by its title." Scott precedes this definition of the author's purpose by placing his work within the context of current similar writing in religion; Scott states that "for this accomplishment alone John L. Esposito and company's scholarly anthology merits the attention of serious students of religion and politics, and justifies the book's own claim to making a 'seminal contribution.'"

The elucidation portion of book reviews often provides additional information about the author. Scott has not included such information about Esposito in his review, but it would be helpful to know, for example, if Esposito has written other books on the subject, has developed a reputation for exceptional expertise on a certain issue, or is known to have an ideological bias. How would your understanding of this book be changed, for example, if you knew that its author was a leader of ISIS or the Taliban? Include information in your book review about the author that helps the reader understand how this book fits within the broader concerns of religion.

Once you explain what the book is attempting to do, you should tell the reader the extent to which this goal has been met. To evaluate a book effectively, you will need to establish evaluation criteria and then compare the book's content to those criteria. You do not need to define your criteria specifically in your review, but they should be evident to the reader. Your criteria will vary according to the book you are reviewing, and you may discuss them in any order that is helpful to the reader. Consider, however, including the following among the criteria that you establish for your book review:

- How important is the subject to the study of religion and theology?
- How complete and thorough is the author's coverage of the subject?
- How carefully is the author's analysis conducted?
- What are the strengths and limitations of the author's methodology?
- What is the quality of the writing? Is it clear, precise, and interesting?
- How does this book compare with others on the subject?
- What contribution does this book make to religion?
- Who will enjoy or benefit from this book?

When giving your evaluations according to these criteria, be specific. If you write, "This is a good book; I liked it very much," you tell nothing of interest or value to the reader. Notice, however, how Scott's review helps clearly define the content and the limitations of the book by contrasting the volume with what he describes as an ideal primary text for a course in Islamic religion: "By way of noting what it does not cover, readers may consider that although it is sufficient for its purposes as it stands, the volume could be a primary text in a course on Islamic religion if it included four additional chapters."

Read & Write 6.3 Review a New Religion or Theology Book

Format and Content   The directions for writing papers provided in chapters 1 through 3 apply to book reviews as well. Some further instructions specific to book reviews are needed, however. List on the title page, along with the standard information required for religion papers, data on the book being reviewed: title, author, place and name of publisher, date, and number of pages. The title of the book should be in italics or underlined, but not both.

Reflective or Analytical Book Reviews   Instructors in the humanities and social sciences normally assign two types of book reviews: the *reflective* and the *analytical*. Ask your instructor which type of book review you are to write. The purpose of a reflective book review is for the student reviewer to exercise creative analytical judgment without being influenced by the reviews of others. Reflective book reviews contain all the elements covered in this chapter, but they do not include the views of others who have also read the book.

Analytical book reviews contain all the information provided by reflective reviews but add an analysis of the comments of other reviewers. The purpose is, thus, to review not only the book itself but also its reception in the professional community.

To write an analytical book review, insert a review analysis section immediately after your summary of the book. To prepare this section, use the *Book Review Digest* and *Book Review Index* in the library or online to locate other reviews of the book that have been published in journals and other periodicals. As you read these reviews, take the following steps:

1. List the criticisms of the book's strengths and weaknesses that are made in the reviews.
2. Develop a concise summary of these criticisms, indicate the overall positive or negative tone of the reviews, and mention some of the most commonly found comments.
3. Evaluate the criticisms found in these reviews. Are they basically accurate in their assessment of the book?
4. Write a review analysis of two pages or less that states and evaluates steps 2 and 3 above, and place it in your book review immediately after your summary of the book.

Length of a Book Review   Unless your instructor gives you other directions, a reflective book review should be three to five typed pages long, and an analytical book review should be five to seven pages long. In either case, a brief, specific, and concise book review is almost always preferred over one of greater length.

6.4 HOW TO WRITE A LITERATURE REVIEW

Your goal in writing a research paper, homily, or exegetical analysis, is to provide an opportunity for your readers to increase their understanding of the subject you are addressing. They will want the most current and precise information available. When you are writing a traditional religion or theology research paper, you must know what has already been learned in order to give your readers comprehensive and up-to-date information or to add something new to what they already know about the subject. If your topic is interdenominational relations, for example, you will want to find out precisely what interdenominational relations efforts are being made, who is conducting them, and how successful they are. When you seek this information, you will be conducting a *literature review*, a thoughtful collection and analysis of available information on the topic you have selected for study. It tells you, before you begin your paper, what is already known about the subject.

Why do you need to conduct a literature review? It would be embarrassing to spend a lot of time and effort preparing a study, only to find that the information you are seeking has already been discovered by someone else. Also, a properly conducted literature review will tell you many things about a particular subject. It will tell you the extent of current knowledge, sources of data for your research, examples of what is *not* known (which in turn generate ideas for formulating hypotheses), methods that have been previously used for research, and clear definitions of concepts relevant to your own research.

Let us consider an example. Suppose that you have decided to research the following question: "How are the attitudes of a congregation affected by political sermons?" First, you will need to establish a clear definition of the phrase "political sermons"; then you will need to find a way to measure attitudes; finally, you will need to use or develop a method of discerning how attitudes are affected by sermons. Using research techniques explained in this and other chapters of this manual, you will begin your research by looking in the library, on the Internet, and through other resources for studies that address your research question or similar questions. You will discover that many studies have been written on members' attitudes and the effects of sermons on them. As you read these studies, certain patterns will appear. Some research methods will seem to have produced better results than others. Some studies will be quoted in others many times, some confirming and others refuting what previous studies have done. You will constantly be making choices as you examine these studies, reading very carefully those that are highly relevant to your purposes, and skimming those that are of only marginal interest. As you read, constantly ask yourself the following questions:

- How much is known about this subject?
- What is the best available information, and why is it better than other information?
- What research methods have been used successfully in relevant studies?
- What are the possible sources of data for further investigation of this topic?

- What important information is still not known, despite all previous research?
- Of the methods that have been used for research, which are the most effective for making new discoveries? Are new methods needed?
- How can the concepts being researched be more precisely defined?

You will find that this process, like the research process as a whole, is recursive. Insights related to one of the above questions will spark new investigations into others, these investigations will then bring up a new set of questions, and so on.

Read&Write 6.4 Write a Religion or Theology Literature Review

Your instructor may request that you include a literature review as a section of the paper that you are writing. Your written literature review may be from one to several pages in length, but it should always answer the following questions for the reader:

- Which previously compiled or published studies, articles, or other documents provide the best available information on the selected topic?
- What do these studies conclude about the topic?
- What are the apparent methodological strengths and weaknesses of these studies?
- What remains to be discovered about the topic?
- According to these studies, what appear to be the most effective methods for developing new information on the topic?

Your literature review should consist of a written narrative that answers—not necessarily consecutively—the above questions. The success of your own research project depends in large part on the extent to which you have carefully and thoughtfully answered these questions.

7

LEARNING EFFECTIVE
RESEARCH SKILLS

7.1 INSTITUTE AN EFFECTIVE RESEARCH PROCESS

Your skills as an interpreter of details, an organizer of facts and theories, and a writer of clear prose all come together in a research paper. Building logical arguments on the twin bases of fact and hypothesis is the way things are done in religion, and the most successful religion scholars are those who master the art of research.

Students new to the writing of research papers sometimes find themselves intimidated by the job ahead of them. After all, the research paper adds what seems to be an extra set of complexities to the writing process. As any other expository or persuasive paper does, a research paper must present an original thesis using a carefully organized and logical argument. But it also investigates a topic outside the writer's own experience. This means that writers must locate and evaluate information that is new, thus, in effect, educating themselves as they explore their topics. A beginning researcher sometimes feels overwhelmed by the basic requirements of the assignment or by the authority of the source material being investigated.

As you begin a research project, it may be difficult to establish a sense of control over the different tasks you are undertaking. You may have little notion of where to search for a thesis or how to locate the most helpful information. If you do not carefully monitor your own work habits, you may find yourself unwittingly abdicating responsibility for the paper's argument by borrowing it wholesale from one or more of your sources.

Who is in control of your paper? The answer must be you—not the instructor who assigned you the paper, and certainly not the published writers and interviewees whose opinions you solicit. If all your paper does is paste together the opinions of others, it has little use. It is up to you to synthesize an original idea from a judicious evaluation of your source material. At the beginning of your research project, you will, of course, be unsure about many elements of your paper. For example, you will probably not yet have a definitive thesis sentence or even much understanding of the shape of your argument. But you can establish a measure of control over the process you will go through to complete the paper. And if you work regularly and systematically, keeping yourself open to new ideas as they present themselves, your sense of control will grow. Following are some suggestions to help you establish and maintain control of your paper.

Understand Your Assignment

It is possible for a research assignment to go badly just because the writer did not read the assignment carefully. Considering how much time and effort you are about to put into your project, it is a very good idea to make sure you have a clear under-standing of what your instructor wants you to do. Be sure to ask your instructor about any aspect of the assignment that is unclear to you—but only after you have read it carefully. Recopying the assignment in your own handwriting is a good way to start, even though your instructor may have already given it to you in writing. Before you dive into the project, consider the following questions.

1. **What is your topic?** The assignment may give you a great deal of specific in-formation about your topic, or you may be allowed considerable freedom in establishing one for yourself. In a course in which you are studying church management, your professor might give you a very specific assignment—for example, a paper examining the difficulties of establishing a viable church recruitment strategy in the wake of declining membership nationwide—or he or she may allow you to choose for yourself the issue that your paper will address. You need to understand the terms, as set up in the assignment, by which you will design your project.

2. **What is your purpose?** Whatever the degree of latitude you are given in the matter of your topic, pay close attention to the way your instructor has phrased the assignment. Is your primary job to *describe* a current situation or to *take a stand* on it? Are you to *compare* denominations, and if so, to what end? Are you to *classify*, *persuade*, *survey*, or *analyze*? To determine the purpose of the project, look for such descriptive terms in the assignment.

3. **Who is your audience?** Your orientation to the paper is profoundly affected by your conception of the audience for whom you are writing. Granted that your main reader is your instructor, who else would be interested in your paper? Are you writing for the members of a particular community? A paper that describes the proposed revision of denominational hermeneutics may justifiably contain much more technical jargon for an audience of theology professors than for students in introductory religion courses.

4. **What kind of research are you doing?** You will be doing one if not both of the following kinds of research:

    -   *Primary research*, which requires you to discover information firsthand, often by conducting interviews, surveys, or polls. In primary research, you are collecting and sifting through raw data—data that have not already been interpreted by researchers—which you will then study, select, arrange, and speculate on. These raw data may be the opinions of experts or of peo-ple on the street, historical documents, the published letters of a famous theologian, or material collected from other researchers. It is important to carefully set up the methods by which you collect your data. Your aim is to gather the most accurate information possible, from which you or other writers using the material will later make sound observations.

- *Secondary research*, which uses published accounts of primary materials. Although the primary researcher might poll a community for its opinion on the outcome of a recent school board decision to allow prayers at athletic events, the secondary researcher will use the material from the poll to support a particular thesis. Secondary research, in other words, focuses on interpretations of raw data. Most of your college papers will be based on your use of secondary sources.

Primary Source	Secondary Source
A published collection of Martin Luther's letters	A journal article arguing that the volume of letters illustrates Luther's attitude toward political revolution
An interview with the bishop	A character study of the bishop based on the interview
Material from a questionnaire	A paper whose thesis is based on the results of the questionnaire

Keep Your Perspective

Whichever type of research you perform, you must keep your results in perspective. There is no way that you, as a primary researcher, can be completely objective in your findings. It is not possible to design a questionnaire that will net you absolute truth, nor can you be sure that the opinions you gather in interviews reflect the accurate and unchanging opinions of the people you question. Likewise, if you are conducting secondary research, you must remember that the articles and journals you are reading are shaped by the aims of their writers, who are interpreting primary materials for their own ends. The farther you are removed from a primary source, the greater the possibility for distortion. Your job as a researcher is to be as accurate as possible, which means keeping in view the limitations of your methods and their ends.

In any research project, there will be moments of confusion, but you can prevent this confusion from overwhelming you by establishing an effective research procedure. You need to design a schedule that is as systematic as possible, yet flexible enough so that you do not feel trapped by it. By always showing you what to do next, a schedule will help keep you from running into dead ends. At the same time, a schedule can help you retain the focus necessary to spot new ideas and new strategies as you work.

Give Yourself Plenty of Time

You may feel like delaying your research for many reasons: unfamiliarity with the library, the press of other tasks, a deadline that seems comfortably far away. But do not allow such factors to deter you. Research takes time. Working in a library seems to speed up the clock, so that the hour you expected it would take you to find a certain source becomes two. You must allow yourself the time needed not only to find material but also to read it, assimilate it, and set it in the context of your own thoughts. If you delay starting, you may well find yourself distracted by the deadline—that is, you will have to keep an eye on the clock while trying to make sense of a writer's complicated argument.

The following schedule lists the steps of a research project in the order in which they are generally accomplished. Remember that each step is dependent on the others and that it is quite possible to revise earlier decisions in light of later discoveries.

After some background reading, for example, your notion of the paper's purpose may change, which may in turn alter other steps. One of the strengths of a good schedule is its flexibility.

Note that this schedule lists tasks for both primary and secondary research; you should use only those steps that are relevant to your project.

1. Do Background Reading

Whether you are doing primary or secondary research, you need to know what kinds of work have already been done in your field.

Warning: Be very careful not to rely too heavily on material in general encyclopedias such as *Wikipedia* or *Encyclopedia Britannica*. Students new to research are often tempted to import large sections, if not entire articles, from such volumes, and this practice is not good scholarship. You may, if you wish, consult one for an overview of a topic with which you are unfamiliar, and *Wikipedia*, for example, can be a very good place to obtain quick information on a potential research topic. But one of the features of this website is that its contents are edited by its readers, which means its essays sometimes lack the academic rigor of sources that are written, vetted, and published by qualified scholars in the subject field. One major reason your instructor has assigned a research paper is to let you experience the kinds of books and journals in which the discourse of religion and theology is conducted. Encyclopedias are good places for instant introductions to subjects; some include useful bibliographies of reference works at the ends of their articles. But to write a useful paper, you will need much more detailed information about your subject. Once you have learned what you can from a general encyclopedia, move on to the academic articles that you will find by following links on your college library's web page. When you locate two or three good articles on your topic, you will find that the bibliographies at the end of the articles will be rich sources of other articles and books of academically acceptable quality.

2. Narrow Your Topic and Establish a Working Thesis

The process of coming up with a viable thesis for a paper involving academic research is pretty much the same as for a paper that doesn't require formal research, though the need to consult published sources may seem to make the enterprise more intimidating. (Chapter 1 offers general tips for finding a successful thesis for a paper.) For a research paper in a course in the sociology of religion, Charlotte Goble was given the topic category of grassroots attempts to legislate morality in American society. She chose the specific topic of textbook censorship. Here is the path she took as she looked for ways to limit the topic effectively and find a thesis.

General Topic	Textbook censorship by religious organizations
Potential Topics	How a local censorship campaign gets started
	Funding censorship campaigns
	Reasons behind textbook censorship
	Results of censorship campaigns
Working Thesis	It is disconcertingly easy in our part of the state for a religious organization to launch a textbook censorship campaign.

As with any paper, it is unlikely that you will come up with a satisfactory thesis at the beginning of your research project. You need a way to guide yourself through the early stages of research as you work toward discovering a main idea that is both useful and manageable. Having in mind a *working thesis*—a preliminary statement of your purpose—can help you select the material that is of greatest interest to you as you examine potential sources. The working thesis will probably evolve as your research progresses, and you should be ready to accept such change. Do not fix on a thesis too early in the process, or you may miss opportunities to refine it.

3. Conduct Interviews

Your research may benefit from information obtained through interviews. Establish a purpose for each interview, bearing in mind the requirements of your working thesis. In what ways might your interview benefit your paper? Write down your description of the interview's purpose. Estimate its length, and inform your subject. Arrive for your interview on time and dressed appropriately. Be courteous.

Before the interview, learn as much as possible about your topic by researching published sources. Use this research to design your questions. If possible, learn something about the backgrounds of the people you interview. This knowledge may help you establish rapport with your subjects and will also help you tailor your questions. Take with you to the interview a list of prepared questions. However, be ready during the interview to depart from your list in order to follow any potentially useful direction that the questioning may take.

Take notes. Make sure you have extra pens. Do not use a recording device because it will inhibit most interviewees. If you must use a recording device, *ask for permission from your subject* before beginning the interview. Follow up your interview with a thank-you letter and, if feasible, a copy of the paper in which you used the interview. For additional tips about conducting an interview, revisit section 5.1 of this manual.

4. Design and Conduct a Survey

If your research requires a survey, there are instructions for designing and conducting surveys, polls, and questionnaires in chapter 5.

5. Draft a Thesis and Outline

No matter how thoroughly you may hunt for data or how fast you read, you will not be able to find and assimilate every source pertaining to your subject, especially if it is popular or controversial, and you should not unduly prolong your research. You must bring this phase of the project to an end—with the option of resuming it if the need arises—and begin to shape both the material you have gathered and your thoughts about it into a paper. During the research phase of your project, you have been thinking about your working thesis, testing it against the material you have discovered, and considering ways to improve it. Eventually, you must formulate a thesis that sets out an interesting and useful task, one that can be satisfactorily managed within the limits of your assignment and that effectively employs much, if not all, of the material you have gathered.

Once you have formulated your thesis, it is a good idea to make an outline of the paper. In helping you determine a structure for your writing, the outline is also testing the thesis, prompting you to discover the kinds of work your paper will need to complete the task set out by the main idea. Chapter 2 discusses the structural requirements of the formal and the informal outline. If you have used note cards, you may want to start outlining by organizing your cards according to the headings you have given them and looking for logical connections among the different groups of cards. Experimenting with structure in this way may lead you to discoveries that will further improve your thesis.

No thesis or outline is written in stone. There is still time to improve the structure or purpose of your paper after you have begun to write your first draft or, for that matter, your final draft. Some writers prefer to write a first draft before outlining and then study the draft's structure to determine what revisions need to be made. *Stay flexible*, always looking for a better connection or a sharper wording of your thesis. All the time you are writing, the testing of your ideas continues.

6. Write a First Draft

Despite all the preliminary work you have done on your paper, you may feel a reluctance to begin your first draft. Integrating all your material and your ideas into a smoothly flowing argument is indeed a complicated task. It may help to think of your first attempt as only a rough draft, which can be changed as necessary. Another strategy for reducing reluctance to start is to begin with the part of the draft about which you feel most confident, instead of with the introduction. You may write sections of the draft in any order, piecing the parts together later. But however you decide to start writing—*start*.

7. Obtain Feedback

It is not enough that you understand your argument; others have to understand it, too. If your instructor is willing to look at your rough draft, you should take advantage of the opportunity and pay careful attention to any suggestions for improvement. Other readers may also be of help, although having a friend or a relative read your draft may not be as helpful as having it read by someone who is knowledgeable in your field. In any event, be sure to evaluate any suggestions carefully. Remember, the final responsibility for the paper rests with you.

Read&Write 7.1 Write a Religion or Theology Research Proposal

Do you aspire to a professional career? Professor? Pastor? Church Administrator? Entrepreneur? Doctor? Lawyer? Engineer? School Principal? Nurse? Architect? Marketing Director? Research Director? The ability to write a high-quality *research proposal* may well be one of the most useful and profitable skills you acquire on route to your BA or BS. Research proposals are written by the hundreds in public and private agencies and by innovators and entrepreneurs every day. A long-standing motto of entrepreneurs of all sorts is a simple guide to commercial success: "Find a need and fill it." From the lightbulb to the iPhone, this principle has been a guiding motivation for thousands of successful inventors, entrepreneurs, CEOs, volunteers, and medical missionaries. Remember that a *need* is both a problem that someone wants to solve and an opportunity for you to make a contribution by solving it.

How does writing a research proposal foster success in this process? Simple. Most new ventures require *funding*. Most sources of funding (government agencies, nonprofit organizations, investors) require you to submit a *plan* or *feasibility study* that demonstrates (1) the need for a particular project, (2) the economic viability of the project, and (3) the identification of the talent, expertise, and experience needed to successfully undertake the project.

Why do students of religion and theology write research proposals? A research proposal is the first step in acquiring the authorization to conduct the research—that is, to affirm the need for and feasibility of the project. The proposal is also necessary to acquire funding. Theses and dissertations, articles, and books may well require funding for travel, access to archives, copies of documents, and other items. If your topic is American evangelism in Uganda, for example, travel for interviews, documents, and personal observation could be quite expensive. University and foundation grant applications supported with strong research proposals are more likely to succeed than applications without them.

Research proposals, therefore, are sales jobs. Their purpose is to "sell" the belief that a research study needs to be done. Before conducting a research study for a private foundation, you will need to convince someone in authority that a study is necessary by accomplishing the following seven tasks:

1. Prove that the study is necessary.
2. Describe the objectives of the study.
3. Explain how the study will be done.
4. Describe the resources (time, people, equipment, facilities, etc.) that will be needed to do the job.
5. Construct a schedule that states when the project will begin and end, and gives important dates in between.
6. Prepare a project budget that specifies the financial costs and the amount to be billed (if any) to the government agency.
7. Carefully define what the research project will produce, what kind of study will be conducted, how long it will be, and what it will contain.

The Content of Research Proposals: An Overview   In form, research proposals contain the following four parts:

1. Title page
2. Outline page
3. Text
4. Reference page

An outline of the content of research proposals appears below:

I. Need for a study
   A. An initial description of the current problem
      1. A definition of the problem
      2. A brief history of the problem
      3. The legal framework and institutional setting of the problem
      4. The character of the problem, including its size, extent, and importance
   B. Imperatives
      1. The probable costs of taking no action
      2. The expected benefits of the study

II. Methodology of the proposed study
    A. Project management methods to be used
    B. Research methods to be used
    C. Data analysis methods to be used

III. Resources necessary to conduct the study
    A. Material resources
    B. Human resources
    C. Financial resources

IV. Schedule for the study

V. Budget for the study

VI. Product of the study

A Note on Research Process and Methods   Your research proposal will briefly describe the steps you will take to find, evaluate, and draw conclusions from the information that is pertinent to your study. The research process normally proceeds in these steps:

1. Data (information) collection: gathering the appropriate information
2. Data analysis: organizing the data and determining their meaning or implications
3. Data evaluation: determining what conclusions may be drawn from the data
4. Recommendation: A concise description of the study that needs to be undertaken

A Note on the Anticipated Product of the Study   In the final section of the proposal, you will describe the anticipated product of your study. In other words, you will tell the persons for whom you are writing the proposal exactly what they will receive when the project is done. If you are writing this paper for a class in religion or theology, you will probably write something like the following:

> The final product will be a research study from twenty-five to thirty pages in length and will provide an analysis of the problem and an evaluation of alternative new policies that may solve the problem.

7.2   EVALUATE THE QUALITY OF ONLINE AND PRINTED INFORMATION

The saying "Winning isn't everything; it's the only thing" may not have originated with Green Bay Packers coach Vince Lombardi, but he certainly popularized it. In terms of academic scholarship, to say "Credibility isn't everything; it's the only thing" is not an exaggeration, because the importance of what is written cannot be underestimated. As you do religion scholarship, assume correctly that if your work lacks credibility, it has no value at all. And the credibility of your writing depends on the credibility of your sources. Here, therefore, are some guidelines to assess the credibility of the sources you will employ in a paper.

Base Choice on Reputation

In general, reputation of information conforms to a clear hierarchy, described here in descending order of credibility. Here is a list of high-quality sources:

- *Articles in academic journals*, though not foolproof, have a huge credibility advantage. They conform to the research and writing standards explained throughout this manual. They often require months, if not years, to write, allowing for revision and refinement. They often employ a team of several authors, each of whom can assess the quality and accuracy of the others' work. Once submitted to a journal for publication, they are distributed (blind) to experts in the articles' topics for review and comment. Once published, they are exposed to widespread readership, providing an additional quality filter.

- *Research studies by recognized think tanks* (research institutes) are often of exceptionally high quality. They are not exposed to the same extent of external review prior to publication as academic journals, and the institutions that produce them often have a known ideological perspective. Yet whether they are conservative, liberal, or libertarian in orientation, their writers know that the credibility of their work depends on maintaining consistent high quality.

- *Research studies by government agencies* are much like think tank papers but are likely to be controversial because their findings will always annoy people who are unhappy with their conclusions. They can be very powerful, however, if they are used by the president or by Congress to adopt public policies.

- *Reports in high quality nonpartisan magazines and television journalism* are often highly reliable in both research and reporting. Examples of sources include periodicals like the *Economist*, the *Atlantic Monthly*, the *New Yorker*, the *American Scholar*, *Foreign Affairs*, and *Foreign Policy*, and PBS journalism in features such as *Frontline* and *The American Experience*.

- *Articles in high-quality newspapers* like the *New York Times*, the *Wall Street Journal*, the *Washington Post*, and the *Christian Science Monitor* cite authoritative sources.

- *Pieces in high-quality partisan magazines* like the *Nation* and the *National Review* can provide relatively reliable, if slanted and selective, information.

Low-quality sources are of several sorts, and all are to be read for quickly secured unverified "facts" and amusement rather than education. Here are some low-quality sources:

- *Wikipedia* provides much information quickly and some tolerable overviews of topics, but it is notoriously vulnerable to contributors who provide unverified and even deliberately false information.

- Partisan blogs like the *Huffington Post* are fun and provide an interesting array of perspectives and insights, but any information you find on them must be verified by more credible sources.

- Commercial TV news sources like CNN and, especially, Fox News are so sensational and clearly biased that their value is little more than entertainment.

The following elements of information sources are essential to assessing content quality.

- *Author.* What are the credentials and reputation of the author of the publication?
- *Information sources.* What sources of information does the author of a particular article use? Are these sources recognized individuals or institutions?
- *Writing quality.* Is the article well written? Is it clear and cogent? Does it use a lot of jargon? Can you understand it?
- *Quantity of information.* Is the article sufficiently comprehensive to substantiate its thesis?
- *Unsupported assumptions.* When an author writes, for example, "Statistics prove that Protestant congregations in rural areas enjoy a more authentic religious experience than congregations in urban churches," does the author identify the statistics? Does the article define what is meant by "a more authentic religious experience"?
- *Balance.* Does the article cover all relevant aspects of a subject?

Develop a Working Bibliography

As you begin your research, you will look for published sources—essays, books, or interviews with experts—that may help you. This list of potentially useful sources is your *working bibliography*. There are many ways to develop this bibliography. The cataloging system in your library will give you sources, as will the published bibliographies in your field. The general references in which you did your background reading may also list such works, and each specialized book or essay you find will have a bibliography that its writer used, which may be helpful to you.

It is from your working bibliography that you will select the items for the bibliography that will appear in the final draft of your paper. Early in your research, you will not know which of the sources will help you and which will not. But it is important to keep an accurate description of each entry in your working bibliography so that you will be able to easily tell which items you have investigated and which you will need to consult again. Establishing the working bibliography also allows you to practice using the bibliographical format you are required to follow in your final draft. As you make your list of potential sources, be sure to include all the information about each one, in the proper format and using the proper punctuation. (Chapter 3 describes in detail the bibliographical formats most often required for religion papers.)

Request Needed Information

During your research, you may need to consult a source that is not immediately available to you. Working on a Hindu worship ceremonies paper, for example, you might find that a packet of potentially useful information may be obtained from a local Hindu congregation or the American Hindu Foundation. Or you may discover that a needed book is not owned by your university library or by any other local library, or that a Hindu temple in another state has established a library of sources on worship ceremonies. In such situations, it may be tempting to disregard potential sources because of the difficulty of consulting them. If you ignore this material, however, you are not doing your job.

It is vital that you take steps to acquire the needed data. In the case mentioned above, you can simply write to the American Hindu Foundation or another Hindu organization. Remember that many religious organizations want to share their information with interested citizens; some have employees or entire departments whose job is to facilitate communication with the public. Be as specific as possible when asking for such information. It is a good idea to outline your own project briefly—in no more than a few sentences—to help the respondent determine the types of information that will be useful to you.

Never let the immediate unavailability of a source stop you from trying to consult it. And be sure to begin the job of locating and acquiring such long-distance material as soon as possible to allow for the various delays that often occur.

Read&Write 7.2 Write a Bibliography with a Dozen High-Quality Sources

Assume you are going to write a ten-page paper on a topic of your choice. Locate and list, in either *CMS* or *JAAR* bibliographical format, a dozen high-quality sources for your paper.

8

STUDY THE HISTORY
OF RELIGION

8.1   STUDY THE ORIGINS OF RELIGION

Atop the Acropolis, the imposing hill that overlooks Athens and its harbor, sit the remains of the Parthenon, a temple to the patron goddess Athena. Many call this structure the most perfect building ever constructed. Its palisade of fine marble columns, its perfect proportions, its cathedral-like aspiration lifting the human spirit to the heavens: All these—plus a perfect deceit—earn it preeminence in the annals of architecture.

Deceit?

The wealth and leadership of the Delian League, an alliance of coastal towns, was derived from Athens' port. People came to Athens primarily by sea, and Athenians, knowing the value of first impressions, took care to provide visitors a moment of singular astonishment. The Parthenon's architects knew that from out at sea the curvature of the earth creates an illusion: Straight architectural horizontal lines appear concave. If they wanted the Parthenon to look perfectly straight, and they did, they would need to make the temple's platform slightly convex, and they did. This slight deceit provided observers approaching the city a glimpse of perfection.

Religions attempt to provide observers with an apprehension—a glimpse—of perfection. A primary tool in the struggle of a religion to achieve perfection is *myth*, in the classical sense of the word. Classical myth is by no means untruth. It is precisely the opposite: complete truth. Myth comprises metaphors for great mysteries, realities we experience but lack the mental capacities to confront directly, understand, and explain. Viewing a solar eclipse directly damages our retinas, so we view it indirectly through instruments or with a visual shield. When it comes to viewing God, we must look away and describe our experience in metaphors: always imperfect, always at least slightly distorted, and therefore always constituting, in one respect, a deceit.

But this defect in no way demeans the way myth directs our personal tribulations into the flow of universal human experience. For the crime of divulging some of Zeus's secrets, for example, the Greek Judges of the Dead condemned Sisyphus to roll a boulder to the top of a hill, from which it would roll back down to its original position, where Sisyphus had to begin again—and again and again, for eternity—the process of rolling it up the hill. We are not Sisyphus, and our boulders are not literal.

Still, many of us feel akin to Sisyphus when we try to pay off our credit cards. And others know his despair when we write a paragraph.

Further, myth's inherent element of distortion in no way dampens our zest for creative ontology, that is, for creating our own realities. Human beings are often better at creating reality than perceiving it. We do not question that a mountain, a lake, or an ocean is real. Neither do we question that money is real. If we think about it, however, we must admit that the effective value of money exists simply in our imaginations. If at any moment we all ceased to believe in the value of a dollar, its "reality" would disappear. The same is true of nations. Until the end of the Middle Ages, nations as we now know them did not exist. They emerged as alliances of principalities in the succeeding centuries. If we chose to disregard them, the borderlines on our world maps would simply vanish.

If our imaginations can create entities as powerful as international financial regimes and nations, surely our minds can create anything, including as many gods as we want. And the list of the thousands of gods who are fervently embraced the world over assures us that we do. In addition, the scores of Christian denominations, and hundreds of separate religious institutions within them, testify to the fact that, though there may be only one God, there is very little agreement about the nature of that God's character.

But does all this disagreement, and all the confusion that it causes in the world, serve as proof that no God exists? No. And that is one thing that makes the study of religion and theology so engaging. What's more, myths are important because, from the swirling cosmic chaos of billions of stars, they create realities that increase our stature and can enfold us in a genuinely experienced and welcome asylum. Creative ontology is therefore powerful. If our neighbor believes his or her god is real, then, for all practical purposes, that god is real, and we would do well not to underrate that god.

The American mythologist Joseph Campbell has postulated that the earliest accounts of humankind's origin and our relationship to the natural world can be traced back to two great mythic streams.[1] One stream originated during the Lower Paleolithic era (2,500,000–200,000 BCE) in the broad grasslands of the temperate zones, where life revolved around the hunt. Small tribes of humans followed the migrations of great herds of grazing animals and competed with ferocious predators for their bounty. A key idea shared by myths out of this primitive *hunting zone* is that death is only a phase, or "a passing back and forth of an immortal individual through a veil." Campbell quotes Najagneq, a North Alaskan native, to summarize the ultimate message of this mythic complex: "Be not afraid of the universe."[2] Another phenomenon common to the hunting zone is *shamanism*, in which an individual is seized or called out from the normal life of the tribe—often through dreams, visions, or highly eccentric behavior—to act as a witness or guide to a transcendent reality that provides unique and timely guidance. Mythic strains from the hunting zone often feature masculine or animal deities personifying great natural forces, and heroic figures whose wandering adventures through many dangers and difficulties result in great boons for the tribe or for all humankind. Campbell sees examples of hunting zone influences in a variety of creation accounts preserved by indigenous tribes throughout Siberia and North America. The Ostayaks from the Yenisei River area depict their creator as a great

---

[1]   Joseph Campbell, *The Masks of God: Primitive Mythology* (New York: Viking, 1959).
[2]   Ibid., 350.

shaman who, hovering over the primeval sea and finding nowhere to rest, uses water-fowl to retrieve Earth from beneath the waters and create an island that becomes the first land. North American tribes attribute the same Earth-building activities to their trickster-hero deity, identified variously as the Old Man, Coyote, Raven, or the Great Hare. Counterparts to this trickster deity are found throughout the world. Many of us may be familiar with his African form, popularized by Walt Disney: Br'er Rabbit.[3]

The second great mythic stream originated much later, during the Neolithic era (10,200–2000 BCE), from "that broad equatorial zone where the vegetable world has supplied not only the food, clothing and shelter of man since time out of mind, but also his model of the wonder of life—its cycle of growth and decay, blossom and seed, wherein death and life appear as transformations of a single, super ordinated, indestructible force."[4] The primitive hunting cultures dealt with the reality of death and the necessity of killing the animals that they both required and revered by see-ing them as spiritual partners and willing victims whose death was only a temporary transition. But in the emerging agricultural societies the plant world provided a new model: In order for new life to emerge, existing life must die, decay, and fertilize the soil. Creation accounts from this zone begin with premortal, presexual ancestral beings living in eternal innocence. This era of innocence ends with the murder of an ancestral being, at which time both death and sexuality enter the world. Finally, from the body of this being—murdered, cut up, and planted into the earth—springs the food and material needed to sustain life. Ritual activities to conform to this model have included shockingly brutal forms of human sacrifice. Although we are now rightly horrified by these accounts, they should be understood in the full historical and cultural context of the perceived reality being affirmed: Individual human life, like all life, is part of the perennial cycle in which apparent death and decay are nec-essary precursors to new life.

Read&Write 8.1   Explore Cosmos and History in South America

Teupeu the creator, together with the feathered spirit Gucumatz, thought deeply, and from their concentrated imaginations arose the world, a place that needed grateful caretakers. Their first creatures, snakes, birds, panthers, and deer, lacked voices with which to worship, so they set out to make man. The first man, made of wet clay, crumbled. The second men, havering, empty-headed wood beings, were not sufficiently appreciative of their benefactors. The creators then made four worshipful and thoughtful white and yellow corn men, and made women for them, and so they lived on.

—Mayan creation myth[5]

The indigenous peoples of Central and South America generated substantial and vigorous societies with locally inspired and emotionally sustaining creation myths that became vibrant and vital parts of their daily lives. Write a research paper in which you compare three Central and/or South American creation myths. What are their commonalities? To what extent do they express different values, perceptions, and aspirations?

---

3   Ibid., 275–76.
4   Ibid., 137.
5   Angie Shumov, "Creation Myths from around the World," in "Creation," an episode of *The Story of God with Morgan Freeman*, National Geographic, accessed March 17, 2017, http://channel.national geographic.com/shows.

8.2 STUDY THE HISTORIES OF MODERN RELIGIONS

Sometimes it helps to orient yourself to a new subject by looking close to home. Before proceeding abroad, let's take a quick look at some aspects of the development of American Christianity. Because the diverse religious landscape in the United States today often appears as a diorama of discord, a wrangle of intermeshing quarrels, it may be surprising to discover it did not always appear that way.

In his classic work *Democracy in America*, French aristocrat Alexis de Tocqueville provides a colorful and insightful portrait of this nation's culture two decades before the Civil War. While traveling from one community to the next and taking copious notes, Tocqueville became impressed with two surprising qualities of American life in general: a passion for equality, and a certain kind of religious unanimity.

One day Tocqueville found himself in a courtroom in upstate New York. A witness, called to testify, was instructed to swear on the Bible that he was about to tell the truth. The witness declined, declaring he did not believe in the Bible. The judge dismissed him, declaring that the witness's lack of faith nullified his credibility. But it is what Tocqueville reported next that surprises us today: "The newspaper reported the incident without further comment."[5] Imagine the reaction a lawyer for the American Civil Liberties Union would have upon reading this sort of report in a newspaper today!

But even a little less than a half century later, a cultural shift was fueled by conflicts between Anglo Americans and Roman Catholic immigrants that would change the cultural landscape. In the presidential election of 1884, Democrats were accused of being the party of "Rum, Romanism, and Rebellion." So much for Tocqueville's "religious unanimity." But far more pervasive changes in worldview were afoot. By the turn of the twentieth century, it was common for the intellectual elite from that era to regard religion as an anachronism, a primitive relic that would surely fade away under the inevitable progress of scientific understanding. And after the Russian Bolsheviks came to power in 1917, it became fashionable to decry religion as a pernicious danger to global peace and human progress.

But the tide turned again after World War II. In 1947 Billy Graham and Oral Roberts began their evangelism crusades. They and others sparked a two-decade religious revival. In the postwar years, the United States became a predominant world power. Booming from sea to sea and confronted by the rise of global communism, America became the new Moses, delivering to the world unparalleled freedom, hope, and prosperity—and pulpits across the land affirmed its glory.

Then in November 1963, three gunshots in Dallas, Texas, brought about the collapse of the Kennedy "Camelot." Shortly afterward, the American civil rights movement threw a world spotlight on the deep, pervasive racism and frequently accompanying violence that characterized much of the nation but was especially pernicious in the American South. Horrors continued to mount. Not even the napalm-seared bodies of Vietnamese children on the evening news could compel President Nixon, fearful of losing a war, to end a deeply divisive Asian conflict. With America's widely assumed postwar moral perfection under increasing challenge, religion had serious new work to do.

And the work goes on. Though Martin Luther King Jr. has fallen, his nonviolent torch still burns.

[5] Alexis de Tocqueville, *Democracy in America*, trans. Henry Reeve (New York: Bantam, 2004), 1:355.

⋮Read&Write 8.2 Chronicle the Recent History of an Asian Religion

As we proceed through the histories of our own religious traditions, we may begin to place those traditions within a broader context: a global perspective. Let's consider one aspect of the interaction of religions and human events: violence.

America has survived deep cataclysms. The Civil War shook the nation to its foundations, and the twentieth century's two world wars swept us into vortexes of fury. The Great Depression and the Cold War are among other obstacles and dangers we have successfully survived.

Other nations and continents, however, have faced destruction that makes North America's woes pale in comparison. Historians will never accurately estimate the casualties of genocides, but those led by Adolf Hitler exceed ten million; those of Joseph Stalin, twenty million; and those of Mao Zedong, fifty million. Turning specifically to Asia, we note that, beyond Mao, Asia has also seen the massacres of three million in Cambodia and countless atrocities in Bangladesh, Indonesia, and Myanmar.

What role has religion played in dealing with such traumas? In the aftermath of these tragedies, how is religion faring in Asia today? Select an Asian religion and write a paper of three to five pages summarizing its major challenges, successes, and defeats since World War II.

8.3 COMPARE RELIGIONS

We are all closely related, and we are all ultimately African. In September 2016 the *Washington Post* published a summary of new studies that were based on DNA testing of populations in Australia and elsewhere, and indicated that "all non-African humans can trace their ancestry back to . . . [a] . . . single, massive exodus from Africa some 72,000 years ago."[6]

It's a remarkable fact that all faith traditions that have grown beyond their native ground to establish themselves as "world religions" have originated from only two basic nurseries: (1) the so-called Fertile Crescent, stretching from the ancient lands of Mesopotamia to the Levant along the eastern coast of the Mediterranean Sea, and (2) the subcontinent of India. In each of these zones a group of indigenous religious strains coalesced and refractured repeatedly over millennia to eventually establish a potent tribal or national religious culture, and each of these in turn gave birth to offshoots that proved to be transplantable to a wide variety of cultures, climes, and ideologies.

The Fertile Crescent

In the Levant region, the religious fountain was *Judaism*, which gave birth in turn to Christianity and Islam, and each of these has gone on to permeate large parts of the globe. In the Judeo-Christian-Islamic triad we find religions of separation and distinction. The Hebrews were God's *chosen* people. In the generations following

---

[6]   Rachel Feltman, "Aboriginal DNA Points to an Earlier Human Exodus from Africa," *Washington Post*, September 22, 2016, https://www.washingtonpost.com/news/speaking-of-science /wp/2016/09/22/aboriginal-dna-points-to-an-earlier-human-exodus-from-africa.

the exodus, God commanded the Hebrews to keep themselves apart from neighboring peoples—that is, to remain unpolluted by alien rituals and gods. Distinct beliefs and practices arose as revelations to the priestly Levites and were continued in the Promised Land.

The Indian Subcontinent

To the east, Hindu scriptures revealed an opposite spiritual conception. In the Hindu *Bhagavad Gita*, we find a remarkable event unfolding.

Prince Arjuna sits in despair in what is to become a great battlefield. The dispute is a family affair. Among the opposing soldiers are cousins, other relatives, and friends. The god Krishna appears to console the conflicted and irresolute commandant. Krishna tells Arjuna to have the unique courage that comes from understanding the ultimate unity of the universe. All things are one; division and separation are only illusions. Arjuna and his foes coexist in an eternal unity. He may fight, or he may fall back; the eternal reality is the same.[7]

Today's Hinduism—or the *Sanatana Dharma* (eternal teaching), the term increasingly preferred by its native adherents—has strains reaching far back into the Neolithic past, preserved in some of humankind's oldest collections of religious literature. Like all major religions, the Sanatana Dharma is today encrusted with various practices that sometimes carry its message far from the insights that inspired it. One such practice is the caste system, a social construct that takes distinction to an extreme.

The Sanatana Dharma's most prominent offspring is Buddhism, a faith based on the Buddha's Four Noble Truths and the Eightfold Path (both listed here in oversimplified terms).

The Four Noble Truths

1. *Dukkha*, the composite cause of the spectrum of life's discomforts, holds us captive.
2. *Dukkha*'s potency results from our need to control or eliminate life's discomforts.
3. *Dukkha* is undone by Nirvana, the eternal flame of the conscious, perpetual, infinite existence.
4. Nirvana is entered via an eightfold path that brings an awakening to one's ever-present true nature.

The Eightfold Path

1. Perfect vision-understanding; we see and truly know.
2. Perfect emotion-aspiration; we feel and desire true perfection of passion.
3. Perfect speech; unadulterated, uplifting communication.
4. Right action: relational ethics perfected.
5. Right livelihood: moral occupation.
6. Complete vitality: spontaneous wholeness, health, creativity.

---

[7] Mohandas Gandhi, *The* Bhagavad Gita *according to Gandhi* (Albany Hills, CA: Berkeley Hills Books, 2000), 30–33.

7. Complete mindfulness: perfect awareness.

8. Complete concentration: absorption into Truth.[8]

After an initial blossoming in the subcontinent, Buddhism found more fertile ground in surrounding lands, including Tibet, China, the Malay Peninsula, Sri Lanka, and Japan. And after more than two millennia of regional development, strains of Buddhism have, since the late nineteenth century, asserted a growing influence in the West and across the globe. Today, Buddhism has spawned several national forms, each with unique expressions that have reshaped the cultures of its adopted homelands. Among these are Ch'an Buddhism in China, Zen in Japan, Vajrayana Buddhism in Tibet, and Theravadan Buddhism in Myanmar, Thailand, and Malaysia.

One broad stream of enduring Hindu influence (and commercial success) around the world today is the tradition of yoga. *Yoga*, which is related to the English word "yoke," refers, like the word *religion* itself, to a spiritual discipline by which we "link back" to a deeper reality. Archeologists have found ritual artifacts in the Indus Valley dating from 2000 BCE or even earlier that depict figures in yogic poses. In Ch'an and Zen Buddhism, a form of the ancient practice *zazen*, or sitting meditation, has been developed into an exacting technique for making the mind "one-pointed" and clear.[9] The *zazen* practice has in turn inspired a whole aesthetic tradition, reflected in architecture, landscaping, music, and dance, that has come to embody much of the national character of each people. Similarly, in Vajrayana, indigenous Tibetan worship forms have been adapted as symbolic vehicles for channeling and refocusing conscious thought into intense emotional energy. This energy produces a radical transformation of the mind, opening a path to permanent enlightenment. Various art forms have been inspired by Vajrayana practice, especially the well-known colored-sand mandalas, which are laboriously and meticulously constructed only to be summarily swept up upon completion.

Read & Write 8.3   Compare the Rituals, Doctrines, or Practice of Two African Religions

Comparing religions can be an invigorating activity, providing many new insights and varied perspectives on universal questions. But religions, with their systems, traditions, and histories, present such multifaceted fields of study that it is crucial, especially when comparing religions, to find effective ways to limit your inquiry in order to make it manageable and to produce useful results. One reasonable method of achieving a fruitful comparison is to focus on the ways in which a certain mode of expression might differ within the target religions. Most if not all religions share certain modes. Here are three universal ones:

- Scripture
- Doctrine
- Expressions of faith or practice across time

[8]   There are many versions of the Eightfold Path. See, for example, John Allan, "The Eight-Fold Path," *Buddhist Studies: Basic Buddhism*, Buddha Dharma Education Association and BuddhaNet, http://www.buddhanet.net/e-learning/8foldpath.htm.

[9]   Mary Pat Fisher, *Living Religions: Eastern Traditions* (Upper Saddle River, NJ: Prentice Hall, 2003), 134.

Another way to set up a framework for a coherent comparison is to adopt a single specific lens to focus your inquiry. A list of such lenses includes:

- The *sociology* of religion: how specific ethnicities and traditions of gender, family, and social cohesion affect belief and practice
- The *psychology* of religion: how primal, deliberative, and perceptive mechanisms of the mind affect belief and practice
- The *politics* of religion: how apparatuses and processes of power and control—institutions, ideologies, charisma—affect belief and practice
- The *economics* of religion: how the machineries of production, accumulation, distribution, and concentration of wealth affect belief and practice

Your task in this exercise is to write a paper, seven to ten pages long, in comparative religion. First, identify a topic of interest by scanning news media and other online and print publications for an idea or phenomenon that you find interesting and worthy of study. Then select a mode of religious expression—perhaps one from the above list—to serve as the focus of your comparison of two world religions. You may also find it useful to employ one of the lenses listed above, to help narrow your field of inquiry.

You may wish to practice a prewriting technique or two, such as freewriting or brainstorming (see section 2.2 of this manual), to help launch your research.

9

DISCOVER SOME CONTEMPORARY APPROACHES TO THE STUDY OF RELIGION

9.1 SOCIOLOGY OF RELIGION

Scholar Spotlight

On October 4, 2007, one of America's most eminent sociologists of religion, Princeton University professor Robert Wuthnow, addressed the Heritage Foundation, a conservative think tank, on the topic of myths about American religion. Wuthnow had a lot to say. He commenced his talk with a note about his qualifications to address his topic: "I have spent more than thirty years studying American religion. I've designed and conducted more than a dozen major national studies on various aspects of American religion, analyzed dozens of other national surveys, and collected in-depth interview transcripts [of personal] faith journeys."[1]

We, the authors of this manual, wish to take a moment to note the astonishing resource that US (and world) scholars provide, and the surprising availability of their works. If you visit Professor Wuthnow's Princeton website, you will find a link to his curriculum vitae (CV), which includes a twenty-one-page list of scholarly accomplishments, including scores of books, book chapters, and articles. Here are titles of just some of his books:

> *In the Blood: Understanding America's Farm Families*
> *Rough Country: How Texas Became America's Most Powerful Bible-Belt State*
> *The God Problem: Expressing Faith and Being Reasonable*
> *Red State Religion: Faith and Politics in America's Heartland*
> *Remaking the Heartland: Middle America Since the 1950s*
> *Boundless Faith: The Global Outreach of American Churches*
> *America and the Challenges of Religious Diversity*
> *Saving America? Faith-Based Services and the Future of Civil Society*

---

[1] Robert Wuthnow, "Myths About American Religion," Lecture #1049 on Religion and Civil Society, Heritage Foundation, October 18, 2007, http://www.heritage.org/research/lecture/myths-about-american-religion.

All in Sync: How Music and Art Are Revitalizing American Religion
Creative Spirituality: The Way of the Artist
Growing Up Religious: Christians and Jews and Their Journeys of Faith
After Heaven: Spirituality in America Since the 1950s
The Crisis in the Churches: Spiritual Malaise, Fiscal Woe
Christianity and Civil Society: The Contemporary Debate
God and Mammon in America
Producing the Sacred: An Essay on Public Religion
The Struggle for America's Soul: Evangelicals, Liberals, and Secularism
The Restructuring of American Religion: Society and Faith Since World War II
Experimentation in American Religion
The Consciousness Reformation[2]

Why do we present this information about Professor Wuthnow? First, simply by reading through a partial list of his books, you can get an idea of the breadth of the subdiscipline of the sociology of religion. Second, we want to note the accessibility of many of America's greatest minds. If you locate (e.g., in your college's library catalog) an interesting article by a living scholar, you can find in the article the author's institutional affiliation. From there you can find his or her university website and an email address. Most scholars reply to student emails. If you have a brief question, do not hesitate to word it politely and send it via email (see "Read & Write" sections 4.1 and 4.2 of this manual). If you find yourself interested in the scholar's work, you may be able to meet this person at an annual national or regional meeting of a discipline's associations. In the case of sociology of religion, the websites of the American Academy of Religion and the American Sociological Association will provide meeting programs that may indicate participation by the scholar in whom you are interested. Academic associations most often provide discounted fees for student attendance and participation.

Let's come back to Professor Wuthnow's address to Heritage. He continues his address with the following comment: "There is an enormous amount of misinformation out there about American religion. . . . [Here] are ones I happen to believe are especially misleading."[3]

Wuthnow identifies five myths about American religion. Here they are, with selected comments about each one.

1. America is in the midst of a religious and spiritual awakening.
    The best data . . . show that there has been no growth in church attendance over at least the past three decades, if not longer.
2. There is no secularization.
    Overall, between 5 and 6 percent fewer Americans participate regularly in religious services now than in the early 1970s.
3. Politics is driving people from the church.
    [Wuthnow asserts that some people claim that] American religion was hijacked in the 1980s by the "religious right." Jerry Falwell, Pat Robertson,

---

[2]   Robert Wuthnow, "Curriculum Vitae," Princeton University Sociology Department, accessed December 27, 2016, http://sociology.princeton.edu/files/faculty/cv/WuthnowCV2015.pdf.

[3]   Robert Wuthnow, "Myths About American Religion."

and others politicized religion to the point that people who disagreed with them—political moderates and liberals—eventually said a plague on all of it. . . . But [the reduction in participation is] driven mostly by the demographics of growing up, getting married, and settling down—all of which are happening later—more so than by disaffiliating from religion because of politics.

4. Membership in evangelical denominations is growing.

   Evangelicalism is not experiencing the huge growth suggested by figures from stories about megachurches. As a proportion of the population, it remains at only about 25 percent.

5. The culture war is over—or never happened.

   [Wuthnow argues that culture wars (as the term has been used notably by University of Virginia professor James Davison Hunter) wax and wane, but are neither over nor nonexistent. In his conclusion, Wuthnow states that] there are signs of serious erosion in such standard measures of religious vitality as church attendance and religious affiliation. The reason for these declines seems not to be that people are leaving because of religious involvement in politics . . . [but] that far more younger Americans are single and childless than was true a generation ago . . . [and they] are not settling into religious congregations at the same rate as their parents did in the 1970s.[4]

Resource Spotlight

As we see from Professor Wuthnow's contributions, exploring the contributions of scholars can bring many rewards. We can also see that Professor Wuthnow bases his arguments on data rather than speculation, a practice that contributes to his credibility as a scholar. Though numerous sources of good data exist for the study of the sociology of religion, one of the best is the Pew Trust. The religion section of the Pew Trust's website (at the time of this writing) begins with the following statement:

Pew studies and analyzes issues at the intersection of religion and public affairs by conducting surveys, demographic analyses, and other research about the practice of religion and its place in American life. Recent work includes a major portrait of Jews in America and interviews with 38,000 Muslims around the globe to provide a more complete understanding of the beliefs and political views of members of the world's second-largest religion.[5]

The section also features a wealth of easily accessible and understandable studies, reports, articles, and news items. An item appearing under the title "Religion in Everyday Life" featured this byline:

A new Pew Research Center study [April 12, 2016] of the ways religion influences the daily lives of Americans finds that people who are highly religious are more engaged with their extended families, more likely to volunteer, more involved in their communities and generally happier with the way things are going in their lives.[6]

4   Ibid.
5   "Religion," Pew Charitable Trusts, accessed December 28, 2016, http://www.pewtrusts.org/en/topics/religion.
6   Ibid.

Here are other titles that were found on this web page:

"How Africa Is Changing Faith around the World"

"Where the Public Stands on Religious Liberty vs. Nondiscrimination"

"One-in-Five US Adults Were Raised in Interfaith Homes"

"Choosing a New Church or House of Worship"

"Trends in Global Restrictions on Religion"

"Evangelicals Rally to Trump, Religious 'Nones' Back Clinton"[7]

Read&Write 9.1 Welcome to Pew Trust Religion Studies

Your task in this exercise is to write a research paper in which you accomplish the following tasks:

1. Select a study or report form the Pew Trust's current religion web page.
2. Summarize the findings of the study you have selected.
3. Identify a dozen other scholarly sources on the topic of the Pew study.
4. Write a paper providing a general discussion of the topic, concluding with a presentation of any consensus of scholars on the topic's history, importance, and likely future trends.

9.2 PSYCHOLOGY OF RELIGION

Like the study of sociology, anthropology, philosophy, political science, and other academic disciplines, the study of religion is becoming an increasingly interdisciplinary enterprise. Two fields profoundly influencing the study of religion are evolutionary psychology and neurology. One contribution of evolutionary psychology to religious studies is religion professor Todd Tremlin's *Minds and Gods.*[8]

Minds and Gods applies the cognitive science of religion to the data of evolutionary psychology to explain how and why people invent gods. A caveat is in order here: Tremlin's work addresses human behavior, not the existence of God. It in no way attempts to prove or disprove the objective existence of any god. He does make a powerful argument, however, for the proposition that human beings are evolutionarily inclined to perceive deities because doing so satisfies natural proclivities that prove to be powerful instruments for survival.

This chapter section presents a brief and informal elaboration of the fundamentals of Tremlin's findings. Let us begin by recalling that, according to archaeology and anthropology, the human brain assumed its current capacity around fifty thousand years ago. We may therefore infer that a baby, snatched from its family five millennia ago and brought up in an adequately supportive family today, could reasonably be expected to graduate from college. We may also assume that our current mental structure retains sufficient "primitive" capabilities that a baby snatched today from a hospital nursery in Chicago and taken back five millennia to an African savanna could survive there as well.

---

[7] Ibid.

[8] Todd Tremlin, *Minds and Gods: The Cognitive Foundations of Religion* (Oxford: Oxford University Press, 2006).

Survival, Tremlin reminds us, requires group life. Among the mental faculties required for group life are "cognitive capacity" (the mental equipment to recognize the requirements of social life) and "strategic thinking" (the ability to use cognitive capacity to contribute to and compete in social life). Next, we encounter what evolutionary psychologists call "theory of mind"—more simply, "mind-reading" or "the ability to put oneself in the mind of another." Theory-of-mind capacity is essential in social life because it allows us to perceive the intentions of others.

Remember a point made a little earlier about the time frame of the brain's development: Our human mental capacities evolved within a "primitive" environment far different from what we experience today, and our brains still operate with those same mechanisms developed in primitive times. Tremlin explains that a basic reason people survive successfully is that their brains evolved in the form of "mental modules," including capacities to detect predators, select appropriate foods, choose mates, raise children, and establish kinship, alliances, and friendship.

According to Tremlin, the brain has intuitive capacities (in other animals we call them *instincts*). Humans have *intuitive biology* (we can distinguish various sorts of plants and animals), *intuitive physics* (we can handle basic modes of solidity and fluidity, motion, and causality), and *intuitive psychology* (we can attribute attitudes and motives of other animals and people, and we can discern various sorts of patterns in our social and physical environments).

At this point in Tremlin's book the discussion shifts from environments to gods. Two more concepts are put in play: Agency Detection Device (ADD) and Theory of Mind Mechanism (ToMM). Tremlin's discussion of these two fascinating concepts is lengthy and detailed. The following scenario attempts, in the interest of brevity, to paraphrase this part of Tremlin's argument. The fictional characters in the scenario have been added by the authors of this writer's manual in an effort to enhance the argument's clarity.

Imagine two fiftieth-century BCE savanna dwellers we shall call Yves and Maddie. Each day they emerge from their rock shelter with one preeminent goal: survival. Most immediately, survival requires safety and food. Their brains are equipped with ADD, the ability of a phenomenon to make its own decisions. They see a stream and know that, even though in the monsoon season it can be dangerous, it lacks agency—in other words, the stream follows its course of least resistance, making no decisions for itself. This morning the current is low and slow and therefore safe. Maddie spots a female lion, a beast that *has* agency, because she can make her own decisions, and motive, because she hunts for her pride. Yves's and Maddie's brains instantly engage ToMM, a set of assumptions our brains make about phenomena with agency. Yves and Maddie note that the pride is yet unfed, so it will be wise to avoid the lions until after lunch. Through ToMM, Yves and Maddie know to avoid coming between an elephant and her calf, to hide their supply of berries from their neighbors' kids, and to fight hyenas with fire.

In today's world we understand that some people possess an incredibly keen sense of ToMM. Politicians like former president Bill Clinton and former British prime minister Margaret Thatcher, for example, seem to be able to read voters like an open book. On the opposite extreme are people afflicted with autism, a condition creating a "mind-blindness" by which autistic people, though often brilliant in other ways, appear incapable of intuitively perceiving the thoughts and feelings of others.

Back to intuition: Our minds are both intuitive and counterintuitive. While navigating the practicalities of life depends upon accurate intuitions, our minds enjoy imagining the counterintuitive: mice who govern magic kingdoms, horses that talk, people who fly, and inventors who go back or forward in time. Gods belong to the counterintuitive in this way; they are most often imagined as having supernatural qualities and talents. People are also social animals, and religions are social constructs. As such, minds and religions provide mechanisms to manage *conditions of exchange* (how we shall share), *reciprocity* (mutuality in sharing), *fairness* (whom we can trust), and *identity of interested parties* (who is in the group). Religions provide to human beings a discernible woven fabric of consciousness. They connect each of us with one another and connect our intuitive beings (our clearly perceptive practical selves) with our counterintuitive natures (our yearning for transcendence, truth, justice, salvation, and magic).

Okay, so how do we connect gods to ADD and ToMM? Through religion. Here, once again, is a loose interpretation of Tremlin's substantial argument.

Let's return once more to Yves and Maddie. Within their clan they consciously navigate the flow of social interactions with vibrant, intuitive ToMMs. They get their needs met through subtle or abrupt gestures. They negotiate their status and secure their piece of the savanna's pie. But a part of their intuitive natures (re everyday life on earth) intersects with their counterintuitions (re their grasp of the mysterious beyond). While the cosmos at times appears chaotic (through floods, fires, and earthquakes), its dependable rhythms (through dawn, day, dusk, night; spring, summer, winter, fall; new moon, crescent moon, first-quarter moon, gibbous moon, full moon) suggest a cosmic order that requires an intelligent agent. That agent is a god. It can be nothing less. And if we are relational, so is our God. When we initiate relations with God (ceremony, ritual, sacrifice, prayer) we perceive a cosmic agent. When our counterintuitive ToMM kicks in, we perceive an agent who first reflects ourselves, providing and demanding, soothing and frightening, provoking and responding. We further perceive an agent who transcends our capacities with faculties sufficient for cosmic management. Yves and Maddie's counterintuitions, therefore, supply them with the comfort of relationship and a source of hope-inspiring strength.

Read&Write 9.2 Encounter *Minds and Gods*

Read and review *Minds and Gods* (see section 6.3 of this manual for pointers on how to review a book). Conclude your review by providing some personal reflections concerning how *Minds and Gods* has affected your personal beliefs.

9.3 NEUROLOGY AND RELIGION

Plants lean toward the sun. Single cells divide to become two. Quartz crystals grow inside geodes. Are these phenomena forms of consciousness?

The concept of consciousness has long been controversial. An ancient yet ongoing dispute is, "Does the brain *create* consciousness, *perceive* consciousness, or *both*?" If the brain can perceive consciousness, can it perceive spiritual phenomena?

One of today's most popular consciousness questions is, "Will artificial intelligence ever duplicate or supersede human consciousness?" The basic question that underlies all these controversies is "What is consciousness?" Asking this question draws theologians and religion scholars into the depths of ontology, epistemology, psychology, and neurology, and answering it requires a still un-achieved precise knowledge of how the brain works, and what, exactly, is "mind." Pursuit of such knowledge has spawned a number of recent interdisciplinary conferences.

The *New York Times* reported on a May 2016 panel sponsored by the New York Academy of Sciences, in which New York University researcher David Chalmers declared, "The scientific and philosophical consensus is that there is no nonphysical soul or ego, or at least no evidence for that."[9] The report also stated that Princeton University neuroscientist Michael Graziano compared consciousness to a kind of con game the brain plays with itself.

> The brain is a computer that evolved to simulate the outside world. Among its internal models is a simulation of itself—a crude approximation of its own neurological processes. The result is an illusion. Instead of neurons and synapses, we sense a ghostly presence—a self—inside the head. But it's all just data processing. "The machine mistakenly thinks it has magic inside it," Dr. Graziano said. And it calls the magic consciousness. It's not the existence of this inner voice he finds mysterious. "The phenomenon to explain," he said, "is why the brain, as a machine, insists it has this property that is nonphysical."[10]

Chalmers and Graziano are two voices on one side of the great divide in consciousness studies: those who believe that the brain *manufactures* its own phenomena, and those who believe that it *perceives* phenomena so far undetected by scientific instruments. But Chalmers, Graziano, and their academic allies have not silenced some determined opposition. A fascinating discussion of consciousness is unfolding as scholars in the disciplines of religion and theology employ science to formulate other potential models of consciousness.

In their book *The Mystical Mind*, Eugene d'Aquili and Andrew Newberg, drawing in part on their own pioneering work with SPECT (Single Photon Emission Computed Tomography) imagery of meditating subjects, present a detailed neurological analysis of the human brain at work during a prototypically *religious* activity. D'Aquili and Newberg build on their findings and related research to propose a "neurotheology" that in many ways turns the classic reductionist critique of mind and soul on its head. Rather than explaining *away* religious experiences as *epiphenomena*, the authors propose that brain science provides powerful support for the "reality" and epistemological utility of spiritual phenomena.[11]

D'Aquili and Newberg describe how the human brain goes about producing meditative states. They find that higher mental functioning, whether it relates to logic, emotions, imagination, or willful action, involves an almost infinitely complex series of interactions across a host of neural structures. As a result, it is impossible to simplistically assign any given mental state to a particular brain part or function. Instead, higher mental states must be seen as the activity of the *whole* brain interacting in a dynamic process within an encompassing human physical and mental environment.[12]

9   George Johnson, "Consciousness: The Mind Messing with the Mind," *New York Times*, July 4, 2016, http://www.nytimes.com/2016/07/05/science/what-is-consciousness.html.
10   Ibid.
11   Eugene d'Aquili and Andrew B. Newberg, *The Mystical Mind: Probing the Biology of Religious Experience* (Minneapolis: Fortress Press, 1999), 126.
12   Ibid.

This understanding leads them to at least entertain the possibility that unverified forms of consciousness may exist. While d'Aquili and Newberg do not claim to prove that a "higher reality" exists in fact, they do find support for the possibility that "a mind can exist without an ego and that awareness can exist without a self."[13]

Read & Write 9.3   Explore Experiences of Spiritual Consciousness

The intersection of religion and science is not always pacific, as illustrated by the success of Pastafarianism (the Church of the Flying Spaghetti Monster) in countering intelligent design theory, a topic discussed in section 1.5 of this manual. Technological advances are allowing neurologists to provide insights into human behavior that span a host of disciplines. While some religious groups counter attacks by denying the validity of science, others are more circumspect in their approach.

The research of d'Aquili and Newberg discussed above is one example of recent advances in neurotheology, which seeks an accommodation between religion and science. Another example of such a study is an article published in the journal *Zygon* by Arizona State University senior lecturer Michael Winkelman, "Shamanism as the Original Neurotheology."[14] Winkelman's abstract asserts, in part,

> Neurotheological approaches provide an important bridge between scientific and religious perspectives. . . . Cross-cultural studies establish the universality of shamanic practices in hunter-gatherer societies around the world and across time. These universal principles of shamanism . . . provide a basis for an evolutionary theology. . . . This approach reveals that universals of shamanism such as animism, totemism, soul flight, animal spirits, and death-and-rebirth experiences reflect fundamental brain operations and structures of consciousness.[15]

Although neurotheology will not convince all its critics that theology has a valid role in advancing scientific knowledge, it does at least provide new opportunities for understanding spiritual phenomena.

Your task in this exercise is to examine an aspect of an exceptional spiritual experience, perhaps a personal experience or the visions of Black Elk or the sorts of phenomena long known in shamanism. Identify, describe, and explain this experience from the varieties of studies you find in scholarly literature and your personal observations.

9.4   POLITICS AND RELIGION

In fall 2016, America's evangelical Christians found themselves on the horns of a dilemma. While they deplored the crass language and behavior of Republican presidential candidate Donald Trump, many of them also abhorred certain policy (e.g., pro-choice, pro–gay marriage) positions of Democratic presidential candidate Hillary Clinton. The plight of these evangelicals gives proof of the old saying that politics is rarely free of religion and religion is rarely free of politics.

---

[13]   Ibid.
[14]   Michael Winkelman, "Shamanism as the Original Neurotheology," *Zygon* 39, no. 1 (March 2004): 193–217.
[15]   Ibid., 193.

One irony of this feature of life is that religion is occasionally a major force in humankind's perpetual attempt to rid life of politics. This phenomenon can be noted in the disputes between the Greek philosopher Plato (427–347 BCE) and his protégé Aristotle (384–322 BCE). Socrates (470–399 BCE), the protagonist of Plato's seminal political work *The Republic*, constructed an ideal regime, the objective of which was to rid Athenian society of politics. In Socrates' vision, a group of philosopher kings, the wisest people of the land, would rule over the guardians, the courageous and athletic military class, and the craftsmen and tradesmen who composed the large body of citizenry. Philosophic rule would result in happiness for everyone, because all citizens would be provided what each desired most. Socrates held that disputes over resources and benefits, status and stations, honors and privileges—the substance of politics itself—would disappear from society. Aristotle fired back that Plato's pie-in-the-sky plan was impractical and dangerous. The younger philosopher championed the healthy if sometimes chaotic drama of political debate and resolution, a phenomenon best accomplished by a middle class that was moderate in means and attitude.

This philosophic debate continued, within both secular politics and religion, down through the centuries. The Roman Republic (intermittently from 509 to 27 BCE) championed expanded, if limited, political participation; it established a senate, courts, and other institutions that later inspired America's Founding Fathers. But at roughly the same time that the Roman experiment took place, antipolitical movements were at work in other parts of the world.

One of these was inspired in China by Lao-tzu ("Old Master"), the name given to the person who wrote, probably in the sixth century BCE, the spiritual meditations known as the *Tao Te Ching*. A sublime and therapeutic lesson in eliminating stress from life, the *Tao* demolishes traditional logic and ethics by turning common conceptions back upon themselves. It eviscerates politics by turning it on its head:

The highest virtue is not virtuous; therefore it truly has virtue.
The lowest virtue never loses sight of its virtue; therefore it has no true virtue.[16]

The spiritual path of the *Tao* is known as the Way, a reversal of the normal course of life:

When the world has the Way, ambling horses are retired to fertilize [fields].
When the world lacks the Way, war horses are reared in the suburbs.
Of crimes—none is greater than having things that one desires;
Of disasters—none is greater than not knowing when one has enough.
Of defects—none brings more sorrow than one's desire to attain.
Therefore, the contentment one has when he knows that he has enough, is abiding contentment indeed.[17]

In the Way, power is the responsibility to liberate:

The Way gives birth to them, nourishes them, matures them, completes them, rests them, rears them, supports them, and protects them.
It gives birth to them but doesn't try to own them;
It acts on their behalf but doesn't make them dependent;

---

[16] Lao-tzu, *Te-Tao Ching*, trans. Robert G. Henricks (New York: Modern Library, 1989), 7.
[17] Ibid., 16.

It matures them but doesn't rule them.
This we call Profound Virtue.[18]

But the *Tao* goes even further than specifying a different path. It turns the normal flow of the means and ends of politics on its head:

The reason why rivers and oceans are able to be the kings of the one hundred valleys is that they are good at being below them.
For this reason they are able to be the kings of the one hundred valleys.
Therefore in the Sage's desire to be above the people,
He must in his speech be below them.
And in his desire to be at the front of the people,
He must in his person be behind them.
Thus he dwells above, yet the people do not regard him as heavy;
And he dwells in front, yet the people do not see him as posing a threat.
The whole world delights in his praise and never tires of him.
Is it not because he is not contentious,
that, as a result, no one in the world can contend with him?![19]

The Stoic philosopher Epictetus (50–120 CE) also dealt a philosophically deadly, if practically untenable, blow to the heart of politics with a relatively simple concept. For this spiritual Roman thinker, the only power anyone can exercise over us is our own fear. If we have no fear of someone, that person has no power over us. A famous vignette illustrates Epictetus's actual exercise of this principle. In his youth Epictetus was the slave of a Roman freedman who, on one occasion, tortured the future philosopher by wrenching his leg. A smiling Epictetus calmly warned his master that, if he continued, the leg would break. When Epictetus's leg did break, he remained composed, saying simply to his master, "There, did I not tell you that it would break?"[20] Epictetus's response to political power, therefore, was a sort of apathy driven not by mental numbness but by mental strength aided by a spiritual confidence. In his discussion "How to Behave toward Tyrants," he presents the following tyrant-citizen discussion:

For when the tyrant says to a man, "I will chain your leg," he that values his leg says, "Nay, have mercy." But he that values his will says, "If it seems more profitable to you, chain it."
"Do you pay no heed?"
No, I pay no heed.
"I will show you that I am master."
How can you? Zeus gave me my freedom. Or do you think he was likely to let his own son be enslaved? You are master of my dead body. Take it.[21]

---

[18]   Ibid., 21.

[19]   Ibid., 36.

[20]   Keith H. Seddon, "Epictetus (55–135 C.E.)," *Internet Encyclopedia of Philosophy: A Peer-Reviewed Academic Resource*, accessed December 29, 2016, http://www.iep.utm.edu/epictetu.

[21]   Epictetus, *The Discourses and Manual, Together with Fragments of His Writings*, trans. P. E. Matheson (Oxford: Clarendon Press, 1916), in *The Stoic and Epicurean Philosophers*, ed. Whitney J. Oates (New York: Random House, 1940), 258, transcribed by John Bruno Hare, Internet Sacred Text Archive, June 2009, accessed December 28, 2016, http://www.sacred-texts.com/cla/dep/dep020.htm.

During the Pax Romana, the Roman Empire brought comparative peace within the Mediterranean world from the third decade of the first century BCE through the end of the second century of the Common Era. Driven in part by nostalgia for the Pax Romana, the Roman Catholic Church claimed supreme political and ecclesiastical authority from the Middle East through Europe for the millennium spanning 400 to 1400 CE. But if a goal of the Catholic Church was to pacify Europe's feuding principalities and ethnicities, it was never entirely successful. And the Catholic Church did not make the latest attempt to eliminate politics from human interaction. Karl Marx intended communism to result in the withering away of the state, producing a society defined by the principle "from each according to his abilities, to each according to his needs,"[22] and in which no government was necessary. But the result was a series of totalitarian states in which politics, instead of disappearing, was consolidated in the hands of one or a few. And, not unlike totalitarian regimes, the Church, in its efforts to eliminate politics, has at times become the embodiment of politics itself.

Anyone who has ever been a member of a church, temple, mosque, or other religious entity, knows that the internal politics of these institutions can at times be brutal. This simply affirms Aristotle's dictum that people are political animals. Family politics, neighborhood politics, church politics—all social and public life is bound by this basic human propensity. When religion can be politically useful, it will be.

If politics is inescapable, then does religion have special resources to deal with it, or will religion be inescapably ensnarled with politics? Should religious leaders, aware of politics' dark side, embrace and make the best of politics, as John Calvin advocated (see section 1.5 of this manual)? Or should religions follow the path of the Amish and the Mennonites and establish small communities where, it is hoped, life is lived closer to God?

Read & Write 9.4   Consider the Politics of Religion

Within Christianity, the theological debate with respect to faith and politics came to its apex with the contrasting views of French sociologist and lay theologian Jacques Ellul (1912–1994) and German theologian Jürgen Moltmann (1926–). Ellul, concerned with what he called the "political temptation," believed that the kingdom of God envisioned by Jesus transcended politics through self-sacrifice and a focus on the needs of others rather than one's own desires. If the kingdom is to have a temporal effect, it must come by means of walking away from politics, not embracing it. Moltmann, known for his "theology of hope," believed that the actual transformation of society was the essence of Jesus's kingdom of God and that, since politics defines social life, only political means can transform it.

This exercise is your opportunity to clarify your own understanding of the relationship of religion to politics. Focusing on an actual and difficult political situation, such as the plight of evangelicals described in the introduction to this section, identify and analyze various facets of the dilemma and then come to your own resolution. You may be an insider (an evangelical, as in our example) or an outsider (in this case a nonevangelical), but either way, you will have an opinion. Write an essay in which you make your case.

---

[22] Karl Marx, "Critique of the Gotha Programme," Marxists Internet Archive, accessed December 28, 2016, https://www.marxists.org/archive/marx/works/1875/gotha.

9.5   POSTMODERN APPROACHES TO RELIGION

Carved in Stone

After the Civil War, across America's Midwest and West, land-grant universities in three predominant forms sprang up: flagships, agriculture schools, and teachers' colleges. Old North, a sandstone building facing west from the western boundary of the campus of the University of Central Oklahoma (UCO), is the state's oldest building for public higher education. Constructed in 1893 and originally the home of the state's teachers' college, the building features above its main door a stone engraved with a single word, in all capital letters: NORMAL.

Why NORMAL?

Read on.

An Era of Uncertainty

The background to our story goes like this. The *modern* era was characterized by an essentially unified worldview in which science and the scientific method provided the key to understanding and the control of an environment seen as objective and independent of human concern. In stark contrast, *postmodernism* has challenged virtually all claims by modernity and its science to a unified and authoritative epistemology. In its place, postmodernism asserts that the objects of inquiry cannot be separated from the investigating agent. The human mind is viewed not as a passive receptacle of the "external" world, but instead as actively shaping and essentially *constructing* the world from elements preselected from a potentially infinite array. Thus, there are no bare "facts." All human understanding is interpretive, and therefore, no interpretation is definitive, authoritative, or final. Instead of facts, insights, or authorities, postmodernism looks for perspectives, constructs, and *narratives.* Hence the *ultimate* nature of reality (if such a construct is even meaningful) is regarded as either ambiguous or unknowable.

Many streams of thought have contributed to the postmodern worldview, but the input of linguistic analysts, including Ferdinand de Saussure, Edward Sapir, B. L. Whorf, and Ludwig Wittgenstein, has proven particularly influential. More recently, the work of Michel Foucault and Jacques Derrida has triggered parallel investigations in fields as far-ranging as political science and art history. Perhaps the central feature of postmodernism is the premise that all human thought is produced and ultimately limited by the cultural and linguistic forms through which that thought is expressed. The human mind can never claim access to an ultimate reality because no reality is possible that has not been "pre-strained" and conditioned by its local form of expression.

One outcome of postmodern thought has been a rigorous critique of the entire Western intellectual canon, increasingly viewed as the limited or even perverse product of a self-aggrandizing male European elite. Received "truths" of modernity such as "reason," "civilization," and "progress" are revisited with an eye not only to its beneficiaries, but also to those left behind or marginalized. The marginalized include, most notably, women, non-Europeans, working classes, indigenous cultures, and, more recently, sexual minorities. Postmodernism's broader critique comprises abuses of other life-forms and environmental impacts of human activities across the entire planet. In certain analyses, postmodern thinkers view the very attempt to impose *any* form of overarching conceptualization of the world, humanity, or history as not only self-deceptive but potentially destructive.

One outcome of the postmodern critique has been the development of a "hermeneutics of suspicion," in which the major thrust of intellectual activity is to "deflate pretensions, expose ulterior motives, explode beliefs, and unmask appearances."[23]

Ironically, an old false confidence in the "superior" abilities of modern knowledge, technique, or sensibility, has been replaced by postmodernity's "special" awareness of the limits of knowledge and its recognition of covert "metanarratives." Still, the postmodern milieu has shown itself to be conducive to a number of positive cultural developments. The fact that no religious, scientific, or philosophical perspective has the upper hand has encouraged unprecedented intellectual flexibility and cross-fertilization and invited open conversations among different understandings, vocabularies, and paradigms.

Perhaps no discipline stands to benefit from the postmodern perspective more than religious studies. An openness to cross-cultural and interdisciplinary perspectives holds great promise, providing a broader context for the understanding of religious experience and for integrating these insights into creative dialogue with other religious traditions as well as secular institutions. In this regard, the prophetic message of many religious traditions offers a natural context for integrating the postmodern deconstruction of false or destructive cultural narratives into a more inclusive and self-sustaining world vision.

Yet despite its positive contributions, many observers find postmodern thought fragmented and unfulfilling. If it asks many important questions, it provides few salutary answers. Especially in religious communities, some commentators, seeking a way to find a new common ground for the fragmented peoples of the world, believe that postmodernity's lack of intellectual authority and cohesion has allowed a host of dangerous subcurrents and festering ancient wounds to break out, threatening global peace and progress. For every unjust or unjustifiable paradigm exposed, new intellectual evasions and pretensions are advanced that threaten to recapitulate the old errors in new garb. Thoughtful theologians and philosophers conclude that the corrective needed is precisely what postmodernism cannot provide—a rooted common vision: a "metanarrative" (or perhaps a "meta-metanarrative") that cuts through the solipsistic din of competing individual or tribal perspectives, interests, and claims.

Read&Write 9.5 Behold the Panopticon

French postmodernist philosopher Michel Foucault (1926–1984) wrote several volumes of what he called "genealogy." He was not interested in tracing family trees. Instead, he attempted to trace patterns of political power as they emerged in society. He was most interested in identifying how political power is created and wielded and how people perceive it and are affected by it. He conducted extensive studies of how power is exercised in medicine, criminal justice, and education. His studies led him to conclude that political

23 Richard Tarnas, *The Passion of the Western Mind* (New York: Ballantine Books, 1991), 401.

power is much more pervasive than many people assume. To illustrate this principle, he borrowed the concept of the panopticon, a curiously designed building proposed by the eighteenth-century British utilitarian philosopher Jeremy Bentham.

Bentham wanted to reform the British penal system. As Foucault notes in his book *Discipline and Punish* (1991), in 1791 Bentham proposed a new, more humane, and more efficient prison design than was in use in the eighteenth and nineteenth centuries: a building constructed in such a way that all its inhabitants could be observed at all times by a supervisor. In his book, Foucault explains how Bentham's panopticon is a metaphor for the instruments of political power in our lives today:

> Bentham's Panopticon is the architectural figure of this composition. We know the principle on which it was based: at the periphery, an annular building; at the centre, a tower; this tower is pierced with wide windows that open onto the inner side of the ring; the peripheric building is divided into cells, each of which extends the whole width of the building; they have two windows, one on the inside, corresponding to the windows of the tower; the other, on the outside, allows the light to cross the cell from one end to the other. All that is needed, then, is to place a supervisor in a central tower and to shut up in each cell a madman, a patient, a condemned man, a worker or a schoolboy. By the effect of backlighting, one can observe from the tower, standing out precisely against the light, the small captive shadows in the cells of the periphery. They are like so many cages, so many small theatres, in which each actor is alone, perfectly individualized and constantly visible. The panoptic mechanism arranges spatial unities that make it possible to see constantly and to recognize immediately. In short, it reverses the principle of the dungeon; or rather of its three functions—to enclose, to deprive of light and to hide—it preserves only the first and eliminates the other two. Full lighting and the eye of a supervisor capture better than darkness, which ultimately protected. Visibility is a trap.
>
> To begin with, this made it possible—as a negative effect—to avoid those compact, swarming, howling masses that were to be found in places of confinement, those painted by Goya or described by Howard. Each individual, in his place, is securely confined to a cell from which he is seen from the front by the supervisor; but the side walls prevent him from coming into contact with his companions. He is seen, but he does not see; he is the object of information, never a subject in communication. The arrangement of his room, opposite the central tower, imposes on him an axial visibility; but the divisions of the ring, those separated cells, imply a lateral invisibility. And this invisibility is a guarantee of order. If the inmates are convicts, there is no danger of a plot, an attempt at collective escape, the planning of new crimes for the future, bad reciprocal influences; if they are patients, there is no danger of contagion; if they are madmen there is no risk of their committing violence upon one another; if they are schoolchildren, there is no copying, no noise, no chatter, no waste of time; if they are workers, there are no disorders, no theft, no coalitions, none of those distractions that slow down the rate of work, make it less perfect or cause accidents. The crowd, a compact mass, a locus of multiple exchanges, individualities merging together, a collective effect, is abolished and replaced by a collection of separated individualities. From the point of view of the guardian, it is replaced by a multiplicity that can be numbered and supervised; from the point of view of the inmates, by a sequestered and observed solitude (Bentham, 60–64).
>
> Hence the major effect of the Panopticon: to induce in the inmate a state of conscious and permanent visibility that assures the automatic functioning of power. So to arrange things that the surveillance is permanent in its effects, even if it is discontinuous in its action; that the perfection of power should tend to render its actual exercise unnecessary; that this architectural apparatus should be a machine for creating and sustaining a power relation independent of the person who exercises it; in short, that the inmates should be caught up in a power

situation of which they are themselves the bearers. To achieve this, it is at once too much and too little that the prisoner should be constantly observed by an inspector: too little, for what matters is that he knows himself to be observed; too much, because he has no need in fact of being so. In view of this, Bentham laid down the principle that power should be visible and unverifiable. Visible: the inmate will constantly have before his eyes the tall outline of the central tower from which he is spied upon. Unverifiable: the inmate must never know whether he is being looked at at any one moment; but he must be sure that he may always be so. In order to make the presence or absence of the inspector unverifiable, so that the prisoners, in their cells, cannot even see a shadow, Bentham envisaged not only venetian blinds on the windows of the central observation hall, but, on the inside, partitions that intersected the hall at right angles and, in order to pass from one quarter to the other, not doors but zig-zag openings; for the slightest noise, a gleam of light, a brightness in a half-opened door would betray the presence of the guardian. The Panopticon is a machine for dissociating the see/being seen dyad: in the peripheric ring, one is totally seen, without ever seeing; in the central tower, one sees everything without ever being seen.[24]

Let us first understand that, although Bentham's panopticon is an actual physical prison, Foucault's panopticon is an allegory for society, or for a subculture of it. We shall apply Foucault's metaphor to a college campus. If you are a male student, you will probably not wear a tutu to history class today. A female wearing a tutu to a ballet class will appear normal, but if a male wears one to his history class, he needs to be en route to his drama course or his part-time job in stand-up comedy.

Virtually everyone in college classrooms, if you think about it, wears a uniform. Professors wear professor uniforms, and students wear student uniforms. The range of dress may seem wide, but if you imagine the available modes of attire—throughout history and around the world—you will likely admit that the range of choices exhibited in a college classroom is narrow indeed. But if it is well known that a tutu-attired male student's career choice is stand-up comedy, he may be cajoled by his history classmates, but he will not risk damage to his credibility.

To the point: If you are a student working for a college degree, your central objective in getting that degree is *credibility*. Virtually everything you do from the time you get up in the morning until the time you go to bed at night is affected, if not entirely controlled, by what others may think of you. Though you may sometimes defy convention, you are very aware that your defiance carries risk.

And so you should not be surprised that the word literally carved in stone above Old North's main entrance is NORMAL. It is not difficult to imagine Foucault pointing to the inscription and saying, "The builders meant exactly what they said: The main objective of secondary education in the nineteenth century was to produce *normal* students—students conforming to community standards of thought and behavior." For Foucault, the concept of normal is a mechanism of control, a power play. And in the nineteenth century, that meant church, manners, respect for authorities, and respectability.

Now, write an essay in which you describe and evaluate—from your own personal experience or from secondary research—a religion, a denomination, or a single congregation's *panopticon effect*, that is, the extent to which this group conditions its members to monitor

---

[24] Michel Foucault, *Discipline and Punish*, trans. Alan Sheridan (New York: Vintage, 1995), 200–203. The page numbers Foucault cites from Bentham come from "Panopticon; or, the Inspection House," in *The Works of Jeremy Bentham*, ed. John Bowring, vol. 4 (Edinburgh: William Tait, 1838–1843).

and manage their own and others' beliefs and behaviors. As you write, contemplate the following questions:

- To what extent is any member of this religious group an inmate of a Foucaultian panopticon—as a guard, a prisoner, or both?
- What are the boundaries of acceptable expression and behavior within this group?
- What can be done to enhance the freedom of expression and individuality within this group, if such enhancement is necessary?
- To what extent are the members of this religious group prisoners of their own devices?

10

ENGAGING SCRIPTURE

10.1 ENGAGING HERMENEUTICS

We live in an exciting era. Elements of a rapidly evolving global economy intermingle like light waves, infusing cultures with stressful challenges and vibrant opportunities. At times they amplify our common understanding; at others they dampen it as we digress into confusion and conflict. Nowhere is this activity more apparent than in our discourse regarding religion. According to Professor Diane Eck of Harvard's Pluralism Project,

> Our religious traditions are not boxes of goods passed intact from generation to generation, but rather rivers of faith—alive, dynamic, every-changing, diverging, converging, drying up here, and watering new lands there. We are all neighbors somewhere [or some way], minorities somewhere, majorities somewhere. This is our new geo-religious reality. There are mosques in the Bible Belt in Houston, just as there are Christian churches in Muslim Pakistan. There are Cambodian Buddhists in Boston, Hindus in Moscow, Sikhs in London.[1]

In this environment many traditions have sought to demonstrate or reestablish their relevance through an appeal to special revelation, by linking to a higher authority or providing insight into a higher reality. For all the world's great religions, these special revelations have been preserved in the form of writings regarded as authoritative and transformative. These writings, or *scriptures*, document the initial revelatory experiences and their subsequent development in the thinking and actions of the individuals and groups most influential in the preservation of a particular tradition. However, because these writings are usually of great antiquity, they frequently rely on customs, outlooks, and means of expression that are difficult for contemporary readers to fully comprehend. In order to access the key message or insights of these scriptures, a means of interpretation, or a *hermeneutic*—a set of general principles upon which to understand scriptures—is required.

There are nearly as many hermeneutic traditions as faith traditions. For the

---

[1] Diane Eck, "A New Geo-Religious Reality," quoted in Mary Pat Fisher, *Living Religions: Eastern Traditions* (Upper Saddle River, NJ: Prentice Hall, 2003), 215.

ancient Greeks, hermeneutics involved attempts to decipher the fragmentary and ambiguous messages of the oracles. Rabbinic tradition exemplified in the *Baraita of Rabbi Ishmael* establishes specific logical rules of inference. One such rule is that the particular must be clarified by the general and the general must be clarified by the particular. Another is that when two passages contradict each other, the difference must be resolved by referring to a third passage. *Vedic* hermeneutics, such as the *Purva Mimansa Sutras*, also establish logical rules of inference, but they add careful definitions of key terms and they relate passages to discussions of differing ritual practices. *Buddhist* hermeneutics aim at extracting the most effective means of achieving spiritual enlightenment.

Biblical hermeneutics since the Christian era also have a lengthy history, albeit little known outside of academic institutions. One principle applied since the time of the Church Fathers and fully articulated by Augustine in *De Doctrina Christiana* is that the Bible should be approached with a spirit of profound humility and knowledge of "signs," that is, the Platonic inspiration that any "thing" has an immediate literal reality but can also potentially serve as a symbol (a "sign") referring beyond itself to a more encompassing reality.

The biblical hermeneutics of the Church Fathers of centuries past have traditionally distinguished four different modes or approaches to scriptural interpretation: the literal, the moral, the allegorical, and the analogical. While the literal mode adheres to the "plain meaning" of scripture, the moral interpretation seeks the underlying moral lessons of a passage. Allegorical readings frequently look for "types" in key figures, places, or events that point to larger patterns or themes. Analogical interpretations look for esoteric mystical patterns, such as numerical values, that reveal hidden patterns in scripture that can predict future events.

Modern biblical hermeneutics date from the pioneering works of "Higher Criticism," most notably by Ferdinand Christian Baur (1792–1860) and Julius Wellhausen (1844–1918). This method of *historical-critical* interpretation sought to resolve apparent redundancies, inconsistencies, or ambiguities by identifying earlier source documents and literary forms contained in the final accepted biblical texts. Some scholars, including most notably Rudolf Bultmann (1884–1976), have used higher criticism as part of a program to "demythologize" or provide historical or naturalistic explanations for biblical accounts that feature miraculous or supernatural occurrences. Later Higher Criticism was combined with or supplanted by a more purely *literary* analysis that attempts to elucidate the text in terms of its narrative style and structure.

In the nineteenth and twentieth centuries hermeneutics emerged as a philosophical and literary discipline with influence far beyond any particular religious tradition or even literary criticism as commonly understood. In the works of Martin Heidegger, Karl Popper, Hans-Georg Gadamer, and Karl-Otto Apel, hermeneutics takes on the broader role of examining all human understanding and the limits of our abilities to process and communicate our experience. Contemporary theorists have extended hermeneutical analysis to architecture, the environment, and international law. Indeed, hermeneutics is at the center of a much broader intellectual current that is seen by many as characteristic of our entire postmodern era.

To serve as an example of hermeneutics (again, sets of general principles upon which to understand scripture), here are some hermeneutics of the Presbyterian Church, paraphrased from a position statement called the *Presbyterian Understanding and Use of Holy Scripture* (1983):

- Scripture is intended for theological, not scientific purposes, and is not a source of answers to scientific questions.
- Scripture is to be understood as unifying, not separating theology and religious practice.
- Scripture is superior to all other theological authorities, including church doctrine and practice, although its interpretation pays due respect and consideration to them.
- The authority of scripture is based on the witness of the Holy Spirit alone.
- Although Christ is central to understanding scripture, it is Christ within the contexts of the Old and New Testaments.
- Selected texts, even including the words of Christ himself, are not to be placed above and beyond Scripture as a whole.
- The foundation of scripture is love of God *and* others, not God alone.
- New scriptural insights must not be disparaged out of hand, and no scriptural interpretation is ever final.[2]

Each of the above statements presents an arguable proposition about critical aspects of scriptural interpretation. You will find different statements on the same issues among Protestant denominations and in Roman Catholic doctrine. A document published alongside the *Presbyterian Understanding and Use of Holy Scripture* reports the results from *The Presbyterian Panel*, an opinion research document that asks people to consider a key hermeneutic, the character of the authority of the Bible. Here is a paraphrase of five opinions that, according to the *Panel*, best represents the range of opinions among Presbyterians regarding biblical authority. Which of the opinions seems most reasonable to you?

- The Bible, although of human authorship, is flawless with respect to theology, history, and science.
- The Bible, although of human authorship, is perfect and flawless with respect to theology, but not with respect to history and science.
- The Bible is a human document inspired by God.
- Some of the Bible may not have been inspired by God.
- The Bible records parts of Christian and Hebrew religious history.[3]

Read&Write 10.1   Construct a Personal Hermeneutic

You can construct a personal hermeneutic whether you are a Christian, Buddhist, or Pastafarian; an agnostic; or an atheist. Consider the chart below, which poses sets of questions within several basic conceptual categories. Write an essay in which you first provide your own personal answers (as you understand them at the present moment) to the "Potential

2   *Presbyterian Understanding and Use of Holy Scriptures: A Position Statement Adopted by the 123rd General Assembly (1983) of the Presbyterian Church in the United States* (Louisville, KY: Office of the General Assembly, 1983), https://www.pcusa.org/site_media/media/uploads/_resolutions/scripture-use.pdf.

3   *Biblical Authority and Interpretation: A Resource Document Received by the 194th General Assembly (1982) of the United Presbyterian Church in the United States of America* (Louisville, KY: Office of the General Assembly, 1983), https://www.pcusa.org/site_media/media/uploads/_resolutions/scripture-use.pdf.

Theological Questions" in the chart's final column, addressing also any similar questions that you find relevant.

Chart of Philosophical-Theological Questions

Set	Concept	Generic Basic Questions	Potential Theological Questions
1	Theological Ontology	What exists?	Is there a god? If so, what are the characteristics of this god?
2	Theological Epistemology	How do we know what exists?	On what authority do we base our answers to the questions in set 1?
3	Theological Anthropology	What is human nature?	What are our preeminent human characteristics? To what extent are we spiritual beings? On what do we base our answers? Scripture? Evolution? Personal Experience?
4	Theological Psychology	What can our minds perceive?	With respect to spirituality, what can we perceive and experience?
5	Theological Sociology	How do we organize and relate?	What is the best role for religion in society?
6	Theological Politics	What is legitimate authority?	Who should be authorized to represent God? What are the scope and boundaries of this authority?
7	Theological Ethics	How should we treat each other?	What principles should guide our conduct with each other?

Next, revise the paraphrased hermeneutics of the Presbyterian Church listed above to accord with the answers to the questions you have just written. In this part of your essay you may find that you agree entirely with the Presbyterian statements, reject all of them (and provide your own theological/philosophical substitutes), or adopt some approach in between. The result will be your own personal hermeneutic. You may find it interesting to place a copy of your essay in a safe place and refer to it every decade or so for continuing personal insight about your own spiritual or philosophical journey.

10.2   ENGAGING EXEGESIS

Across America citizens hear a continuous stream of calls to enshrine the Ten Commandments in civic centers, to teach the Bible in public schools, and to reflect biblical norms regarding abortion policy and other issues. We are engaged in an ongoing debate about whether our civic mores depend upon a Judeo-Christian foundation or upon a secular creed of separation of church and state. Even in our global village, with its clash of customs, values, and ideals, many groups continue to view contemporary social issues through the lens of venerable religious traditions. And these traditions are generally preserved in sacred scriptures, regarded as authoritative guides for individual and social life. But embedded in this view are deeper questions about the scriptural sources of disputed religious values.

In any case, the definitive "moral" position we take on a public issue will be defined, consciously or not, by our hermeneutic, which can be the general set of principles by which we understand not just scripture, but all other sources of moral authority as well. With respect to scripture, for example, our hermeneutic will tell us the extent to which scripture is inspired by God, and if its authority extends beyond matters of faith to science and history.

Since the Reformation (i.e., the late fifteenth century), many adherents of Protestant tradition following the reformers—most notably Luther and Calvin—have placed great emphasis on *sola scriptura* (scripture alone) instead of on the Roman Catholic Church's doctrinal authority as the bedrock of Christian belief. This hermeneutic reflects a determination to free Christian thought and action from the strictures of what some view as a corrupt, even heretical, clerical superstructure. But one consequence of this sole reliance on scripture has been a dogmatic insistence that the Bible is largely, if not entirely, "self-interpreting," that is, clear, consistent, and immediately applicable to all intellectual, social, and personal concerns. Large segments of Christian adherents continue to uphold this doctrine of biblical inerrancy. But, beginning even with reforming voices like Erasmus, this doctrine has been consistently challenged by a rationalistic critique that has pointed to many instances of textual ambiguity, inconsistency, and even apparent contradiction. With the advent of Higher Criticism in the nineteenth century, the challenge to literal inerrancy has broadened into wide-ranging analyses of philology, history, literary forms, and comparative religion.

Although much of this work originated with German Protestant academics, Catholic scholarship received crucial support from Pope Pius XII in 1943. His encyclical *Divino Afflante Spiritu* encouraged biblical scholars to make use of all methods of language study, historical research, and archeology, because, in the words of the encyclical, "the investigation carried out on this point during the past forty or fifty years with greater diligence and care than ever before, has more clearly shown what forms of expression were used in those far-off times, whether in poetic description or in the formulation of laws and rules of life or in recording the facts and events of history."[4] In this eloquent defense of the rigors and products of biblical criticism, Pope Pius XII affirms by inference the need for skillful exegesis.

And why do we need exegesis? Whereas hermeneutics provide theological *strategy* (principles for our general approach to scripture), exegesis provides *tactics* (specific rules for interpreting particular passages of text). Here are some common Christian exegetical principles:

- Sound exegesis is done utilizing scholar-selected Hebrew and Greek texts.
- Sound exegesis provides a clear, direct sense of what is written.
- Following a common theological adage, "A text without a context is a pretext," sound exegesis understands text within its scriptural, cultural, and historical contexts, and perceives the purpose for which it was written.
- When a pericope (a selection of text) from one source (a Gospel) is longer than a similar one from another source, the more complete of the two is to be preferred.

Exegesis is both art and skill, and, because our minds have a strong tendency toward bias, it demands an excruciating integrity. We as exegetes must be determined to discover *what the text says*, not *what we want it to say*.

---

4   Pope Pius XII, *Divino Afflante Spiritu*, para. 36, quoted in Lawrence Boadt, *Reading the Old Testament: An Introduction* (New York: Paulist Press, 1984), 13.

With this imperative in mind, it is common for theology students to exegete portions of scripture in order to determine *exactly* what the scripture says, and this quest is often challenging and, more than occasionally, disappointing. According to Matthew 26:27, for example, at the Lord's Supper, Jesus drinks from a cup. He then passes it to his disciples, telling them to *all drink of it*. No, no . . . wait; wait. At the Lord's Supper, Jesus, after drinking from a cup, passes it to his disciples, telling them to *drink all of it*. Which is it?

The answer is important when conducting communion services. Some Christians, following the first version, make sure that everyone present gets to drink some of what is served. Others, following the second version, make sure that the last person to drink consumes the last drop. Who is right? Decide for yourself. Of the more than fifteen thousand ancient Greek New Testament texts, no two are identical, and yet no two disagree on the fundamental elements of doctrine. And so, in questions of how to proceed with the communion cup, different texts may produce different answers. A second difficulty in translating Greek is that it has no punctuation, no periods, no commas, no paragraphs. Ancient (common, everyday) Greek is just a continuous series of letters that the reader must parse into words, and some combinations of letters may be made into more than one set of words. Add to this the fact that in Greek many words compose complete sentences, and you have manuscripts that defy exact translation by providing several legitimate interpretive options.

The problem is more complicated still. The word βαπτίζω (baptize) in Greek, for example, is like many English words in that it can have several meanings, anything from complete immersion to a sprinkle, and Christian practice reflects this span of interpretation in its diverse practice of baptisms.

All this is not to say, of course, that exegesis is a fruitless exercise. Much understanding is to be gained from its practice. And it provides a profound insight: Scriptural texts are as likely to encourage liturgical and devotional freedom as to demand a singular uniformity.

Read&Write 10.2   Practice Exegesis

Let's return to the exegetical principles stated above. We shall assume that you have not acquired language proficiency in ancient Greek or Hebrew, and yet it is profitable to understand some of the challenges that exegesis entails.

Bible translations differ in ways that may not appear to contrast substantially yet may produce some interesting and perhaps significant variations. Consider the following translations of Luke 23:2:

- *King James Version:* And they began to accuse him, saying, We found this fellow perverting the nation, and forbidding to give tribute to Caesar, saying that he himself is Christ a King.

- *The Bible in Basic English:* And they made statements against him, saying, This man has to our knowledge been teaching our nation to do wrong, and not to make payment of taxes to Caesar, even saying that he himself is Christ, a king.

- *The Common English Bible:* began to accuse him. They said, "We have found this man misleading our people, opposing the payment of taxes to Caesar, and claiming that he is the Christ, a king."

- *The Complete Jewish Bible:* where they started accusing him. "We found this man subverting our nation, forbidding us to pay taxes to the Emperor and claiming that he himself is the Messiah—a king!"

Your first task in this exercise is to locate a religious scripture of your choice in any convenient translation. Browse through it until you locate an interesting pericope, perhaps a parable, a poem, or a lamentation.

Next, find some alternative translations of your selected text. If your scripture is within the Christian Bible, for example, you will find Bible Study Tools (biblestudytools.com), operated by the Salem Web Network, to be wonderfully helpful.

On your electronic device, follow the steps provided by Bible Study Tools, and bring up the list of translations for the first verse in your pericope. Compare the translations of this verse and the subsequent verses you have selected with respect to the extent to which each translation operates in accordance with the exegetical principles listed above—that is, "provides a clear, direct sense of what is written," and "understands the text within its scriptural, cultural, and historical contexts and perceives the purpose for which it was written."

Now, write an essay in which you select one translation as superior to the others with respect to these exegetical principles, and defend your selection. You will need to read the text preceding and following your selection, and you will benefit from the biblical commentaries.

ENGAGING THE HISTORY
OF THEOLOGY

11.1   TRACING THE COURSE OF
A TRADITION'S THEOLOGY

A common misperception holds that religion is primarily about esoteric, *heavenly* matters that have little to do with the often messy and entangling business of living in human society. But an honest review of the history of any faith tradition makes it clear that religion is at least as much about earthly struggle as heavenly bliss. This struggle takes many forms. Initially the founders of great faith traditions struggle to deal with a sense of alienation or displacement from their culture of origin. Moses finds himself "a stranger in a strange land" after his impulsive act of solidarity with an oppressed minority shatters his life of privilege in the Egyptian court. Siddhartha Gautama similarly rejects a proffered life of power and prestige that fails to provide answers to his questions. Muhammad is stricken by the nagging voice of the angel Gabriel commanding him to "Recite!" He finds the message both terrifying and incomprehensible.

But witnessing and articulating the founding revelation is only the beginning of the struggle. As the original revelation is communicated more widely, each emerging tradition struggles to integrate it into a consistent lifestyle. The result of this struggle is theology. Once the founders and the original generation of the faithful have departed, questions of leadership and succession must be addressed. At this phase the tradition often encounters resistance from the surrounding culture, which often compels the new group to separate itself either physically (the Jews into Sinai, the Muslims from Mecca to Medina, the Buddhist Sangha into monastic life) or by means of special dress, rituals, or language.

Upon reaching a stage of broad cultural or national acceptance, the tradition faces a host of new challenges as broader cultural matrices threaten to dilute or even eclipse the original revelation.

At each stage of the tradition matters of organization and discipline must be addressed: How are new members to be chosen and initiated? How will transgressions from accepted norms be handled? If the tradition endures long enough to become a world historical faith, it will pass through many intervals of stagnation, corruption, reevaluation, and reinvigoration. At this mature stage, it often becomes necessary to sort through the accumulated forms and expressions of the faith, compare them with the original revelation, and reestablish doctrinal priorities. This can be a painful and divisive process, often leading to schism and, not infrequently—especially when coercive governing establishments become involved—to violent social upheavals. These periods are all the more disturbing in light of the original visions of peace and social cohesion of the faith communities and their founders. In fact, such periods of violence are frequently cited as evidence against the very faith claims of the tradition. But it is difficult to find comparable long-standing cultural movements, religious or otherwise, that have not gone through such trials.

This brings us back to our original premise—namely, that religion and human struggle are thoroughly intertwined. Thus any attempt to ignore or sanitize the developmental history of a tradition can ultimately succeed only in draining it of relevance and vitality. If we can't ignore or discount our histories, perhaps we should instead attend to the difficult business of becoming *intimate* with them and seek after the larger lessons they unfold. Once again, understanding is achieved most clearly through writing. And, in the case of religion, this writing is known as theology.

Read & Write 11.1   Trace the Course of a Religious Tradition's Theology

Theology (literally, "words about God") is an attempt to explain and defend a religion's beliefs. Major religions produce an array of competing theologies. Select a religious tradition with which you are not acquainted and then, in a research paper of at least ten pages, summarize the history of its most influential theologies. In your conclusion, summarize the theological themes that are consistent across that tradition and the major theological cleavages that have both developed through time and remain today.

11.2   COMPARING PRACTICES AND DOCTRINES

Religious practices are vast in number and variety, and some are simply fantastic. Are you carrying baggage from a past spiritual experience? If you think you are, your belief is not uncommon. In fact, religious rituals designed to free us from the distress of damaging events are universal. If you are a Scientologist you may employ technology in your purification quest. Some Scientologists believe you can use an "e-meter" (a device that measures the electrical properties of human skin) to discover spiritual inconsistencies. Although e-meters were designed for use on humans, they also revealed, according to L. Ron Hubbard, the founder of Scientology, that tomatoes scream when they are sliced.[1]

---

[1]   This notorious claim is discussed in "Scientology Mythbusting with John Atack: The Tomato Photo!" The Underground Bunker, accessed February 11, 2017, http://tonyortega.org/2013/02/02/scientology-mythbusting-with-jon-atack-the-tomato-photo.

Most rituals have ancient roots. The Old Testament describes numerous animal sacrifices employing sheep, goats, bulls, and birds. The purpose of the sacrifice is to remind the person conducting it of the gravity of sin and the cost of absolving it. Transferring the penalty to the animal, the sinner becomes aware of both the iniquity and the penalty for his or her sin and then, after the animal's life is sacrificed, experiences relief from guilt and gratitude to God for the pardon. A small minority of Jews still practice *kaparot*, a ritual enacted on the eve of Yom Kippur, in which a chicken is sacrificed and its body then donated to the poor.[2]

Practices such as these elicit our curiosity and, occasionally, bemused derision. But perhaps we should be more willing to contemplate their content as creative expressions of human nature. The popular 1980 film *The Gods Must Be Crazy*, for example, depicts the reactions of a group of isolated African natives who first encounter the outside world via a Coke bottle casually thrown out of a passing airplane. The humor and charm of the story revolve around its revelation that what *we* regard as perfectly normal and obvious can be anything but that for someone outside our own culture or tradition.

For many steeped in the rationalistic worldview that reached its culmination in the late nineteenth and early twentieth centuries, *religion* itself—and especially ancient narratives describing key religious events—came to be increasingly regarded as a realm of curious attitudes, beliefs, and behaviors that were dismissed either as naïve anachronistic relics or, at best, phenomena that needed to be decoded and explained.

That attitude was gradually modified as anthropological evidence surfaced and indicated the ubiquity and similarity of religious practice across history, geography, and culture. Still, it is very natural for us to regard *our* faith tradition as normal and desirable while viewing the traditions of others with suspicion or, at best, curiosity.

Once we accept that religion is a natural and defining characteristic of the human species, it becomes clear that studying the distinctive ways in which humanity has expressed its religious impulses over the millennia will illuminate a good deal about the range and variety of human behavior itself. We will find ourselves looking critically into the meanings we assign to life, death, our natural world, human society, conflict, morality, and our development as tribes, nations, and eventually civilizations. And we will find that each faith tradition offers insight into the possible ways that the religious impulse can be translated into artistic expression, social organization, and human knowledge. Delineating these differing adaptations provides us with a laboratory from which to view the *ecology* of faith over a range of conditions.

Within this laboratory we are able to note the means by which a defining revelation was expressed. Was this revelation communicated during a single experience to a single individual or to a number of people over time? Buddhism builds on the insight of a single individual, Siddhartha Gautama, on a single, very special occasion. Islam was formed around a *series* of messages from the angel Gabriel to the prophet

---

2   "The Kaparot Ceremony," Chabad.org, accessed February 11, 2017, http://www.chabad.org /holidays/JewishNewYear/template_cdo/aid/989585/jewish/Kaparot.htm.

Muhammad. By contrast, while much of the core of Judaism reflects the singular encounter of Moses with Yahweh on Mount Sinai, there is an extensive series of protorevelations narrated in the biblical book of *Genesis* and two whole *additional* sections of the *Tanach* (the Hebrew bible)—namely, the *Nevi'im* (the Prophets) and the *Kethuvim* (the Writings)—that extend, refine, and provide context to the original revelation.

Returning to our laboratory, we might ask, "How did the founder or founding group come to accept the initial message, or did he, she, or they resist at first?" Initially, Muhammad and many of the Hebrew prophets were terrified and tried to deny or flee from their revelations. Even the Buddha, for a time, considered keeping his insight to himself. On the other hand, Christian tradition holds that Jesus was foreordained as the Logos (Word of God) from all eternity, and Jesus appeared to understand his destiny from early childhood. Yet even the Christian tradition holds that, after his baptism by John and anointing by the Holy Spirit, Jesus retreated to the desert, where he was subject to temptation by the devil before beginning his pronouncement of the "kingdom of God."

Looking further we might consider how the original message was spread to a wider group.

The first Muslim was Muhammad's wife Khadija, who calmed him, reassured him that he wasn't going crazy, and convinced him to heed his visions. Jesus left his hometown of Nazareth and recruited a core group of like-minded young men from the Galilean lake town of Capernaum to share his message and mission. Similarly, the Buddha first shared his new revelation at a deer park in Sarnath with five companions who had shared his earlier attempts at extreme asceticism. By contrast, in the more ancient traditions of Judaism and Hinduism, this particular early phase of development is shrouded in the mist of tribal memory and time.

We might continue our study with a number of related investigations. Were there any members of the founding group who deserted or apostatized? At what stage in the tradition did observances or liturgies emerge that were distinct from the surrounding culture? When did distinctive lifestyles, such as specific diets, dress, or behavioral codes, develop? How did the surrounding culture react to the new tradition? When and how did the emerging tradition acquire governing influence or authority? How was the original revelation preserved and developed into a comprehensive philosophy of life? How was order and discipline maintained? Did the founder(s) designate a successor or successor group? Was a clergy or hierarchy established? Is there a single contemporary leader?

The answers to these and similar questions provide the raw data from which the student of religion can gain perspective on the current status and future prospects of any particular tradition or religious expression in general. In the course of this study it will become apparent that no tradition is completely unique or separated from the broader contours of human culture. Instead, each tradition will reveal its distinctive character as an adaptive, evolving response to the perennial search for meaning and structure in our human existence.

Read & Write 11.2 Compare Doctrines of Two Major Sects within a Major Religious Tradition

Doctrines are the pillars of religious faith. They comprise the core values and beliefs of particular religions or sects. Here's an opportunity to explore some core doctrines of unfamiliar religious communities. Choose a theme, such as the character of God, salvation, or the nature of the sacred, and write a ten- to twenty-page research paper comparing the doctrines of two sects or religions. The discussion above was designed to focus your attention on a basic question: How do religions choose to encounter the challenges and opportunities of human existence? In your conclusion, discuss how the doctrines of your selected groups reveal similarities and differences about human nature and the human condition.

12

WRITING FOR WORSHIP AND SHARING LIFE

12.1   THE CRAFT OF HOMILETICS

At first glance, it might seem easy to view our contemporary era as a unique "golden age" for communication of every sort. Each of us holds in the palms of our hands exponentially more information than in prior ages was possessed by entire civilizations. And we have the means to sort this information and deliver our own message to millions simultaneously across the planet—a truly remarkable achievement. Yet the very magnitude and ubiquity of the messaging process pose challenges that we are only beginning to understand. How do we prioritize this flood of information? How do we distinguish fact from fiction, the helpful from the malicious? And how do we gauge the impact of our communications? Does the number of "friends" or "likes" we garner provide a reliable metric of the value or effectiveness of our messages?

It seems fair to note that this brave new world of information has not relieved the world of conflict, misunderstanding, exploitation, or general human suffering. Instead, *misinformation* and *disinformation* seem to have found rich new fields in which to grow, propagate, and infect their victims. So perhaps the mere quantity or availability of information is an insufficient means to evaluate the state of human intercommunication. A more critical perspective might begin to consider the *effects* that various messages have, and this focus, in turn, might lead to a consideration of the intent and the context of our communication. This whole tangle of approaches is directly relevant to the primary genre of religious communication: *homiletics.*

A *homily* is a religious discourse (a sermon, perhaps, or a lecture) that attempts to articulate the purpose, concern, or special focus of a group assembled (or otherwise identified) for religious observance. A homily is intended to facilitate understanding of the larger aims of a tradition and, more importantly, to encourage commitment to those aims. Our era presents new opportunities for the development and transmission of homilies—and very significant new challenges. We have access to a vast store of information regarding the sources and exegetical resources of our traditions that allow us sharpen and support our message, and we have sophisticated systems to address assemblies directly or through electronic media. But we must also recognize that any message from the pulpit may be received through the filters of a postmodern worldview. Younger listeners in particular tend to look skeptically at all messages advancing universal claims or absolute norms. This skepticism is even more intense when the message is identified with groups that have historically wielded (and often abused) power and privilege.

The postmodern impulse is to look for unacknowledged bias or self-interest lurking behind any truth claim. While it's often impossible to categorically dismiss these suspicions, a complete surrender to them would lead us to dilute our messages to the point of vacuity or fall into a deadening cynicism. There is an alternative approach that does not abandon truth claims altogether but works to integrate them into a variety of other perspectives. This approach makes certain demands. We must first make every attempt to understand and accurately represent our faith tradition to the community. This may include suitably selecting from primary scriptural sources and commentaries and appropriately extracting and summarizing the relevant message. But even more important, we must then bring this message to life by sensitively relating it to the questions, problems, and conflicts posed by our own experience. This demands that we be willing to share our own excitement and understanding, but also—and honestly—our fears, doubts, and frustrations, and we must also be emphatically aware of similar feelings within our assembly.

Turning to practicalities, a homily is an exercise in rhetoric, an ancient and venerable practice. Today's clergy, attorneys, and public officials owe much to its professional practitioners in ancient Athens and Rome. Although many rhetorical principles and techniques have been developed over time, for this chapter's writing exercises we ask you to focus your attention on three aspects of your homily: your audience, your purpose, and rhetorical proficiency.

Is your audience composed of the faithful? If so, your role is that of a team captain. Affirmation, encouragement, direction, inspiration, dedication, and the worthiness of goals are the primary components of your message. Dr. Martin Luther King Jr.'s "I Have a Dream" speech is a good model. Your homily may not be as dramatic, but your commitment to a vision should be clear.

Is your audience composed of potential converts? Evangelism is often successful when composed of a carrot, a stick, and repetition. There is a sense in which the thousands of sermons preached by the twentieth century's great evangelist, Dr. Billy Graham, contained a single clear, repeated message: Death is universal, and without commitment your prospects for a positive afterlife are tenuous at best. But acceptance of the sacrifice of Jesus on your behalf guarantees salvation to eternal life.

Evangelist Oral Roberts was highly persuasive because he offered both hope and a sense of personal dignity. Inaugurating healing crusades, Roberts prayed personally for thousands of people in despair with difficult health problems. Later in his career he found success in what he called "seed faith." Making a financial contribution to his ministry, he claimed, was like planting a seed that would accrue to the donor's financial benefit. But behind the surface message was a more profound and effective one. When people donated to a Roberts ministry, lives would be touched, souls would be saved, and the suffering would be healed. By donating, the giver was providing a valuable service. With valuable service came dignity, often in moments when little dignity was otherwise to be found.

To edify is to awaken new thoughts, images, and discoveries in your listeners' minds. You are hoping less to point them in a certain direction than to open them up, usually to new dimensions of something already familiar. Do you want them to perceive more clearly or deeply the effects of their own acts of kindness? Do you want them to appreciate new facets of a particular pericope in scripture?

Your purpose, therefore, follows from assessing the needs of your audience. Will you attempt to encourage, edify, or persuade? You may easily wish to accomplish all three goals, but focus on one at a time. Part of the perennial popularity of religion is its salutary effect on personal mental health. The difficulties of life demand affirmation and hope, neither of which tends to be excessively abundant. On the other hand, do you want the members of your audience to alter, if only slightly, their paths? Do you want them to contribute, support, counter, or become aware of a challenge or opportunity in their spiritual lives?

Irrespective of the nature of your audience, there are some things that contribute to the effectiveness of any homily. First, have a clear central idea, and repeat it. "Tell them what you are going to say, say it, and tell them what you said" is sage advice and has much merit. Second, you will find homilies easier to write if you follow a common rule: Make your argument, whatever it is, in three succinct points. Preachers, politicians, and psychologists have long known that the human memory stores information readily if it is received in sets of three ideas or themes. Religion is full of triads: Abraham, Isaac, Jacob; Father, Son, Holy Spirit; the three wise men. Politics has its own favorite threesomes: executive, legislative, judicial branches of government; the Marxist proletariat, bourgeoisie, and aristocracy. Phrasing your homily in three succinct points can give balance, clarity, and weight to your argument.

Note: For generations Protestant evangelists have sharpened their three-point sermons by using alliteration (the repetition of the same letter or sound at or near the beginning of words in an utterance) to phrase each point. A typical sermon preached at a revival meeting might, for example, focus on the *p*ower, the *p*reeminence, and the *p*eace that a relationship with the deity affords. While alliteration can be an effective mnemonic device, it is easy to misuse it by settling in your homily for a less-than-appropriate key word only because it happens to alliterate with your other key words. Should you use alliteration to help shape your homily? If you consider alliteration as a strategy, be aware that there is much discussion of alliteration as a possible aid—or detriment—to homiletic texts online.

Read & Write 12.1   Write Words to Inspire

Choose a date or an occasion of special significance to your faith tradition (e.g., Easter, Yom Kippur, Eid al-Fitr). Identify scriptural references appropriate to the occasion and carefully review exegetical resources and commentaries. Draft a homily of no more than ten minutes in length. Remember to first carefully consider your intended audience and purpose. Is your aim simply to clarify, as objectively as possible, a point in scripture? Or are you trying to persuade your reader of the truth of your interpretation? Review and edit your draft, shaping its overall structure and flow, looking especially for answers to these six questions with regard to your narrative:

1. Does its beginning appropriately introduce the occasion and engage the assembly?
2. Does it address and clearly explicate (but not slavishly repeat!) any scriptural reference?
3. Does it relate the scripture to the occasion and any relevant issues facing the assembly?

4. Does it contain an appropriate call to action or reflection?
5. Does it contain any abrupt or confusing transitions?
6. Does it contain any awkward, confusing, or inappropriate words or phrases?

After finally editing your draft, arrange to deliver your homily to a selected group, such as your classmates, instructors, or some members of your faith community. Provide your audience members with a form on which they can offer feedback on your homily. After delivering your homily and collecting comments from your audience, review the written feedback and revise the homily accordingly.

12.2   THE CRAFT OF CELEBRATION

Celebration is the heart of culture and the soul of faith. We celebrate birthdays, anniversaries, great people, great events, graduations, and even sometimes phases of the moon. For millennia, local communities have celebrated the bounty of successful harvests, jubilation at hunting or military success, and the inauguration of new rulers. Religious ceremonies often reenact sacred events: Christian communion, Ramadan, Passover, Ganesh Chaturthi, and Bodhi Day reenact, respectively, the Last Supper of Christ, the revelation of the Qur'an to Muhammad, the liberation of the Hebrews from Egypt, the birth of Shiva (Hindu), and the day when the Buddha experienced enlightenment.

Universally, people celebrate birth and commemorate death. But, almost universally, we reserve our greatest celebratory energies for marriage. Perhaps this is because, although birth represents life's ongoing potential and death brings to mind life's accomplishments, marriage has the potential to inaugurate our most profound and enduring happiness. Following a myriad of patterns from silence to cacophony, from simple to highly formal, from poetic to mundane, people express in weddings their hopes, love, and joy. Weddings present unparalleled opportunities for music, food, fun, aspiration, and affirmations of personal and communal commitment.

Unfortunately, however, increasing specialization and technical sophistication have left us increasingly removed from many of the natural contexts for celebration. When we have little or no direct involvement with the food we consume, feelings of joy surrounding planting or harvest activities become increasingly remote. In place of more natural contexts for celebration we now have a bewildering array of messages seeking to link our natural desire to celebrate with the consumption of goods or services offered by an increasingly invasive *cyber* society. This ubiquitous messaging has produced an escalating desire for sensation and spectacle, and yet it appears to be yielding diminished returns of real joy and community. Nowhere is this trend more obvious than in the frenzied field of wedding planning. While a sizable industry has developed around the production of ever more elaborate (and expensive) *designer* or *destination* weddings, many religious professionals lament the increasing difficulty of even getting the attention of the participants, let alone relating the proceedings to a larger religious context.

Conducting a *religious* celebration assumes a responsibility to relate a special occasion to the vastly larger context of a faith tradition. It is the celebrant's role to make clear to those gathered that they represent and participate in a drama larger than themselves, that their dance is a universal dance. In a culture marked by diversion and distraction, the religious celebrant is called to restore focus and reestablish priorities. Above all, the religious celebrant is charged with shaping an occasion of joy into a more lasting expression of solidarity and hope for the future.

Compared with funerals and sacred event days (Christmas, Passover), wedding homilies are normally brief. Some traditions view weddings (and births and deaths) as opportunities for evangelism, and speakers in this vein infuse their messages with hope of the joys of relationship within their spiritual life patterns. In some traditions the presiding clergy or official provides a bit of practical personal advice to the new bride and groom, in comments such as this one:

> On this occasion we want to talk about how to keep a marriage happy, and I have an idea for the bride and groom. Imagine that you, Chris and David, each have a backpack on your back. In these backpacks you each carry your own hopes and dreams—your aspirations, the ideas of what you want out of life. Perhaps there is something you can do to have a happier marriage. Take your backpacks off and lay them down. Then pick up your partner's backpack and put it on. It's amazing how much lighter it will feel. You forget about your own hopes and dreams and focus your efforts on doing everything you can to make sure that your partner realizes his or her hopes and dreams. And he or she will do the same for you. Now the load for each of you is lighter, and the future you share is brighter.

Among other encouraging elements of wedding celebrations are the personalized pledges of commitment made by the partners to each other. Unique expressions of devotion and expectation bring the relational energies of the couple involved to the center of the collective experience of all who are joined on a day of life and love.

Read & Write 12.2 Write Words to Unite in Joy

Design a wedding ceremony for yourself, a family member, or a friend. Incorporate features of your faith, family, and cultural traditions, including settings, music, movement into and out of the ceremony, homilies, blessings or benedictions, food or beverages, and mementos or commemorative items. Review the plan with a group of classmates or your instructor. If practical and appropriate, actually arrange and conduct your ceremony.

12.3 THE CRAFT OF HEALING

Our pain at the loss of a loved one is commensurate with the intensity of joy that the person brought to our lives. Premature and unexpected death inflicts especially deep emotional wounds. Our thoughts on these occasions are directed to a single preeminent purpose: healing. We heal by celebrating the joy of that person's presence among us and experiencing the grief of the loss of his or her love together with family and friends.

In this effort we have help. We may begin by remembering that our most compelling literature, from ancient sagas to contemporary memes, builds on the drama occasioned by abrupt interruption of our day-to-day lives. All the major faith traditions announce themselves as a response to an essentially tragic human condition. For the Abrahamic faiths we are the heirs of a primeval fall from divine grace. For the Buddhist we live in a world that is *dukkha* (see section 8.3), apparently misaligned and infused with suffering. For the Hindu we are lost in *maya*—illusion and ignorance—that blinds us to our essential divine nature.

In addition to religion, popular culture has much to contribute to our healing journey.

Psychology provides a common guide to assuaging durable grief, a set of five stages in the process of emotional restoration: denial and isolation, anger, bargaining, depression, and acceptance. Psychology also tells us that avoiding pain increases its durability, and that to accept and experience pain allows it to pass more directly. Our culture's music and literature abound with expressions of these stages. A famous poem by Dylan Thomas, excerpted here, amply expresses anger at our inevitable fate:

Do not go gentle into that good night,
Old age should burn and rave at close of day;
Rage, rage against the dying of the light.

Though wise men at their end know dark is right,
Because their words had forked no lightning they
Do not go gentle into that good night.[1]

Among popular songs of grieving are Eva Cassidy's "I Know You by Heart," Eric Clapton's "Tears in Heaven," and Sting's "Fields of Gold."

At the heart of our grieving and healing traditions is the conviction that, while the harsh reality of our temporal existence cannot be eliminated or avoided, it can be viewed from a larger context. The great faith traditions testify that our individual suffering, frustration, or failure is not the last word, but that we participate in a larger reality. These traditions can offer the greatest possible consolation: that we are not isolated, suffering specks in an abyss, but that we stand together—at birth, throughout every phase of life, and in death—in understanding, compassion, and solidarity.

Read&Write 12.3 Write Words to Console in Bereavement

A funeral is a celebration of the life of a person who has died. It is an opportunity to get healing under way by joining friends and family in a unified grieving community. In May 1910, responding to the death of England's King Edward VII, Oxford divinity scholar Henry Scott Holland (1847–1918) delivered a poetic and comforting sermon entitled "Death Is Nothing at All," part of the text of which has been recast in verse:

Death is nothing at all.
It does not count.
I have only slipped away into the next room.
Nothing has happened.

Everything remains exactly as it was.
I am I, and you are you,
and the old life that we lived so fondly together is untouched, unchanged.
Whatever we were to each other, that we are still.

[1] Dylan Thomas, "Do not go gentle into that good night," *The Collected Poems of Dylan Thomas 1934–1952* (New York: New Directions, 1971), 128.

Call me by the old familiar name.
Speak of me in the easy way which you always used.
Put no difference into your tone.
Wear no forced air of solemnity or sorrow.

Laugh as we always laughed at the little jokes that we enjoyed together.
Play, smile, think of me, pray for me.
Let my name be ever the household word that it always was.
Let it be spoken without an effort, without the ghost of a shadow upon it.

Life means all that it ever meant.
It is the same as it ever was.
There is absolute and unbroken continuity.
What is this death but a negligible accident?

Why should I be out of mind because I am out of sight?
I am but waiting for you, for an interval,
somewhere very near,
just round the corner.

All is well.
Nothing is hurt; nothing is lost.
One brief moment and all will be as it was before.
How we shall laugh at the trouble of parting when we meet again![2]

You now have an opportunity to practice, in advance, comforting people who are grieving the loss of someone they love. Select an actual person whom you love or who you know is well loved. Write a homily in which you imagine that person is departed, and in which you (1) remember that person's fine qualities, and (2) foster healing for the mourners present.

---

[2] Henry Scott Holland, "Death Is Nothing at All," Family Friend Poems, http://www.familyfriendpoems.com /poem/death-is-nothing-at-all-by-henry-scott-holland.

GLOSSARY

absolutism
The holding of rigid, literalistic beliefs or preconceptions with regard to the tenets of a religion, philosophy, or political system.

agnosticism
The belief that, if there is a higher power or realm transcending the material universe revealed by science, it is impossible for humans to know it.

asceticism
A mode of life or belief that embraces voluntary self-denial in the pursuit of religious liberation or improvement.

atheism
The belief that there is no deity or higher power transcending the material universe revealed by science.

atman
In Hinduism, the soul or deity within.

Bhagavad Gita
A portion of the Hindu epic scripture the *Mahabharata*, in which Lord Krishna specifies ways of spiritual progress.

bodhisattva
In Mahayana Buddhism, one who has attained enlightenment but renounces nirvana for the sake of helping all other sentient beings in their journey to liberation from suffering.

Brahman
In Hinduism, the impersonal, ultimate principle; a Hindu of the highest caste, assigned to the priesthood.

canon
An authoritative collection of writings or other works that apply to a particular religion or author.

dharma
In Hinduism, moral order, righteousness, or religion. In Buddhism, the doctrine or law revealed by the Buddha; the correct conduct for each person according to his or her level of awareness.

diaspora
Collectively, the practitioners of a faith living beyond their traditional homeland.

doctrine
The official or standard teaching of a religion or by an analogous social, cultural, or political organization.

dogma
A tenet held to be authoritative, normative, or definitive by a religion or by an analogous social, cultural, or political organization.

dualism
The general philosophical or theological view that all reality is composed of and arises from distinct, independent, and antagonistic principles, such as Good and Evil, or Spirit and Matter; also known as *Manichaeism*.

dukkha
According to the Buddha, a central fact of human life, variously translated as dissatisfaction, suffering, frustration, or disjointedness.

ecclesiology
The theological study of the Church, churches, or analogous religious organizations.

ecumenism
The movement that seeks to articulate and restore unity among Christian faiths and that, ultimately, works toward unity with all humanity.

Eid al-Fitr
The annual Muslim festival celebrating the end of Ramadan, the month of fasting.

encyclical
A letter written by the pope and circulated throughout the Roman Catholic Church and beyond.

The Enlightenment
The philosophical movement and historical epoch that reached its zenith in eighteenth-century Europe and America, characterized by its advance of secularism, intellectual freedom, and moral autonomy over the older ideology of monarchy and state religion.

epic	A long narrative in an elevated style, often poetic, that recounts the deeds of legendary or historic figures.
eschatology	A branch of theology concerned with the final events in the history of the world.
exclusivism	A mode of belief that holds that one's own religion is the only valid way.
excommunication	The formal or ritual expulsion of an individual or group from a religious community.
exegesis	A systematic, scholarly, or scientific critique or interpretation of scriptural or other analogous texts.
fideism	An ideology that relies primarily on religious faith rather than reason for understanding the world and humankind's place in it.
fundamentalism	A mode of belief or scriptural interpretation that prioritizes what adherents perceive or represent as the authentic, literal, or historical form or expression of their religion or belief system, in contrast to more contemporary or scientific understandings.
Gnosticism	A mode of belief that holds that enlightenment or personal development can be achieved through an intuitive knowledge of spiritual realities that transcend or supersede the material world.
heresy	Significant deviation from the accepted, standard, or official beliefs of a religion or an analogous social, cultural, or political organization.
hermeneutics	The development and application of methods and rules for interpreting texts.
historicity	A mode of understanding that sees the human condition as being fundamentally set in time and shaped by the movement of history.
homiletics	The skill, method, or practice of writing and preaching sermons.
idolatry	Beliefs or practices that exalt a finite being, power, or principle to ultimate status.
immanence	That which subsists at the heart or core of creation or a created being, usually as applied to the presence of God or the Divine Spirit.
inclusivism	The belief that the core values of all religious beliefs can be accommodated within the tenets of a single religion.
inerrancy	The belief that one's sacred scriptures are either free from factual error of any kind, or alternatively are free from fundamental error with regard to central doctrines or tenets.
infallibility	A doctrine of the Roman Catholic Church that holds that the Church, acting either directly through the Roman pontiff (the pope) or an ecumenical council, is protected from fundamental error with regard to specific teaching about faith or morals.
inspiration, scriptural	The belief that one's sacred scriptures were produced either by the direct action of a divinity or a divine spirit or, alternatively, through divine influence on a human author or group of authors.
juridical	Of or relating to a mode of understanding religious life or the work of religious organizations primarily in terms of laws, obligations, and the duty to obey authority.
karma	In Hinduism and Buddhism, the natural and moral effects of one's actions in this life and on potential future lives.
Koran	*See* **Qu'ran**.
liberalism	An approach to religion that tends to regard tradition as developmental rather than fixed for all time, and views scripture and doctrinal expressions as primarily metaphorical rather than as literal truth or absolute legal imperatives.

Mahayana	The Northern branch of Buddhism, especially prominent in Tibet, China, and Japan, that features a broader and more mystical and expansive interpretation of Buddhist scriptures, traditions, and practices. This branch stresses the importance of altruistic compassion rather than intellectual efforts at individual liberation.
materialism	The philosophical position that nothing exists but the material universe revealed by natural science, and that there are no deeper or encompassing dimensions to life; a mode of life or belief that prioritizes personal possessions and comforts over altruistic, intellectual, or spiritual pursuits.
maya	In Hinduism, the attractive and intoxicating but ultimately illusory and unfulfilling material world.
moksha	In Hinduism, enlightenment or liberation from illusion and suffering (*maya*).
monasticism	A style of life that emphasizes communal dwelling, work, study, worship or contemplation, asceticism, and separation from the larger society.
monism	A mode of belief or understanding that regards life or reality as a unified whole without any fundamental distinction between physical or spiritual states.
monotheism	Belief in a single God, deity, or Higher Power.
mysticism	A mode of consciousness or belief that prioritizes the intuitive perception of spiritual truths, which are viewed as deeper or more encompassing than truths revealed by reason or natural science.
myth	A symbolic story that expresses aspects of a worldview or the values, practices, or history of a people.
Neoplatonism	A late stage of classic Greek philosophy that posits a great hierarchical chain of being in which all lower levels are seen as emanating from the highest level, God or the One, to which all levels strive to return.
nihilism	A state of belief or consciousness in which all beliefs are regarded as baseless, and existence is viewed as senseless and without value.
Nirvana	In Buddhism, the ultimate state of awakening, realization, or transcendence.
nominalism	A branch of medieval philosophy that, denying the reality of universal principles, views every *real* thing as irreducibly individual.
orthodoxy	Consistency with the established traditions, tenets, or practices of a religion or analogous social, cultural, or political entity.
pericope	A selected small portion of text, most commonly from the Bible.
phenomenology	A philosophical discipline that aims at establishing a firm foundation for all human understanding by conducting a rigorous survey of data presented to human consciousness *prior to* or separated from any "presuppositions," that is, any arbitrary operating assumptions or habits of mind, whether conscious or unconscious. This discipline can lead to complex and highly technical analyses of language, logic, and human psychology.
pluralism	A worldview or philosophical perspective that holds that reality is ultimately multiform rather than singular or unified in nature; a state of society in which a diversity of religious, cultural, or political expressions or viewpoints are given equal legal standing.
profane	The realm of ordinary human awareness or experience ("the profane"); as an adjective, nonreligious or secular.
Qu'ran	The scriptures accepted by the Muslim faith tradition as the authoritative revelation of God (Allah) to the prophet Muhammad.
rationalism	A philosophical perspective that prioritizes the role of reason in the pursuit of truth.

realism
A philosophical system that holds that objective or universal truths exist independent from linguistic conventions or individual perceptions.

sacred
A realm or dimension transcending ordinary experience ("the sacred"); as an adjective, holy.

samsara
In Buddhism, Hinduism, and Jainism, the continual cycle of birth, death, and rebirth.

sangha
In Buddhism, the community of those dedicated to the dharma or teaching of the Buddha.

shamanism
A set of religious practices and beliefs about spirits interpreted by shamans, people who have spiritual visions, often in trances.

Shiva
In Hinduism, the deity viewed to comprise the creative, destructive, and liberating aspects of Ultimate Reality.

sola scriptura
The theological view prominently advanced by the Protestant Reformers that "scripture alone," apart from ecclesial teaching or theology, is sufficient to inform and guide individual religious faith and practice.

sutra
A discourse regarded by Buddhist tradition as an authentic teaching of the Buddha.

Tao
In Far Eastern faith traditions, the Way—that is, a nameless ultimate reality.

teleology
A viewpoint or way of thinking that considers the ultimate end (*telos*) or purpose of actions or phenomena.

theism
Belief in a supreme deity or various deities.

Theravada
The southern branch of Buddhism that adheres to the earliest scriptures and emphasizes individual efforts to overcome human suffering.

transcendent
Of or relating to a realm or dimension of reality that supersedes ordinary existence.

ummah
The Arabic term for the collective Muslim faithful.

Upanishads
A group of Hindu scriptures that develop broad philosophical themes regarding ultimate reality and individual human destiny.

utilitarianism
A philosophical perspective that judges human actions primarily in terms of their usefulness or the happiness or pleasure that they bring about.

Vajrayana
A system of meditative practice used by the Tibetan branch of Mahayana Buddhism that makes use of specialized techniques and symbols to concentrate immediate awareness.

Vedas
Ancient scriptures revered as divinely inspired and authoritative in the Hindu tradition.

Vishnu
In Hinduism, the deity viewed as the preserving and incarnating aspect of ultimate reality.

Yoga
One of a number of specific branches of Hindu philosophy or practice aimed toward spiritual realization.

Zen
The Japanese branch of Mahayana Buddhism that emphasizes the true nature (Buddha-nature) of all things, which can only be grasped by releasing the mind from habitual conceptual thinking.

REFERENCES

"About CRL." Center for Research Libraries Global Resources Network. Accessed December 1, 2016. http://www.crl.edu/about.

Adams, John. *Diary and Autobiography of John Adams.* Vol. 3. Cambridge, MA: Belknap Press of Harvard University Press, 1961.

Allan, John. "The Eight-Fold Path." *Buddhist Studies: Basic Buddhism.* Buddha Dharma Education Association & BuddhaNet. Accessed July 27, 2017. http://www.buddhanet.net/e-learning/8foldpath.htm.

Argyriou, A. A., G. Iconomou, A. A. Ifanti, P. Karanasios, K. Assimakopoulos, A. Makridou, F. Giannakopoulou, and N. Makris. "Religiosity and Its Relation to Quality of Life in Primary Caregivers of Patients with Multiple Sclerosis: A Case Study in Greece." *Journal of Neurology* 258, no. 6 (June 2011): 1114–19. doi:10.1007/s00415-010-5894-8.

Asis, Adrian. "10 of the Strangest Religious Rituals around the World." *The Richest*, April 28, 2014. http://www.therichest.com/rich-list/most-shocking/10-of-the-strangest-religious-rituals-around-the-world.

"Associations." SBL: Society of Biblical Literature. Accessed December 15, 2016. http://www.sbl-site.org/aboutus/associations.aspx.

Biblical Authority and Interpretation: A Resource Document Received by the 194th General Assembly (1982) of the United Presbyterian Church in the United States of America. Louisville, KY: Office of the General Assembly, 1983. https://www.pcusa.org/site_media/media/uploads/_resolutions/scripture-use.pdf.

Black, H. K. "Gender, Religion, and the Experience of Suffering: A Case Study." *Journal of Religion and Health* 52, no. 4 (December 2013): 1108–19. doi:10.1007/s10943-011-9544-y.

Boadt, Lawrence. *Reading the Old Testament: An Introduction.* New York: Paulist Press, 1984.

Campbell, Joseph. *The Masks of God: Primitive Mythology.* New York: Viking, 1959.

"Collections with Manuscripts." Library of Congress. Accessed March 7, 2016. https://www.loc.gov/manuscripts/collections.

Dalai Lama. "Countering Stress and Depression." The Office of His Holiness the 14th Dalai Lama, December 31, 2010. https://www.dalailama.com/messages/compassion-and-human-values/countering-stress-and-depression.

D'Aquili, Eugene, and Andrew B. Newberg. *The Mystical Mind: Probing the Biology of Religious Experience.* Minneapolis: Fortress Press, 1999.

Donovan, R., A. Williams, K. Stajduhar, K. Brazil, and D. Marshall. "The Influence of Culture on Home-Based Family Caregiving at End-of-Life: A Case Study of Dutch Reformed Family Care Givers in Ontario, Canada." *Social Science & Medicine* 72, no. 3 (February 2011): 338–46. doi:10.1016/j.socscimed.2010.10.010.

Eck, Diane. "A New Geo-Religious Reality." Quoted in *Living Religions: Eastern Traditions*, by Mary Pat Fisher. Upper Saddle River, NJ: Prentice Hall, 2003.

Edwards, Jonathan. "Sinners in the Hands of an Angry God." Jonathan Edwards Center at Yale University. Accessed November 21, 2016. http://edwards.yale.edu/archive?path=aHR0cDovL2Vkd2FyZHMueWFsZS5lZHUvY2dpLWJpbi9uZXdwaGlsby9nZXRvYmplY3QucGw/Yy44yMToONy53amVv.

Epictetus. *The Discourses and Manual, Together with Fragments of His Writings.* Translated by P. E. Matheson. Oxford: Clarendon Press, 1916. In *The Stoic and Epicurean Philosophers.* Edited by Whitney J. Oates. New York: Random House, 1940. Transcribed by John Bruno Hare. Internet Sacred Text Archive. June 2009. Accessed December 28, 2016. http://www.sacred-texts.com/cla/dep/dep020.htm.

Feltman, Rachel. "Aboriginal DNA Points to an Earlier Human Exodus from Africa." *Washington Post*, September 22, 2016. https://www.washingtonpost.com/news/speaking-of-science/wp/2016/09/22/aboriginal-dna-points-to-an-earlier-human-exodus-from-africa.

Fisher, Mary Pat. *Living Religions: Eastern Traditions.* Upper Saddle River, NJ: Prentice Hall, 2003.

Forster, E. M. *Aspects of the Novel.* New York: Harvest, 1956.

Foucault, Michel. *Discipline and Punish*. Translated by Alan Sheridan. New York: Vintage, 1995.

Gandhi, Mohandas. *The* Bhagavad Gita *according to Gandhi*. Albany Hills, CA: Berkeley Hills Books, 2000.

Gilsinan, Kathy. "Big in Europe: The Church of the Flying Spaghetti Monster." *Atlantic*, November 2016, 23.

Hardman, Ben. *Islam and the Métropole: A Case Study of Religion and Rhetoric in Algeria*. American University Studies. New York: Peter Lang, 2009.

Hartwell, Patrick. "Grammar, Grammars, and the Teaching of Grammar." *College English* 47 (February 1985): 105–27.

Hayford, Sarah R., and Jenny Trinitapoli. "Religious Differences in Female Genital Cutting: A Case Study from Burkina Faso." *Journal for the Scientific Study of Religion* 50, no. 2 (2011): 252–71.

Henderson, Bobby. *The Gospel of the Flying Spaghetti Monster*. New York: Villard, 2006.

"History of the Library." Library of Congress. Accessed March 7, 2016. http://www.loc.gov/about/history-of-the-library.

Holland, Henry Scott. "Death Is Nothing at All." Family Friend Poems. http://www.familyfriendpoems.com/poem/death-is-nothing-at-all-by-henry-scott-holland.

Holmes, Lowell D. *Anthropology: An Introduction*. New York: Ronald Press, 1965.

Holy See Press Office. "11—USA—Washington—24.09.2015—09.20: Congress of the United States of America Visit." United States Conference of Catholic Bishops. Accessed November 28, 2016. http://www.usccb.org/about/leadership/holy-see/francis/papal-visit-2015/media-resources/upload/11-EN-congressional-address.pdf.

Joe-Laidler, K., and G. Hunt. "Unlocking the Spiritual with Club Drugs: A Case Study of Two Youth Cultures." *Substance Use & Misuse* 48, no. 12 (September 2013): 1099–1108. doi:10.3109/10826084.2013.808067.

Johnson, George. "Consciousness: The Mind Messing with the Mind." *New York Times*, July 4, 2016. http://www.nytimes.com/2016/07/05/science/what-is-consciousness.html.

"The Kaparot Ceremony." Chabad.org. Accessed February 11, 2017. http://www.chabad.org/holidays/JewishNewYear/template_cdo/aid/989585/jewish/Kaparot.htm.

Kazantzakis, Nikos. *Zorba the Greek*. Translated by Carl Wildman. London: Faber and Faber, 1974.

King, Martin Luther, Jr. "'I Have a Dream . . .' Speech by the Rev. Martin Luther King at the 'March on Washington.'" National Archives. Accessed November 21, 2016. https://www.archives.gov/files/press/exhibits/dream-speech.pdf.

Kinyua, Johnson. *Introducing Ordinary African Readers' Hermeneutics: A Case Study of the Agikuyu Encounter with the Bible*. Religions and Discourse 54. New York: Peter Lang, 2011.

Kübler-Ross, Elisabeth. "Quotes." Elisabeth Kübler-Ross Foundation. Accessed March 25, 2016. http://www.ekrfoundation.org/quotes.

Lao-tzu. *Te-Tao Ching*. Translated by Robert G. Henricks. New York: Modern Library, 1989.

Lester, Toby. "Oh, Gods!" *Atlantic*, February 2002. http://www.theatlantic.com/magazine/archive/2002/02/oh-gods/302412.

Lincoln, Abraham. "The Gettysburg Address." Abraham Lincoln Online. Accessed March 25, 2016. http://abrahamlincolnonline.org/lincoln/speeches/gettysburg.htm.

Marx, Karl. "Critique of the Gotha Programme." Marxists Internet Archive. Accessed December 28, 2016. https://www.marxists.org/archive/marx/works/1875/gotha.

Mendola, A. "Case Study. Faith and Futility in the ICU. Commentary." *Hastings Center Report* 45, no. 1 (January–February 2015): 9–10. doi:10.1002/hast.409.

Neihardt, John G. *Black Elk Speaks: Being the Life Story of a Holy Man of the Oglalah Sioux, as Told through John G. Neihardt (Flaming Rainbow)*. Lincoln: University of Nebraska Press, 1988.

Pastoral Constitution on the Church in the Modern World. Gadium et Spes, §76. December 7, 1965.

Pearce, Catherine Owens. *A Scientist of Two Worlds: Louis* Agassiz. Philadelphia: Lippincott, 1958.

Pope Pius XII. *Divino Afflante Spiritu*, para. 36. Quoted in Lawrence Boadt, *Reading the Old Testament: An Introduction*. New York: Paulist Press, 1984.

Presbyterian Understanding and Use of Holy Scriptures: A Position Statement Adopted by the 123rd General Assembly (1983) of the Presbyterian Church in the United States. Louisville, KY: Office of the General Assembly, 1983. https://www.pcusa.org/site_media/media/uploads/_resolutions/scripture-use.pdf.

"Program Book [2015]." SBL: Society of Biblical Literature. Accessed December 15, 2016. https://www.sbl-site.org/meetings/Congresses_ProgramBook.aspx?MeetingId=27.

"Reading Religion." AAR: American Academy of Religion. Accessed December 13, 2016. https://www
.aarweb.org/publications/reading-religion.

"Religion." Pew Charitable Trusts. Accessed December 28, 2016. http://www.pewtrusts.org/en
/topics/religion.

RNC Platform Committee. *Republican Platform 2016*, July 18, 2016. https://prod-cdn-static.gop.com
/media/documents/DRAFT_12_FINAL[1]-ben_1468872234.pdf.

Rissanen, Inkeri. "Developing Religious Identities of Muslim Students in the Classroom: A Case Study from
Finland." *British Journal of Religious Education* 36, no. 2 (2014): 123–38. http://dx.doi.org/10.108
0/01416200.2013.773194.

"Scientology Mythbusting with John Atack: The Tomato Photo!" The Underground Bunker. Accessed February 11, 2017. http://tonyortega.org/2013/02/02/scientology-mythbusting-with
-jon-atack-the-tomato-photo.

Scott, Gregory M. Review of *Political Islam: Revolution, Radicalism, or Reform?* ed. John L. Esposito. *Southeastern Political Review* 26, no. 2 (1998): 512–24.

Seddon, Keith H. "Epictetus (55–135 C.E.)." *Internet Encyclopedia of Philosophy: A Peer-Reviewed Academic
Resource.* Accessed December 29, 2016. http://www.iep.utm.edu/epictetu.

Shumov, Angie. "Creation Myths from Around the World." In "Creation," an episode of *The Story of God
with Morgan Freeman.* National Geographic. Accessed March 17, 2017. http://channel.nationalgeo
graphic.com/shows.

"Sikkim Photos (Kandell Collection)." Library of Congress. Accessed December 13, 2016. https://www
.loc.gov/collections/sikkim-photos/about-this-collection.

"Style Guide." General Instructions, *Journal of the American Academy of Religion*, Oxford Academic.
Accessed June 10, 2017, https://academic.oup.com/DocumentLibrary/jaar/style guide.docx.

Tarnas, Richard. *The Passion of the Western Mind.* New York: Ballantine Books, 1991.

Thomas, Dylan. "Do not go gentle into that good night." In *The Collected Poems of Dylan Thomas 1934–
1952.* New York: New Directions, 1971.

Tocqueville, Alexis de. *Democracy in America.* Translated by Henry Reeve. New York: Bantam, 2004.

Todd, N. R. "Religious Networking Organizations and Social Justice: An Ethnographic Case Study."
American Journal of Community Psychology 50 (September 2012): 229–45.

Tremlin, Todd. *Minds and Gods: The Cognitive Foundations of Religion.* Oxford: Oxford University Press,
2006.

US Census Bureau. "Self-Described Religious Identification of Adult Population." *Statistical Abstract of the
United States: 2012.* Section 1: Population, Table 75. Revised November 23, 2015. http://www.census
.gov/library/publications/2011/compendia/statab/131ed/population.html.

University of Chicago Press. *The Chicago Manual of Style.* 16th ed. Chicago: University of Chicago Press,
2010.

Vonk, Levy. "Big in Mexico: The Migrants' Saint." *Atlantic*, June 2016. http://www.theatlantic.com/mag
azine/archive/2016/06/big-in-mexico/480759.

Williams, Daniel K. "Why Values Voters Value Donald Trump." *New York Times*, August 20, 2016. http://
nyti.ms/2bvKvO7.

Winkelman, Michael. "Shamanism as the Original Neurotheology." *Zygon* 39, no. 1 (March 2004): 193–217.

Wuthnow, Robert. "Myths about American Religion." Lecture 1049 on Religion and Civil Society.
Heritage Foundation. October 18, 2007. http://www.heritage.org/research/lecture/myths-about
-american-religion.

———. "Curriculum Vitae." Princeton University Sociology Department. Accessed December 27, 2016.
http://sociology.princeton.edu/files/faculty/cv/WuthnowCV2015.pdf.

Wyse, Marion. *Variations on the Messianic Theme: A Case Study of Interfaith Dialogue.* Judaism and Jewish
Life. Brighton, MA: Academic Studies Press, 2009.

Yardley, William. "Pastors in Northwest Find Focus in 'Green.'" *New York Times*, January 15, 2010. http://
www.nytimes.com/2010/01/16/us/16church.html.

INDEX